P9-EFJ-526

Criminal Justice

Recent Scholarship

Edited by
Marilyn McShane and Frank P. Williams III

A Series from LFB Scholarly

Community Policing
The Challenges of Successful Organizational Change

Joseph A. Schafer

LFB Scholarly Publishing LLC
New York 2001

Library of Congress Cataloging-in-Publication Data

Schafer, Joseph A. (Joseph Andrew), 1973-
Community policing : the challenges of successful organizational change / Joseph A. Schafer.
p. cm. -- (Criminal justice)
Includes bibliographical references and index.
ISBN 1-931202-04-4
1. Community policing--Case studies. 2. Organizational change--Case studies. I. Title. II. Series
HV7936.C83 S37 2001
363.2'3--dc21

2001000573

ISBN 1-931202-04-4

Printed on acid-free 250-year-life paper.

Manufactured in the United States of America.

To my parents,
who loved enough to give me strong roots
and then had the courage to give me wings.

And to Shelby,
my companion and colleague in all that truly matters.

Contents

List of Tables

Acknowledgments

Many faculty members at Michigan State University played important roles in my graduate education. Drs. Dennis Payne, Chris Vanderpool and Daniel Kruger graciously served on my dissertation committee, teaching me a tremendous amount about their disciplines. Dr. Christopher Smith contributed to my professional development with his advice, insights and sense of humor. Dr. Timothy Bynum and Dr. Stephen Mastrofski directed the project which generated this text's data and suggested that it serve as the basis for my dissertation research. They always treated me as a colleague rather than a subordinate, allowing me to learn more than I realized at the time.

The original research project was funded by the National Institute of Justice (NIJ) (Grant # 95IJCX0093). Points of view or opinions expressed in this book are those of the author and do not necessarily represent the official position or policy of NIJ or the U.S. Department of Justice. In the course of preparing this research I received generous financial support from the Robert Trojanowicz Community Policing Endowed Fund. I hope my work contributes to the ideas Dr. Trojanowicz believed in so deeply. I would also be remiss if I did not thank the men and women of the Motor City Police Department for their cooperation, candor, and time.

The men and women of the Ames (IA) Police Department taught me a great deal during my formative years. More recently, Geoff Huff and Jeff Hale have offered important insights and perspectives (JD bbq, anyone?). My esteemed colleagues from Pour Richard's in Cedar Falls, Iowa, started me on this road and have periodically helped me along the way. "Long may you run..."

Dr. Clem Bartollas has been tireless in serving as a mentor and friend, offering me essential encouragement, guidance and advocacy; it has meant more to me than you may know. I look forward to more visits by the roses in the years to come. It would seem R.T. Lewis was right after all. Also, the countless prayers, endless encouragement and unwavering support provided by my aunts, uncles, cousins, and siblings helped me during my journey through graduate school; know that it is appreciated.

Many friends and colleagues have assisted in the preparation of this text. My failure to mention certain people does not diminish my appreciation for their contributions. Elizabeth Bonello, Todd Bricker, and Tracy Varano have been supportive collaborators, comrades, and travel companions. Beth Huebner has been a good friend, a patient instructor and a thoughtful critic in reviewing sections of this text. Sameer Hinduja, Sean Varano, Jeffrey Cancino, Brandon Kooi, John McCluskey and Kall Loper graciously provided additional reviews and comments. Mr. Leo Balk, President of LFB Scholarly Publishing, has patiently and skillfully guided me through the editing process.

My graduate education was greatly enhanced through my association with Dr. David L. Carter. David has been a mentor, advocate, sounding board, counselor, co-author, and (most importantly) a good friend. He has been instrumental in my professional development and survival. I am honored to have been associated with him and am truly indebted for all he has done for me.

Finally, I dedicate this dissertation to the three people who have been most instrumental in my life. My parents, John and Grace Schafer, never allowed me to place limits on what I could achieve through dedication and persistence. My wife, Shelby, tolerated the selfish lifestyle of a graduate student and sacrificed so much to help me realize my goals. Although I know they have not always agreed with the choices I have made, they have given me unwavering support, love and encouragement in this and all other endeavors I have pursued. I find words on paper inadequate to convey what I feel in my heart.

Thank you.

CHAPTER 1
Introduction

Any organization seeking to change its form and/or function is likely to face a number of internal and external challenges. Internally, organizations must be able to manage the needs of their employees, the logistics of planning, and finite resources. Externally, organizations exist in a broader environment which limits and constrains how they operate. Police agencies are not immune to such challenges when they seek to make major organizational changes. When police planners seek to bring change within their organization, they must negotiate a minefield of employee needs and motivations, structural and organizational restrictions, budgetary and personnel constraints, legal obligations, political obstacles, and community desires and demands.

Community policing represents the most significant change to American policing since the professionalization movement emerged in the first half of the twentieth century. Community policing is a major transformation in how the police interact with the public which they serve. Under traditional policing paradigms, the police maintain a distance from their community; the police are viewed as the experts on crime and, as such, take the lead in addressing issues of crime and community order. Community policing is a philosophy which turns this traditional paradigm on its head. The police empower citizens and the public is placed in the proverbial driver's seat; citizens have a voice in determining what the police role and agenda will be within their community.

Community policing is a philosophy, not a program. Police organizations which wish to "do" community policing must do more than just create a small unit of officers who will be charged with working closely with the citizenry. Agencies which fully embrace community policing must undergo a major transformation in terms of their structure, agenda, role orientation, and organizational culture. Adopting a community policing philosophy requires most agencies to rethink how they operate and to reorient their employees. While management and policing literature are replete with rhetoric on how organizations can empower their employees through organizational change, in reality, it may be very difficult to successfully change an organization in a positive direction.

If community policing is ever going to become the dominant philosophical paradigm in American policing, it will be necessary to have an understanding of the common obstacles which may emerge during this transformation. Once obstacles have been identified and understood, it is possible to develop more effective means by which to implement community policing. This text does not explore the merits of community policing as a program or a philosophy. Instead, it focuses on those obstacles which might impede organizational change in police agencies attempting to implement community policing. Specifically, the text explores the change process in a medium-sized police agency seeking to shift from a traditional to a community policing paradigm.

STATEMENT OF THE PROBLEM

Criminal justice scholars and practitioners tend to disagree as to whether the transformation to a community policing paradigm represents a fundamental shift in how police officers have historically performed their duties. This debate aside, in the past decade it has become apparent that police organizations wishing to adopt a community policing philosophy must undergo a certain degree of structural and cultural transformation in order to achieve this objective. While much has been written detailing the wonderful potential community policing may have for generating positive transformations in police-community relations and the quality of life in American cities, experience has shown that bringing this lofty vision to fruition has been a substantial challenge.

A police organization which is seeking to adopt a community policing philosophy must do more than simply change itself on paper. Such a reorientation requires an organization to conduct a self-examination. Such introspective examination might indicate how the agency's structure, organizational inertia, and employee culture, selection, and training need to be altered if effective change is to be realized. Simply changing an organization's rhetoric (i.e., its mission statement, philosophy, goals, motto, etc.) is insufficient to ensure that a proposed change will become a reality.

Thus, the problem is that if police organizations are to undergo a successful transformation to a community policing paradigm, police planners and executives need to have a clear understanding of the barriers to such an organizational change. Having a knowledge of the most common barriers to change does not guarantee that a new program, initiative, or philosophy will ultimately succeed. On the other hand, such knowledge assists police planners in understanding that successful change requires attention to a myriad of issues on all levels of an organization (structure, culture, socialization, operations, etc.). This research identifies the most salient factors which might impede organizational change in police agencies seeking to shift their operational and philosophical orientation from a traditional to a community policing paradigm.

PURPOSE OF THE STUDY

This text considers barriers to successful organizational change through the use of data from an evaluation of an attempted community policing implementation in a medium-sized police organization. The primary source of data is a self-administered survey completed by police officers who were most affected by this planned organizational change. Survey results are supplemented by other findings from this case study, including field observations, semi-structured interviews, and focus group discussions. Specifically, the text: (1) identifies those factors in the individual socialization of employees which might generate resistance to organizational change; (2) determines how organizational culture (collective values, tradition, and beliefs) might contribute to employee resistance to planned change; and (3) defines the role organizational planning might play in how a police agency adapts to change. The author has drawn upon quantitative and qualitative research to identify such factors in the context of planned organizational change in a medium-sized police force. Utilizing the results of this research, police executives may be able to plan organizational changes in a more efficacious manner.

Identifying Individual Socialization Factors

Perhaps the greatest challenge that managers face in planning organizational change is confronting the prior socialization of individual employees. An individual's socialization is the product of a complex network of the employee's personal values and beliefs, their background and past experiences, and their orientation toward the occupation, organization, and work environment. These factors are operationalized using the results of a survey of police officers in the study agency. Specifically, consideration is given to the backgrounds, demographics, and occupational orientations and beliefs of the respondents, and how these factors might relate to support for community policing in general and community policing specifically as it was implemented in the study agency. The available data does not allow for easy determination of the personal values and beliefs of respondents, making this potential factor very difficult to assess.

Identifying Organizational Culture Factors

In addition to being influenced by their own personal values and beliefs, employees may also be influenced by the culture of the organization in which they work. This culture may be composed of the attitudes of other employees, organizational tradition and beliefs, and the way in which new employees are selected, trained, and socialized. These factors are operationalized in two manners to determine the role organizational culture plays in the outcome of planned organizational change. The primary source of information about these factors is derived from focus group discussions, semi-structured interviews, and field observations. Second, to a lesser degree data from the survey of police officers is used to identify various aspects of the organizational culture at the time of the survey, in particular examining those collective beliefs and values toward both community policing and community policing as it was operationalized in the study organization. Combining these various sources allows for the development of a general picture of the organizational culture during the period of time immediately proceeding and during the planned change being studied.

Identifying Organizational Planning Factors

Data were analyzed to assess the role, if any, of organizational planning in the outcome of the change effort under consideration. In the context of organizational change, elements of planning are those factors which are under an organization's immediate control (e.g., structure, policy, procedure, methods of implementation, etc.). This analysis emphasizes the way in which change was planned, introduced, and implemented in the study agency. Similar to the approach used in assessing organizational culture, organizational planning is operationalized in two manners, using findings from both quantitative and qualitative aspects of the available data. Particular attention is given to the role the implementation process may have played in the level of acceptance of the proposed change. In addition, these qualitative findings were complemented with data on employee attitudes toward the implementation process derived from a survey of patrol officer.

Research Objectives

The text relies on data from a case study of police department attempting to change from a traditional to a community policing philosophy. Two objectives are of paramount interest. First, survey data provided by officers affected by an organizational change are used in order to assess how individual level concerns and attitudes may have acted as impediments to securing organizational change. Second, qualitative data (from focus groups, semi-structured interviews, and field observation) aid in the assessment of how organizational culture, as well as organizational action and planning, may have impeded successful organizational change.

Findings from this research allow police planners to be better informed as they begin to consider initiating planned organizational change. Knowing the factors which might impede successful change does not ensure that planned organizational change will be effective. By understanding that successful change requires attention to a variety of considerations existing on a number of levels in an organization, planners may be able to design programs which may be more responsive to the needs created by these various factors. Identifying the most salient obstacles to organizational change allows police executives to be better informed as they seek to reorient their organizations.

DEFINITIONS OF TERMS

This text employs a variety of terms which need to be defined for the reader at the outset. The following terms are operationally defined as applicable to the text.

Community Policing Officer (CPO). An officer assigned to coordinate and administer all community policing activities in a geographic area (significantly smaller than a normal police patrol beat). This officer is general exempt from handling any call outside of his/her assigned neighborhood. In the Motor City Police Department (MCPD), CPO's were members of a unit outside of the Patrol Division. In the context of the officer survey, "CPO" refers to an officer, sergeant, or lieutenant from the Patrol Division who was or had held a Community Policing Officer assignment.

Dual Accountability & Supervision: A key feature in the generalized community policing structure that MCPD implemented was a bifurcated system of supervision and accountability. Line officers were held accountable to a sergeant who supervised their team area and the sergeant(s) who supervised their patrol shift. Patrol sergeants supervised both the line officers who worked their shift and the officers assigned to their team area.

Evaluation of Community Policing as Implemented in the Motor City Police Department. An officer's view of how generalized community policing was operationally defined and implemented within the Motor City

PD. This evaluation may be distinct from an individual officer's perceptions of community policing as a philosophy.

Generalized Community Policing: A structural and philosophical approach which makes the administration of community policing the responsibility of all employees within an agency. A generalized approach is the ideal way to fulfill a community policing paradigm.

Line Officer. The base of an organization's hierarchy; in police agencies "the line" is composed of employees holding the rank of "police officer."

Non-CPO. A line officer, sergeant, or lieutenant assigned to the Patrol Division who had never held an assignment as a Community Policing Officer.

Non-Supervisor. A sworn police employee holding the rank of "officer"; in most cases refers to an officer working in either a patrol or community policing capacity.

Perceptions of Community Policing. An officer's view of community policing as a philosophy. These perceptions may be separate from an officer's attitude toward the use of CPO's or other forms of community policing in the Motor City Police Department. They relate to the individual's reaction to the theory and practice of community policing.

Road officer. A Motor City Police Department term for a sworn employee holding the rank of "police officer" and assigned to the Patrol Division.

Shift Sergeant. A road officer's immediate supervisor on a daily basis. Shift sergeants had temporal responsibility for a squad of patrol officers assigned to a particular precinct during a specific time frame. They were one of the two supervisors to whom an officer was accountable. In addition to their temporal responsibility for a squad of officers working the same shift, shift sergeants also had responsibility for officers assigned to a geographic area (a Team Area).

Specialized Community Policing: A structural approach which makes a limited number of employees responsible for administering community policing within an agency. Such an approach tends to make community policing a program (administered by a few employees) rather than a philosophy (administered by all employees). This is the approach most commonly seen in American police organizations, yet it is not fully consistent with the philosophy of this policing paradigm.

Supervisor. A sworn police employee holding a rank above "officer"; in most cases, refers to a sergeant or lieutenant.

Team Area. A geographic subdivision of Motor City. Each member of the patrol division was assigned to a team area. While on duty and in service, this officer had primary responsibility for any calls for service in the team area (although the officer might handle calls for service throughout their precinct or the city). The long-term quality of life concerns and neighborhood problems in the team areas were addressed by a "team" of police officers under the supervision of a patrol sergeant.

Team Sergeant. A supervisor from the Patrol Division with the responsibility of coordinating problem solving activities within a team area. Team sergeants had the dual responsibility of supervising road officers on a given shift and overseeing their team area's overall quality of life. The team sergeant was expected to facilitate problem solving endeavors using the team of officers who policed the team area around the clock.

Temporal and Geographic Responsibility & Accountability. The ideas that patrol officers and patrol sergeants might hold obligations based on both time and location. Patrol officers were temporally responsible to the sergeants who routinely supervised their shift and were geographically responsible to the sergeant who supervised their team area. Officers were also temporally responsible for handling calls for service throughout their precinct (and on occasion, the city) on a daily basis, while also being geographically responsible for the long-term problems in the team area to which they were assigned. Patrol sergeants were temporally responsible for a squad of officers on a given shift and were geographically responsible for a group of officers assigned to their team area. Sergeants were temporally responsible for making sure operations ran smoothly and that calls were handled during the course of their daily shift; they were also geographically responsible for the long-term quality of life in the team area they supervised.

DELIMITATIONS

The following limitations to the research design and analysis used in this text may limit its results. While every effort has been made to minimize their repercussions upon the research findings, they may still have an unforseen impact. First, the study site was not selected using any form of probability sampling; rather, it was chosen out of convenience. Consequently, these research findings may not be automatically generalized to other settings. Second, it is difficult to determine the degree to which the organization under consideration (the Motor City Police Department) represents what might be experienced in other police organizations. Motor City may not be typical due to the size, diversity, economy, and geography of the community. In addition, the experiences in Motor City may not be found in agencies which differ in size, composition, or organizational culture.

Third, the data were collected during the course of a two and a half year research project. Consequently, the experiences in Motor City may be explained to some degree by history. While the study was being conducted, the Department was in the center of a number of controversies relating to the actions of officers and the general attitude and performance of the agency. It is possible that the attitudes of individual officers may have been shaped to an unknown degree by these controversies, rather than by the organizational change with which this text is concerned. Fourth, the time frame of this study may have been too narrow to reflect success with the organizational change. Data was collected within the first 24 months after the change was initiated. It is not clear how practices and attitudes may have changed after this time. While success did not emerge during this 24-month study period, it may have been achieved later in time.

Fifth, the available data is not a perfect match with the conceptual framework developed through the literature review. It is difficult to determine the true strength of portions of the conceptual framework because ideal measures are not always available. Sixth, data are heavily reliant upon self-reported attitudes (thus the strength of the data is limited by the quality of the instrument and administration methodology) and qualitative research (which is subject to interpretive bias on the part of the research team). While steps were taken to maximize the integrity of the data, flaws may still exist to some degree. Seventh, the survey data was only gathered at one point in time, limiting the findings and making them susceptible to a variety of validity threats. Furthermore, the survey instrument was developed and tested in part using a focus group of purposively selected officers; important dimensions may have been overlooked.

Eighth, Motor City had a long history of experimenting with various forms of community policing, which may be reflected in its organizational culture. A police department attempting an analogous reform from a "fresh" starting point might not have faced an organizational culture with such deeply ingrained attitudes (be they good or bad) toward this philosophy. Ninth, in the interest of their protection, survey participants were not identified, preventing follow-up inquiries of non-respondents. The survey response rate was high, but the response distribution may still inject a degree of bias into the results. Finally, although the survey instrument was subject to a modified form of pretesting, it was not a validated instrument.

BASIC ASSUMPTIONS

The process of conducting social inquiry invariably requires that the researcher make certain basic assumptions. It is critical that the researcher recognizes and acknowledges those assumptions made in order to understand how they may modify or mitigate the research findings. In developing the conceptual and methodological framework for this text, four key assumptions have been made. First, it is assumed that the MCPD's attempt to implement generalized community policing was a failure. Although not empirically proven, it is assumed that the organization's attempt to implement a structure compatible with a broad community policing philosophy was not successful. This conclusion was not derived from predetermined outcome measures; rather, it was based on the overwhelming sentiment from within the organization and its leadership that "this is not working." In addition, the Department's failure to clearly identify expected outcomes of the reorganization would have complicated any efforts to empirically assess the success of the team-based community policing system.

Second, the author assumes that the barriers and impediments identified in the MCPD experience can be generalized to other settings and/or other forms of organizational change. Specifically, it is assumed that many of the barriers observed in Motor City might complicate attempts to implement generalized community policing in other organizations. Third, it is assumed that the research methodology was able to accurately identify and diagnose the most salient issues in the organization and in the change effort. Finally, the author assumes that the primary survey instrument, although never systematically validated, was an accurate and reliable means by which to assess salient employee opinions, experiences, and attitudes.

ORGANIZATION OF THE TEXT

This text examines the role three concepts, individual socialization, organizational culture, and organizational planning, play in the process of organizational change. The salient literature pertaining to these concepts is reviewed and discussed, both in general terms and in the context of police organizations. It should be noted that while conceptually these ideas are each distinctive, analytically they may be difficult to separate. In particular, the socialization of individual employees and an organization's culture may be linked in a nearly inextricable manner. These two concepts are part of a complex network of social phenomena which help to determine an individual's work ethic, work-related behavior, occupational personality, etc.

The relationship between the concepts of individual socialization and organizational culture may be strongly reciprocal in terms of how they impact an individual's work-related attitudes, beliefs and values. As such, separate analysis of their individual influences on such attitudes may be very difficult. Assessing the individual influences of these dimensions was not the objective of the evaluation project which generated the data used in this text. The instrument used to collect data on attitudes and opinions was not designed to clearly distinguish between individual socialization and organizational culture. Therefore, this analysis often treats their impact as a combined factor in shaping employee values, beliefs and attitudes. For the purposes of the literature review organizational culture and individual socialization are discussed as distinctive concepts.

This text is divided into five major sections. First, a brief discussion of traditional and community policing paradigms in law enforcement is provided to properly orient the reader with the type of organizational change examined in this text (Chapter 2). Next, individual consideration is given to each of the three major concepts of analytical importance in this text (Chapters 3-5). Third, the methodological approaches which generated this study's data are described and defined (Chapter 6). Fourth, the conceptual framework is considered using quantitative and qualitative data from a select police agency undergoing organizational change (Chapters 7-9). The text concludes by discussing the implications of the research findings for change in police organizations, for the implementation of generalized community policing, and for organizational research within police agencies (Chapter 10).

CHAPTER 2

Traditional and Community Policing Paradigms

This book examines the process of organizational change, particularly the implementation of community policing. Prior to investigating important dimensions of organizational change, the reader needs to have a basic understanding of historical and contemporary trends in the structure of American police agencies. This chapter provides a brief description of traditional and community-oriented policing approaches. The discussion considers these methods of policing and how these two strategies impact the structure and function of police organizations. The chapter also explores the best modes and means of policing under both perspectives. Finally, consideration is given to the consequences of both traditional and community policing on the front-line police officer.

TRADITIONAL POLICE ORGANIZATIONS

Police departments in the United States have traditionally been very close to purely mechanistic organizations (Kuykendall & Roberg, 1982). These authors note that mechanistic organizations are characterized by: specialization (compartmentalizing tasks and functions), hierarchy (status and rank differentiation), authority (influence derived from one's position), rule orientation (a focus on methods of operation; means are emphasized over ends), and position orientation (emphasizing obeying directions, using accepted means, and displaying loyalty are emphasized).

Others have characterized traditional police organizations as bureaucratic, hierarchical, paramilitary organizations (Bittner, 1970; Cordner, 1978; Franz & Jones, 1987; Jermier & Berkes, 1979; McNamara, 1967).

This traditional organizational structure was not always in place. It has been suggested that during the early decades of their existence, American police officers enjoyed a close relationship with the citizenry they served (Fogelson, 1977; Walker, S., 1977). This close relationship was rooted in the core principles of policing espoused by Britain's Sir Robert Peel (Radelet & Carter, 1994). Included in these core principles were the ideas that the police must seek public support, cooperation, and compliance in order to be effective. Sir Peel's core principles are generally regarded as the ideals upon which early American policing was also based.

Unfortunately, this close relationship between the police and the community resulted in graft, misconduct, abuse and corruption in too many communities. Efforts to reform corruption in police organizations, as well as politics in general, began to emerge during the latter decades of the nineteenth century. During the first decades of the twentieth century here was a push to "professionalize" police officers and to remove them, at least symbolically, from the communities they served. The traditional structure of police organizations emerged during this era as a means to control and regulate the relationship between the police and the public. According to Samuel Walker (1977):

> By the end of the 1930s the dominant feature of modern American police administration had taken shape, large bureaucratic structures organized along hierarchical, semi-military lines, increasingly drawn into a tight knit subculture. Almost no new ideas or techniques were introduced in police administration from 1920s through the mid-1960s. (p. ix).

This separation from the community was reinforced by historical circumstances, including the development and proliferation of automobiles, telephones, and two-way radios.

Supervisors in these traditional organizations sought to maintain a high degree of internal control by creating detailed policies and procedures to define what officers should and should not do, and to control their discretion (Weisburd, McElroy, & Hardyman, 1988). One reason for these strict policies and rules was the widely scattered nature of a police work force. Unlike a factory setting, employees were not in one central location where their actions could be closely monitored. Because of this, supervisors employed written policies, procedures, directives and rules in an attempt to control officer conduct and action.

Patrol officers make up the "backbone" of traditional police organizations (Trojanowicz, Kappeler, Gaines, & Bucqueroux, 1998; Walker, S., 1999). Officers have traditionally been viewed as the front line in the "war on crime." On a daily basis, patrol officers have more direct contact with the public than any other member of a police organization (Crank, 1998). Despite media images and public impressions to the contrary, patrol work tends to be highly routinized and mundane. Extensive studies with widely varying methodologies have been employed to study police activities. The net result of these research endeavors is that their findings "in no way lend support to the headline news vision of police work as a violent running battle between police and criminals" (Greene & Klockars, 1991: 283).

Patrol officers in traditional police organizations spend most of their time waiting for a call for service (Payne & Trojanowicz, 1985). While waiting to be sent somewhere to do something, officers typically engage in preventive patrol (Reiss, 1971); officers attempt to spot some sign of trouble, such as a traffic violation or suspicious activity. When officers are given a call for service, they are typically sent to "take a complaint" from a citizen. All too often, police officers find themselves cast as the adversary in their contact with citizens (Wilson, 1968). When the police are called to intervene in a situation, the result is often that someone will be arrested or given a citation. The person on the receiving end of this sanction may feel animosities toward the officer, even though the officer is only doing his or her job by enforcing the law. As a result, officers often feel a sense of isolation from, and antagonism toward, the community they serve (Manning, 1997b; Rubinstein, 1973; Skolnick, 1994).

Notable police scholars such as David Bayley, Egon Bittner, Carl Klockars, Peter Manning, Albert Reiss, Jerome Skolnick, and William Westley (to name just a few) have spent their careers attempting to describe the consequences of this tension between the police and the citizenry they serve. The elaboration of their writings is not fully germane to this discussion. Suffice it to say that this tension may be a powerful force in socializing officers to adopt particular attitudes and behavioral patterns. By virtue of their social role, police officers are granted unique powers and rights which tend to set them apart from other members of society (Bittner, 1970; Kobler, 1975). This status also tends to reinforce the idea that the police have a monopoly on expertise about crime and community safety (Trojanowicz, Kappeler, Gaines, & Bucqueroux, 1998). The consequence of these collective factors has been a historical divide between police organizations and officers, and the communities which they serve. From a management perspective, this divide may seriously compromise the efficacy of police efforts to address crime and disorder.

The structure of traditional police organizations may have a negative impact on police officers and the quality of work they produce. Traditional police organizations are paramilitary bureaucracies, with clear lines of authority, formalized policies and procedures, command-and-obey relationships, and centralized decision making. As such, patrol officers are at the bottom of the power hierarchy. Paramilitary bureaucracies stifle innovation among their members (Angell, 1977), in particular, line-level employees. Individual employees must closely conform to the organization's expectations. Rewards are enjoyed by those who engage in the activities supported by the bureaucracy; these activities are commonly focused on the quantity of employee outputs in the form of arrests, citations, and calls for service handled. Supervisors at the top of the organization's hierarchy focus on controlling and directing their subordinates, rather than supporting autonomy, creativity and innovation (Trojanowicz, Kappeler, Gaines, & Bucqueroux, 1998).

This traditional structure may lead to the emergence of a number of counterproductive psychological responses among line-level employees. As Cordner observed:

> Among these feelings are demoralization and powerlessness in the lower ranks, a conception of top command as arbitrary, a growing cynicism among supervisory and middle-management personnel, and the subsequent development of a we/they attitude toward top management...Ideas are stifled, officers are not

> confident of the support of top management, and the CYA syndrome takes hold (1978: 30).

Suspicion is engendered between the ranks. Communication slows to a trickle. Distrust begins to grow, particularly of the department's higher echelons. Morale problems emerge at all levels of the organization, most prominently among front-line officers (Franz & Jones, 1987). As the educational level of employees increases, they experience a greater desire to be involved in the decision-making process of their organization (Angell, 1971). The traditional model does not allow for such autonomy and input, leaving officers frustrated, alienated, and resentful.

Individuals typically pursue a career in policing out of a sense of benevolence; they wish to help others in times of need (Meagher & Yentes, 1986). Unfortunately, this noble concept may be stifled by the very nature of the occupation and organization which the individual wishes to join. The new employee soon finds that many of those people they wish to help are less than appreciative, despite good intentions and noble concepts. On a daily basis they work with peers, many of whom have become cynical and jaded. Rather than supporting their efforts, these peers may insist that callous indifference is the only way to survive the rigors of their occupation.

This is compounded by an organizational structure which seeks to control their discretion, stifle their creativity and innovation, and demand their conformity. The once idealistic officer is trapped between a seemingly ungrateful citizenry and an organization devoid of compassion and support. The essence of this situation may be best captured by Trojanowicz, Kappeler, Gaines, & Bucqueroux (1998), observing that "thwarted idealists may struggle against becoming cynics, but cynicism toward the community and toward the police hierarchy may be so potent that few can resist" (p. 269).

AN OVERVIEW OF COMMUNITY POLICING

If traditional policing approximated a purely mechanistic organization, community policing approximates a purely organic organization (Kuykendall & Roberg, 1982). Organizations which are organic are characterized by: generalization (de-emphasizing the specialization of jobs and tasks), collegiality (interactions between members are informal and differences in status and ranks are de-emphasized), power (status and influence determined largely by ability and reputation), situation-orientation (all employees contribute to solving problems; ends are emphasized over means), and goal-orientation (accountability and rewards are linked to quality performance; commitments to organizational goals are emphasized over personal achievements). Although not limited to these characterizations, the organizational structure necessary for successful community policing is far more organic than the mechanistic bureaucracies which have been the hallmarks of traditional police organizations. Before elaborating on the principles and outcomes of community policing, it is necessary to examine the history which surrounded its development.

Substantial efforts to modify police operations and practices were made during the first three-quarters of the twentieth century. Despite attempts to professionalize policing, to improve police-community relations and to promote crime prevention, crime rates and public perceptions of safety seemed to move independently of these efforts. In the aftermath of the President's Commission on Law Enforcement and the Administration of Justice of 1967, police practitioners and scholars had begun to question the fundamental assumptions upon which traditional police operations were based. The result of these inquiries was that the "research had shown repeatedly that traditional police strategies were not working effectively" (Skolnick & Bayley, 1986: 3).

Although some have raised issues regarding the methodologies of individual studies, the overall message of this research was that it was difficult (if not impossible) to prove that traditional policing methods were effective on a variety of outcomes. Skolnick and Bayley (1986) reviewed the most prominent evaluative studies and identified what they believed to be the most significant findings of these research endeavors:

> First, increasing the number of police does not necessarily reduce crime rates or raise the proportion of crimes solved...Second, random motorized patrolling neither reduces crime nor improves chances of catching suspects...Third, two-person patrol cars are no more effective than one-person cars in reducing crime or

> catching criminals...Fourth, saturation patrolling does reduce crime, but only temporarily, largely by displacing it to other areas...Fifth, the kind of crime that terrifies Americans most– mugging, robbery, burglary, rape, homicide– is rarely encountered by police on patrol...Sixth, improving response time to emergency calls has no effect on the likelihood of arresting criminals or even in satisfying involved citizens...Seventh, crimes are not solved– in the sense of offenders arrested and prosecuted– through criminal investigations conducted by police departments. (pp. 4-5).

If the accuracy and validity of these findings are accepted, the tried-and-true methods of policing employed by virtually every American law enforcement agency in the mid-1970's were doing nothing to reduce crime or foster a feeling of safety among the public.

A redefinition of American policing occurred during the last quarter of the twentieth century. The notion of community policing has emerged on the tail end of this effort. In this time frame there has been a growing realization that traditional/professional policing inadvertently "left people out of policing" (Trojanowicz & Carter, 1988: 1), both in terms of the people police organizations served and the people they employed. Police-community relations, crime prevention, team policing...all attempted to reintegrate people into the process of policing. Each of these successive efforts also moved police organizations closer to an organic structure. In addition, each effort was less programmatic and more philosophical than its predecessor.

Community policing is a reform innovation which finally moved beyond a program and crossed over to the realm of organizational philosophy. In its pure form, community policing is carried out by an organization, not by select members. It is integrated into the beliefs, values and actions of all members of an organization. While community policing holds the promise to bring about a positive transformation in American policing, some view it with skepticism because it has evolved from a line of failed organizational strategies (Trojanowicz & Carter, 1988). Perceived as the latest installment for managers who subscribe to the "paradigm of the month club," many front-line officers do not take this philosophy seriously. It is perceived as a temporary phase which will pass in favor of the next wave of innovative policing. This has made it difficult for many agencies to shift to a community policing paradigm, regardless of good intent on the part of police executives.

Despite the abundance of attention it has received in the last 25 years, community policing is still a concept which many do not fully understand. It is a "fundamental change in the basic role of the police officer" which enables officers to "engage in problem-solving activities and to develop new partnerships with ...the community" (Wilkinson & Rosenbaum, 1994: 110). Community policing is based on the notion that police officers and private citizens can work together to creatively solve community problems (Trojanowicz, Kappeler, Gaines, & Bucqueroux, 1998). While these problems may relate to crime, they may also relate to the fear of crime, neighborhood disorder (either social or physical), or quality of life conditions. Rather than viewing themselves as the resident experts on crime, community policing suggests that police organizations and officers should take a more democratic approach. Police organizations, officers, and community residents collaboratively identify problems, establish priorities, and develop and enact solutions in order to address a broad array of social and crime conditions.

Community policing epitomizes a new organizational strategy which allows police agencies to decentralize their services and redefine the structure and role of the patrol function (Skogan & Hartnett, 1997). Police organizations have historically emphasized staffing specialized units, often at the expense of the patrol division. In contrast, community policing places a renewed emphasis and primacy on the patrol division. By reallocating personnel from specialized functions into the more generalized patrol division, agencies engaging in community policing are able to support more community-based efforts (Greene, Bergman, & McLaughlin, 1994). Rather than viewing the patrol division as the reservoir from which specialized units draw personnel and support, community policing views the patrol division as reservoir which specialized units must feed and support.

The focus of this strategy is on supporting the line officer who is assigned to work closely with people and problems in a designated geographic area (Trojanowicz, Kappeler, Gaines, & Bucqueroux, 1998). Community policing may place a heavy emphasis on "establishing geographic responsibility and accountability to police officers, establishing relatively permanent shifts and beats for personnel assignments, and limiting cross-dispatching of officers away from assigned areas" (Weisel & Eck 1994: 65). It is an effort to stabilize the relationship between the individual officer and the geographic area which the officer service. It is a way for the police to strengthen their ties with the citizens and community they serve (Greene, Bergman, & McLaughlin, 1994). By doing so, it is believed that police efforts will be more efficient and effective.

The late Robert Trojanowicz did more than any other scholar or practitioner to define what constitutes "true" community policing and to further the cause of community policing. According to his work (see generally, Trojanowicz & Carter, 1988 and Trojanowicz, Kappeler, Gaines, & Bucqueroux, 1998) , community policing may be defined using the following parameters. Community policing is a philosophy and an organizational strategy, not just a tactic or a program. True community policing is reflected in the attitudes and actions of all officers in a police organization, not just a select few who are relegated to a specialized unit. It shapes all aspects of police operations, not just narrow tasks in limited geographical areas. Community policing is problem-oriented. Police officers and organizations proactively seek out long-term solutions to the conditions which are contributing to crime and disorder in communities. This problem focus cannot occur without input and involvement from the community's residents.

Community policing is working together and sharing power by viewing citizens as partners in the process of bringing about positive change within a community. Citizens are believed to have the knowledge and resources which can make cooperative efforts more successful than efforts initiated by the police alone. Community policing is concerned with the development of trusting relationships. Incidents of corruption and abuses of power, no matter where they occur, can harm the image of the police in any community. Community policing gives a name and a face to the police so that residents will feel that the police are people they can trust and work with. Community policing is creative and innovative, not a static program. It is a fluid response to dynamically changing community needs and issues. To be successful, it must seek out new and different ways to address these problems.

Community policing is broadly focused. While traditional policing centered strictly on quantitative outputs (response time, arrests made, crimes reported, crimes cleared), community policing also considers qualitative outputs (the fear of crime, the level of neighborhood disorder, the quality of community life, the degree of citizen satisfaction). The mandate of the police within the community encompasses a wider range of concerns and responsibilities, making the process of policing a more complex enterprise. Finally, community policing has a strong geographical focus. It is expected that officers who serve the same area every time they work will develop a better knowledge of the people and problems confronting their "beat." As an officer becomes involved in the life of a neighborhood on a day-to-day basis, he or she will become more invested in that area and its quality of life, developing a sense of ownership.

In the last quarter century, a great deal of research and literature has been devoted to the topic of community policing. Despite this abundance there is still a great deal of confusion over what community policing is and is not. In addition to defining community policing, Trojanowicz, Kappeler, Gaines and Bucqueroux (1998) also defined what it is not. This "counter-definition" is instructive as it provides a more comprehensive understanding of what is encompassed by the philosophy of community policing. Community policing is not a technique "that departments can apply to a specific problem, but an entirely new way of thinking about the role of the police in the community" (Trojanowicz, Kappeler, Gaines and Bucqueroux, 1998: 15). Community policing is not public relations, although improved relations with the public is a welcome by-product. Prior attempts at improving police-community relations were largely appearance, while community policing is substance.

Community policing is not soft on crime and does not restrict officers from making arrests or enforcing the law. Officers involved in community policing may make fewer arrests than their traditional counterparts, but this is because they are dealing with a broad range of community concerns and issues, not all of which are criminal in nature. Community policing is not an independent entity within a police department, such as a function assigned to a group of specialized officers. Not every officer in an organization pursuing community policing will work in an assigned beat area every day, but they may still operate in a manner consistent with this philosophy. Community policing is not cosmetic; it is a *genuine* effort to address both criminal and non-criminal matters.

Community policing is not just another name for social work. The police already perform a wide variety of services which have little to do with serious crime and the enforcement of the law. As the only government agency addressing social concerns 24 hours a day, seven days a week, the police must be responsive to requests for information and service which are non-criminal in nature. Finally, community policing is not a panacea. Social problems are dynamic, making it difficult to correct them with simple solutions. Although not a cure for every problem, community policing is the most responsive policing philosophy developed to date.

In its ideal form community policing would be a generalized function within a police department. Every officer would have an assigned beat area which they would service every time they worked. Unfortunately, this is simply not feasible in the majority of American police organizations. Instead, agencies are forced to develop a strategy to integrate community policing specialists with other organizational divisions (Trojanowicz, Kappeler, Gaines, & Bucqueroux, 1998). Specialization has a tendency to reduce communication between parts of an organization. It also tends to alienate officers who are removed from the mainstream. Experience has shown that officers working in community policing units tend to feel marginalized from the remainder of the organization because of the false perception that they are not engaged in "real police work" (Eck, 1992; Sadd & Grinc, 1994).

This gives rise to a fundamental paradox of community policing. Where it is a specialized function, such community policing units may provide "fertile ground for the growth of resentment between traditional patrol officers and [community policing] officers" (Sadd & Grinc, 1994:38). It may not be pragmatically possible to design a police department in which every member holds geographic responsibility. The very nature of policing may necessitate that a certain number of officers must be prepared to provide rapid-response emergency services. The challenge for police planners and executives is to find the balance within their organization which minimizes tension and fosters a sense of cooperation. Particularly daunting may be the challenge of establishing that every police officer has an obligation to operate with a community policing mind-set, regardless of assignment.

Despite periodic criticism of community policing by uninvolved officers, those who spend time working in such an assignment often find it to be a rewarding experience and may be more supportive of this philosophy of policing (Trojanowicz, Kappeler, Gaines, & Bucqueroux, 1998). Employees working in community policing assignments tend to experience increased job satisfaction (Wycoff & Skogan, 1994). Officers also report that they enjoy developing relationships with the community, appreciate the flexibility offered by community policing, and feel they have time to address the problems they encounter (Trojanowicz & Pollard, 1986). Those working in community policing assignments have the opportunity to get to know the "good people" in their assigned area and feel that they had better relationships with the community (Skogan & Hartnett, 1997).

Relationships within police departments may also be enhanced by community policing (More, 1998). Cooperation and communication may increase between various units within a department as these units all work together to respond to neighborhood problems and community concerns. Supervisor-subordinate relationships may improve as front-line officers are granted a voice in their organization and are recognized for their contributions and efforts. Community policing affords employees the opportunity to exercise creativity and innovation, while developing a sense of ownership. It should be noted, however, that not all police officers want to be creative or innovative in performing their duties. It is generally expected that officers who have held a community policing assignment view this philosophy more favorably than do those who have only performed traditional policing duties.

The professional model of policing dominated American policing for the majority of this century. Despite its virtues, this model generated a variety of negative consequences for those officers on the receiving end of its command and control. Community policing has emerged as an alternative way for police organizations to operate. Table 1 contrasts elements of traditional policing with elements of community policing. The major differences between these two paradigms are clear. While it has been defined and operationalized differently from agency to agency, a community policing philosophy emphasizes partnership, prevention, and

Table 1.
Contrasted elements of traditional and community policing.

Element of Traditional Policing	Element of Community Policing
Enforcing the law is the key end that officers/agencies pursue.	Enforcing the law is one means to the ends.
Law enforcement is the paramount goal.	Improving quality of life in the community is the paramount goal.
Reactive.	Proactive.
Short response time is critical.	Short response time is less important.
Officers spend as little time as possible handling assigned calls for service.	Officers invest as much time as is reasonably necessary to handle a call for service by "getting at" the root problem.
Line officers must be controlled and directed.	Line officers must be given freedom and discretion.
Supervisors encourage obedience and conformity.	Supervisors encourage creativity and innovation.
No capacity to accept failure.	Capacity to accept failures made in good faith.
Evaluations quantitatively driven (arrests, citations, calls handled).	Evaluations qualitatively driven (citizen satisfaction, problems addressed).
Supervisors are there to command and control line officers.	Supervisors are there to support efforts of line officers.

Police limit information given to the public.	Police share knowledge with the public.
Police distrust the public.	Police seek to work cooperatively with the public.
Police view themselves as experts on crime in the community.	Police and citizens share expertise on crime in the community.
Police officers view themselves as crime fighters, law enforcers, and crook catchers.	Police officers view themselves as community organizers, community activists, and providers of vital community services.
Police agencies are closed systems.	Police agencies are open systems.

problem solving. Police officers with community policing experience typically report a greater sense of satisfaction in the job they perform and view citizens as partners, rather than as adversaries.

CRITICAL PERSPECTIVES ON COMMUNITY POLICING

Support for community policing has been far from universal in both police and academic circles. This criticism can be divided into two camps: those who are critical of community policing as a theory and those who are critical of community policing in practice.

While the theory behind community policing would seem to be sound, some have questioned its veracity. Community policing assumes that citizens want to work cooperatively with their police (Sadd & Grinc, 1994) and want their police to focus attention and resources on non-criminal matters (Gaines, 1993). Conversely, it might be argued that citizens pay taxes to fund police departments so that they do not have to expend energy actively fighting crime and disorder themselves.

Community policing advocates make the assumption that citizens *want* to be actively involved in issues of crime and justice.

Community policing is concerned with the extent to which citizens fear being the victims of crime in their community. While reducing fear of crime may be a noble endeavor, it is not necessarily correlated with a reduction in actual crime (Mastrofski, 1993). Although community policing might foster a greater sense of safety within the public, it does not necessarily create greater *actual* safety. It has also been suggested that not only do communities need more responsive police agencies, but also more responsive municipal governments (Taylor, Fritsch, & Caeti, 1998). The police do not always have the necessary expertise to deal with certain types of neighborhood problems. At some point, they need other agencies to address some of these non-criminal matters. Agencies engaged in community policing often find that they must struggle to convince other government service providers to work with the best interests of the community in mind.

Given these circumstances, the police may not be the proper arm of the government to spearhead comprehensive improvements in community conditions and government services. It has been observed that in many areas where community policing has been implemented "the police had to take the lead and [hope that] other agencies *might* follow along" (Sadd & Grinc, 1994:50) (emphasis in the original). Even where police organizations have actively pursued a community policing philosophy, such efforts have not always received the necessary support from other governmental agencies and social service providers.

Riechers and Roberg (1990) drew upon the works of a number of authors, as well as their own observations, to develop a list of ten underlying assumptions of community policing. These authors believed that before community policing could be fully embraced by academicians and practitioners, these issues still need to be discussed and resolved. Included in their list of concerns were the assumptions that: it is the responsibility of the police to help in defining and shaping community norms; neglect and disorder lead crime and the perceived lack of safety; the traditionally mechanistic nature of police organizations can be easily adapted to the organic structure necessary for effective community policing efforts; and, that police organizations are the proper means by which to bring about improved quality of life in communities. The point of this and similar arguments is not that community policing is implicitly a bad idea which should be rejected (Hoover, 1992). Instead, these authors content that the assumptions which drive community policing have not been adequately debated on a more fundamental level.

From an evaluation perspective, some contend that the vote is still not in on the efficacy of community policing. "There is precious little empirical evidence that supports the idea that community policing has a positive impact on community perception of the police or crime reduction" (Taylor, Fritsch, & Caeti, 1998: 3). In addition, those benefits which have been measured have been relatively modest and frequently come at a great monetary cost (Findley & Taylor, 1990). In all fairness, many evaluations are linked with community policing experiments funded through federal grants; agencies might be more judicious when they are paying for community policing out of their operating budget.

Another school of thought regarding community policing is composed of those who question the way in which community policing is often practiced. Manning (1997b) refers to community policing as the "Rhetorical Giant" and writes that community policing "is yet another 'presentation strategy,' a means of selectively highlighting some changes in urban policing while suppressing information about others" (p. 15). Klockars (1991) contends that community policing is merely another attempt by the police to obscure the reality of what they do– use force and coercion to deal with citizen problems. Kraska and Kappeler (1997) see part of the rise in police militarization veiled under the legitimacy of community policing efforts. By relaxing control over police officers and reintegrating them into the community they serve, some fear that agencies may invite a return to the corruption police departments worked so hard to overcome during the first half of the twentieth century (Walker, S., 1993; Wycoff, 1991).

The purpose for providing a brief review of literature critical of community policing is to illustrate that, even in the academic community, support for this innovation is by no means universal. This lack of a consensus does not appear to be hampering the idea of community policing from taking hold in American policing to any serious degree. It should be noted, however, that if community policing is going to transform American policing, there may come a time when some of these issues will need to be more fully resolved.

SUMMARY

During the past two decades, countless books, articles, and reports have been written about the community policing philosophy (see generally, Goldstein, 1990; Greene & Mastrofski, 1988; Rosenbaum, 1994; Skolnick & Bayley, 1986; Sparrow, Moore & Kennedy, 1990; Trojanowicz, Kappeler, Gaines, & Bucqueroux, 1998). Various "flavors" of community policing have been studied in cities throughout the country, including: Baltimore, Maryland; Boston, Massachusetts; Denver, Colorado; Detroit, Michigan; Flint, Michigan; Houston, Texas; Madison, Wisconsin; Newark, New Jersey; Oakland, California; Philadelphia, Pennsylvania; and San Diego, California...to name just a few. Many of these studies have been focused on how community policing was received and perceived by the local citizenry. Others have examined how community policing has impacted crime rates and quality of life in those neighborhoods in which is has been implemented. Still more studies have examined how community policing affects the perceptions of police officers charged with carrying it out, usually in a specialized unit.

What is absent from the overwhelming majority of these studies is an examination of how police organizations experience the implementation of community policing. This is typical of evaluation research in policing, which tends to focus on change outcomes (crime reduction, response time, clearance rates, etc.) while overlooking the change process itself (Greene, 1981). More attention needs to be given not just to the outcomes of community policing (i.e., greater citizen satisfaction with police services, enhanced quality of life, job enhancement and enrichment among police officers), but also to the process of change and implementation within the police organization. In other words, what are the processes and problems associated with the shift from a traditional to a community policing organizational structure and philosophy? How is the implementation of community policing experienced by police agencies and those officers most directly affected by this change? What barriers may hamper the success of efforts aimed at retooling the mechanistic structure of modern American police organizations?

This text attempts to fill this void in the research by examining the implementation of community policing as a form of organizational change. Specifically, it examines how three dimensions of a police organization (the individual employee, the collective culture, and the organization's structure) may mitigate efforts to implement community policing and redefine organizational structures and operations. The following literature review will establish the conceptual framework within which the text's analysis is conducted. By examining this problem using multiple dimensions and measures, it is expected that the challenges associated with the successful implementation of community policing may be better understood.

CHAPTER 3

The Role of Individual Socialization

When individual employees enter their work environment, they bring their education, background and experiences (their "individual socialization"). Such dimensions influence the way employees behave in their occupational role and as a member of an organization. Traits of individual socialization are independent of the organization's internal culture, formal and informal training, politics, traditions and norms. These traits might include an employee's: values and beliefs; expectations of what their occupation role will/should be; expectations of how they will/should be treated within the organization; and, attitudes toward co-workers, supervisors, and the people being serviced by the organization (where applicable). Traits of individual socialization are a product of a complex blend of education, race and ethnicity, gender, family traditions and upbringing, age, and life experiences. As such, individual socialization is a very abstract phenomena, making its complete operationalization and measurement challenging, time consuming, expensive, and, perhaps, ultimately elusive.

The following analysis examines some of the most basic elements of individual socialization. First, attention is given to elements which readily lend themselves to measurement, such as an employee's race, ethnicity, gender, education, and seniority. Second, consideration is given to other aspects of an employee's personality (the psychological contract, distrust of management, perceptions of change, and attitudes) which might be particularly salient in determining how individuals respond to change within their employing organization. Finally, a brief discussion of the possible relationship between individual socialization and community policing is provided.

RACE, ETHNICITY AND GENDER

Research on gender- and race-specific attitudes of police officers is relatively limited in light of the fact that female and minority officers have only become active in all areas of policing in recent decades. Much of this literature exploring women in policing is focused on how female police officers experience their occupation (Bartollas & Hahn, 1999). In particular, these works commonly examine sexism and the "glass ceiling" which may confront female officers in some police organizations. Anecdotally, many of the barriers which confronted early female police officers have disappeared in many departments; female police officers frequently report that they are treated as equals by the majority of their co-workers (Fletcher, 1995).

While these studies offer important insights, it remains unclear if female police officers hold differential job-related attitudes. Carpenter and Raza (1987) found little psychological difference in the attitudes expressed by male and female police recruits. Upon entering their new career, these officers had similar outlooks on role and duty expectations within the community they served. Furthermore, Meagher and Yentes (1986) found that both men and women reported pursuing a career in policing for analogous reasons: job security and the desire to help society. This limited body of literature would suggest that although female police officers may experience their career in a fashion somewhat different from their male counterparts, both genders hold similar attitudes about what it does (or should) mean to be a police officer. While specific components of such attitudes may be gender-specific, the overall outlook differs little between male and female officers.

In the past quarter century an increasing amount of research has examined attitudinal and opinion differences between white and non-white police officers. As with studies of the attitudes of female police officers, this body of literature is somewhat limited as truly meaningful career opportunities have only been extended to non-white police officers in recent decades. Buzawa (1981) found significant differences in the work attitudes of African American and Caucasian police officers. The specific issues she explored included attitudes toward: pay and benefits, the social prestige of policing as an occupation, job stress, quality of supervision, opportunities for advancement, and overall job satisfaction. Studies of attitudes of police officers toward community policing, however, show no relationship between such attitudes and an officer's race/ethnicity or gender (Weisel & Eck, 1994). "Neither race nor sex was more likely to be identified with support of community policing...White, black, and other persons of color were equally likely to feel positive about the future of community policing in their agencies" (p. 68-9).

Reviewing the available literature, Dantzker (1995) observes that "it would appear that there is little difference in attitude between genders before and after entering law enforcement" (p. 249). Similar conclusions are made by Bartollas and Hahn (1999) based upon their assessment of existing studies. Both sets of authors also find that (based upon the works of other researchers) there is not a significant difference in attitudinal patterns among officers of different racial and ethnic backgrounds. While officers may hold different views or attitudes on narrow topics based upon their race or gender, the evidence does not suggest that race or gender affects an officer's overall occupational personality, or policing-specific attitudes. Furthermore, there is no evidence that an officer's race or gender has an impact on how an officer does their job as a whole, although there may be differences based on certain dimensions (i.e., the handling of certain types of calls, injury rates, accident rates, etc.) (Bartollas & Hahn, 1999). Overall, the current literature does not suggest police officers hold differing views of organizational change based upon their gender, race, or ethnicity.

AGE AND SENIORITY

Anxiety over proposed organizational change may be more acute among employees who are older and/or who have been with an organization for a longer period of time (Johns, 1973). Older and more senior employees have more invested in their occupation and with their employer. Experienced employees have spent longer periods of time attempting to be good employees with the expectation that they will be rewarded with advancement, raises, and continued employment. In contrast to their less experienced counterparts, these senior employees have invested more time and energy into their professional development and in the success of their employing organization.

Older and more senior employees also have spent a longer period of time growing accustom to the traditional way in which their employing organization operates. They are accustomed to specific means and patterns for performing their job-related duties and relating to their co-workers, supervisors, and clients. It may not be that you "can't teach and old dog new tricks;" rather, the "old dog" may be content with the tricks they have done for so long. In addition, these older employees are more likely to have a family, a spouse with an established career, and established roots within their community. As such, they have more invested in their career, their employer, and the community in which they reside. When they perceive that a proposed change threatens their job stability or occupational status, older employees commonly exhibit more resistance than their younger counterparts because they (potentially) have more to lose.

It is probable that the change from a traditional to a community policing philosophy and structure in a police organization produces less anxiety among employees than change in the corporate and private sectors. Typical corporate change, such as downsizing, may pose a very real threat to the future employment status of employees. Those workers who cannot demonstrate their worth and value to their employer may find that their position has been eliminated. Community policing should not threaten an officer's future employment with his or her department. Many police officers are protected by civil service and/or union standards which make dismissal unlikely in the absence of criminal conduct or substantial rule violations. While adopting community policing may create doubts about future promotions or assignments to specialized units, the change should not create significant doubts that officers will still have a job in another week, month, or year.

In terms of community policing, an officer's age and length of service may play a major role in their support for, or opposition to, community policing (Carter, Sapp, & Stephens, 1989; Skolnick & Bayley, 1988). Weisel and Eck (1994) surveyed officers in six police departments to determine their views on community policing. They found that officers' attitudes toward community policing were significantly different based upon their seniority. Specifically, "support for community policing is higher among newer or younger officers and declines for personnel in subsequent years of service" (p. 68). Although the role of age and seniority in the change process may be less significant among police employees, prior research and experience suggest that it is still an important factor, particularly in the context of community policing.

EDUCATION

One outgrowth of the President's Commission on Law Enforcement and Administration of Justice was a number of programs aimed at promoting college education for police officers. The notion of requiring police officers to poses a college education originated in the 1930's with reformist administrators such as August Vollmer (Carte & Carte, 1975; Klockars, 1985), but the idea gained little inertia during the mid-century professionalization movement. From the late 1960's through the early 1980's, the federal Law Enforcement Education Program (LEEP) helped to fund college educations for thousands of active police officers (Skolnick & Fyfe, 1993). In response, the number of university programs in criminal justice and criminology began to increase dramatically in the 1960's and 1970's. LEEP was a short-lived program, yet its legacy fundamentally transformed educational standards in American policing. Although few departments currently require a full four-year college degree (more than 70 percent require only a high school diploma), in many areas it has become the unofficial norm (Dantzker, 1995).

Soon after LEEP was established, researchers and police executives began to question whether education made a difference in the traits and performance of police employees. In other words, were there identifiable differences between officers with only a high school diploma versus officers with some college education? Subsequent research identified significant differences on a number of different outcome measures. Extrapolating from these findings in might be presumed that a college education will equip officers with a set of skills and attitudes that make them better able to function in an organization which has adopted a community policing philosophy.

Officers with a college education tend to have the ability to see the "big picture" when they respond to a call for service. They may be better prepared to perceive the underlying "illness" (lack of supervision during after-school hours) which is causing the "symptoms" they observe (delinquent behavior in teenagers). These officers also tend to seek out greater challenges, to function more independence, to behave more responsibly, and to exhibit greater innovation and flexibility in dealing with complex problems (Carter, Sapp, & Stephens, 1988). In addition, college-educated police officers tend to generate fewer citizen complaints, perhaps because they are more likely to explore nonphysical options (whenever possible) when confronted with a challenge (Kappeler, Sapp, & Carter, 1992).

To accomplish these ends, research has shown that an officer needs a college experience which goes beyond the traditional "nuts and bolts" of police training. Officers are best served when they take classes from a broad curriculum emphasizing exposure to the social sciences (sociology, psychology, anthropology, political science, etc.), as well as principles of economics, management, and administration (Carter, Sapp, & Stephens, 1988). Diverse curriculums provide exposure to a wide variety of ideas and expand knowledge of how the "real world" operates. Students develop into critical thinkers, problem solvers, and more open-minded individuals. The overall college experience develops important skills, such as self-discipline, task management, improved communication skills, enhanced analytical skills, and the ability to work with others. The result is an officer who is generally better prepared to function in an organization which expects him or her to operate in support of a community policing philosophy.

Current research supports the idea that education plays a major role in how officers respond to community policing (Carter, Sapp, & Stephens, 1988; Skolnick & Bayley, 1986). In at least one study, however, an officer's level of education was not found to impact support for community policing (Weisel & Eck, 1994). "Those personnel with a high school degree were as likely to support community policing as were those with additional years of education, perhaps debunking the popular myth that officers with college educations might be more likely to embrace community policing" (p. 68). Although there is variation from one department to another, most research has indicated that officers with college education have skills and attitudes which will make them better prepared to carry out community policing. Past experience also suggests that officers with a college education tend to be more supportive of community policing.

THE PSYCHOLOGICAL CONTRACT

An employee's psychological contract is the set of beliefs that they hold "regarding promises made, accepted, and relied on between themselves and another" (Rousseau, 1995: 9). It specifies "what the individual and the organization expect to give to and receive from each other in the course of their working relationship" (Schermerhorn, Hunt, & Osborn, 1994: 51). A psychological contract consists of the expectations employees have regarding what they will contribute to their employing organization and what they expect to receive from that organization in return (Moorhead & Griffin, 1998). Psychological contracts are subjectively defined by an individual and are best understood from the perspective of the employee, not the organization (Guzzo, Noonan, & Elron, 1994).

The psychological contract is an implicit relationship between employees and employers and is essential in the functioning of an organization. "It materializes immediately upon the person's joining the police department and affects his morale, motivation, job satisfaction, and job performance" (Trojanowicz, 1980: 245). While individuals may not explicitly understand the elements of their own psychological contract, such expectations are held by the vast majority of employees. For example, a police officer may be willing to contribute loyalty, skills, time, effort, and expertise to the performance of her duties. In return, she might expect pay, benefits, job security, respect, trust, and career and promotional opportunities.

Surprisingly, the vast majority of the elements found in the psychological contracts of employees are non monetary in nature. While employees seek pay and benefits, they also seek the fulfillment of social needs, such as recognition for their achievements and contributions, security, respect, and a voice in their organization. Because the psychological contract is not explicit, identifying individual elements of importance to an employee may present a challenge for managers in an organization. An action which fulfills the psychological contract of one employee may violate the psychological contract of another. Unfortunately, it is all too common for employers to violate the psychological contracts of their employees with some frequency. Such violations may be the result of managerial ignorance, rather than malicious intent. Violations of the psychological contract tend to promote mistrust, anger, and attrition within organizations (Robinson & Rousseau, 1994); in extreme cases, violations might result in increased litigation by employees (Bies & Tyler, 1993).

Employers must always be mindful of the psychological contracts held by their employees. Organizations need to be constantly cognizant of the fact that their employees are human beings with human needs, desires, and motivations. Understanding the psychological contract makes a manager more effective. Managers who are making efforts to provide for the social needs of their employees are likely to enjoy better relationships with subordinates and peers. It is generally expected that when a psychological contract is being honored in the workplace, the result will be a high level of employee satisfaction, job performance, and occupational commitment.

Those proposing organizational changes (for example, implementing community policing) should make efforts to incorporate such considerations into their plans. In the process of bringing about change, organizations are asking their employees to modify attitudes, opinions, behaviors, and patterns of job performance. Employees who are more satisfied with their job and feel positive about relationships with superiors may be more willing to "go out on a limb" and try a new approach. These employees may offer less resistance to the idea of change.

Organizations must bear in mind that an employee's commitment "may change rather abruptly as the result of a reevaluation of the psychological contract, a reevaluation precipitated by a change in work-related conditions" (Guzzo, Noonan, & Elron, 1994: 625). When organizations change, employees may redefine what they expect in this exchange relationship with their supervisors and employer. In addition, the organization's ability to meet elements of the psychological contract may diminish as a result of structural and operational modifications. Consequently, in the process of bringing about change, it is critical that organizations take steps to ensure that they are meeting both the monetary and social needs of their employees. Although the change process offers the opportunity to improve upon efforts to fulfill the psychological contract, it may also threaten healthy employee-employer relationships.

DISTRUST OF MANAGEMENT

American police departments have historically been characterized by a chasm between "street cops" and "management cops" (Reuss-Ianni, 1983). Front-line officers are accustomed to following orders and traditionally express the belief that their superiors are out of touch with the realities they experience "on the street" (Crank, 1998; Rubinstein, 1973). A key element of many current organizational innovations is an attempted reduction in tension between managers and line-level employees (Schermerhorn, Hunt, & Osborn, 1994). These innovations seek to improve relationships, to enhance communication, to foster a sense of team, and to solicit line-level input in the decision making process.

It is difficult to identify the true root of an employee's distrust of management. While distrust may be an element of an organization's culture (discussed in the following section of this chapter), it might also be a manifestation of an individual's biography and experiences. It might be hypothesized that an employee's upbringing (i.e., raised in a union family) might influence their predisposition toward persons of occupational authority. Conversely, an employee with a family member or friend in management may be more empathetic to the challenges and difficulties confronting persons in positions of power and authority. An individual might also be engendered with various attitudinal predispositions as a result of prior job experiences, or prior experiences in their current occupational setting.

Much of the tension and distrust between management and employees may have its roots in where each group sits in the organization and the communication (or lack there of) between these various levels and units within the organization. Because they hold different positions in the organization, with different responsibilities, expectations, and demands, line employees and top management officials may not see eye-to-eye on many operational matters. Failing to understand the reasoning behind decisions made by "the boss," a line-level employee develops the belief that the superior is "out of touch" with employees. By not explaining the reason for their decisions, the actions of managers may seem capricious or whimsical (Blau, 1963). Theorists suggest that employees will be more accepting of management decisions when they have been "sold" on an idea, rather than being "told" what to do (Kuykendall &Unsinger, 1982).

The tendency for employees to distrust managers are generally reinforced through the change process. It is a simple reality that some employees dislike being given orders (Johns, 1973); by it's very nature, the change process has a tendency to increase the flow of orders from supervisors to subordinates. The very essence of traditional planned organizational change is that managers tell subordinate employees how to do their job. The process of change "achieves the uncomfortable (and doubtless unintended) objective of emphasizing the subordinate status of subordinates" (Johns, 1973: 45). Employees who dislike managers, and orders in general, may feel increasingly hostile toward management during times of organizational change.

PERCEIVING CHANGE AS A THREAT

It is common for employees to resist organizational change (Barkdoll, 1998). Despite the fact that organizations are in a constant state of flux, employees often attempt to preserve the *status quo*, for better or for worse. Change threatens stability and patterns of conduct to which employees have become accustom (Greene, 1981). Employees may resist change as a result of the "fear of the unknown" (Johns, 1973). This resistance to change is separate from employee attitudes and perceptions of the proposed alterations. It is not just a matter of employees resisting a particular proposed change within their organization; rather, it is the general tendency of employees to resist all forms of change. It should be noted that this resistance, while common, is not an automatic response to changes in the status quo (Blau, 1963). Many officers resist the principals of community policing, not because they disagree with this philosophy, but because it represents a deviation from traditional policing practices and operations (Sadd & Grinc, 1996).

Individuals enter policing with certain career aspirations (promotions, assignments to specialized units) and with certain expectations about the type of work they will be doing (fighting crime, enforcing the law). The traditional police department, like most organizations, has historically chosen to "select personnel to meet role requirements, train them to fill specific roles, and socialize them with sanctions and rewards to carry out prescribed patterns" (Katz & Kahn, 1978: 714). When community policing is introduced into a traditional police organization, employees may believe that it is a threat to these traditional role requirements, sanctions, and rewards, regardless of whether this is actually the case. Consequently, officers may resist the implementation of community policing out of the belief that it is not the type of work they want to do, were hired to do, or have been trained to do.

Because community policing represents a shift toward an organic organizational structure, it may "flatten" an organization's hierarchy and decrease specialized assignments(Steinman, 1986). Officers may feel threatened by the implementation of community policing based on the perception that it limits their future prospects for career advancement (Weisel & Eck, 1994) and/or special duty. Community policing may be viewed as a threat to the reward structures which officers have pursued throughout the course of their career. By changing "what matters" within the organization, officers may perceive that community policing will inhibit their capacity to be a "good" police officer who deserves opportunities for rewards, advancement and recognition. Officers may view community policing as a threat to their ability to do "real police work" as they assume new duties with the "grin and wave squad."

Any substantial organizational change is likely to require that personnel engage in a "relearning" process (Johns, 1973). Employees must "relearn" how to do their job, how to interact with their superiors, their peers, and their customers, and how they will be evaluated and rewarded under the new organizational structure. This relearning may generate feelings of anxiety and uncertainty, and also requires extra work on the part of employees. For these reasons, they may resist change in order to avoid being forced to relearn how to do their job and how to function in their organization. Although these perceptions of community policing as a threat may be a product of organizational culture, the beliefs of individual employees may also play an important role.

Perceiving community policing as a threat to the nature of one's job or career ambitions are not limited to patrol officers (Skogan & Hartnett, 1997). "Changes in organizational patterns may threaten the expertise of specialized groups...[or] the established power relationships in the system" (Katz & Kahn, 1978: 714). Command staff may feel that community policing threatens the power and territory they have accumulated. Such emotions revive memories of prior failures in innovative policing, in particular the experiences many departments had with team policing during the 1970's (Wycoff & Kelling, 1978). Research on the efficacy of team policing indicated that one reason for the failure of such programs was that supervisory and middle-level managers felt that team policing reduced their power and control. Because this innovation modified the traditional hierarchical, command-and-obey relationship found in the study departments, middle-level managers were engaging in passive and active sabotage (Gaines, 1993; Walker, S., 1993). Those planning for organizational change must consider the ways in which change might be viewed as a threat, and make efforts to pre-emptive such perceptions.

EMPLOYEE ATTITUDE

It has been suggested that employee attitudes and organizational culture are the greatest obstacle to police innovation (Sparrow, Moore, & Kennedy, 1990). Police officers tend to view organizational change with a healthy dose of skepticism; community policing is in no way immune from this tendency. Management strategies, organizational structures, and department philosophies seem to come and go in police organizations. Employees with more tenure are likely to have picked up on such trends and patterns. It is common for officers to label community policing as the "management reorganization of the week" (Sadd & Grinc, 1994: 39). Given this labeling, many officers see community policing as another "phase" which management is going through and which will pass with time. Consequently, officers may not believe that they actually need to modify their attitudes and behaviors in response to a mandate to adopt a community policing philosophy.

Due to the structure of community policing units, the distribution of community policing responsibilities, and the lack of understanding of the goals of community policing, it is common for officers to view this philosophy with distrust and skepticism. When community policing is organized as a specialized unit, it is seen as elite and engaging in tasks other than "real police work" (Eck, 1992; Wilkinson, Stemen, & Allen, 1997). Specialized community policing units often grant officers the ability to flex their work hours, select their leave days, and work at their own direction, without being interrupted by routine calls for service (Wilkinson & Rosenbaum, 1994). Given this arrangement, other officers perceive community policing as a "fluff" assignment; the units are viewed with disdain and, in all likelihood, a healthy dose of jealousy by other officers within the organizations (Walker, S., 1993).

Truly embracing community policing would require many police officers to make fundamental changes in their skills, motivations, and opportunities, and in their willingness to develop partnerships with the community they serve (Sparrow, 1988; Wilkinson & Rosenbaum, 1994). Agencies which ignore personnel attitudes in planning an organizational change run the risk of ensuring failure. Officers forced to accept a new innovation without an understanding of the innovation are likely to respond with apathy, frustration, resentment, fear, and other factors which might impede successful change (Lurigio & Rosenbaum, 1994). Many police officers went into policing to be a "law enforcer" and a "crook catcher" (Gaines, 1993); as such, they may have difficulty adapting to the "service role" created by community policing.

Until the beliefs, perceptions, attitudes, and behaviors of officers are transformed to levels more compatible with community policing, resistance is likely and its success will be limited (Lurigio & Rosenbaum, 1994). Planners and managers must attempt to predict the employees' response to proposed change and to determine the best course of action in light of these circumstances. Employee cooperation can be improved through: allowing participation from those most likely to be affected by the change (Wycoff & Skogan, 1994b); training employees to operate under a new dominant philosophy; clarifying the goals and means by which employees can succeed in carrying out their redefined duties; and, educating employees to understand the rationale and benefits for implementing change. Individual attitudes can shift from a traditional orientation to an orientation more consistent with community policing

(Wycoff & Skogan, 1994a); however, such a transition takes time, forethought, and patients.

INDIVIDUAL SOCIALIZATION AND COMMUNITY POLICING

A number of demographic variables may mitigate how employees respond to change, including police officers being asked to embrace community policing. In addition, the ways in which employees have traditionally viewed their occupation, supervisors, and employing organization may generate automatic responses to certain organizational initiatives. Police officers may resist community policing not because they disagree with this philosophy, but rather because it is a "knee-jerk" reaction to distrust managers, to be apprehensive of modifications in the *status quo*, to perceive change as a threat, and to fear the unknown elements (how do I do my job, to whom am I accountable, how will I be evaluated, how to I work cooperatively, etc.) which accompany major organizational change.

The data analyzed in this text only allow for limited assessment of the role individual socialization might play in organizational change. The quantitative findings provide the race, level of education, gender, and age (in this case, operationalized as years of service) of a group of police officers. These elements have been statistically examined to determine what, if any, affects they have on attitudes toward community policing. Additional insights into the role which individual socialization plays in organizational change may be obtained from various qualitative data sources, including field observations, focus group interviews, and semi-structured interviews.

CHAPTER 4

The Role of Organizational Culture

In recent decades scholars have spent considerable time studying police culture and exploring the notion that there is a distinct "police subculture." Most of these studies have emphasized the extreme elements of police work, such as the use of force, coercion, danger, and corruption (Bittner, 1970; Kappeler, Sluder, & Alpert, 1998; Klockars, 1985; Skolnick, 1994; Skolnick & Fyfe, 1993). While these issues may be of great interest to social scientists, policy makers, and police planners, they overlook the broader themes which define the occupational culture of policing (Crank, 1998). Studies of police culture have tended to view this phenomenon in a pejorative fashion. Because they have been focused upon the "dark side" of policing, they have not emphasized that police officers, like virtually every occupational group, have an occupational culture. At its core, the organizational culture of policing differs little from that of many other occupations.

This section will define and explore organizational culture as a concept important to the social scientific study of organizations. Considerations will be given to the challenges associated with changing organizational culture. The culture of police organizations as it relates to community policing will also be discussed.

DEFINING ORGANIZATIONAL CULTURE

In the past two decades there has been an increase in the level of research into the role organizational culture plays in the study of organizations and their behavior. Despite the emergence of interest in organizational culture across disciplinary lines, there is not a broadly accepted definition of this concept (Moorhead & Griffin, 1998). Van Maanen and Schein (1977) offered one of the earliest definitions in suggesting that organizational culture consists of:

> ...long standing rules of thumb, a somewhat special language and ideology that help edit a member's everyday experience, shared standards of relevance as to the critical aspects of the work that is being accomplished, matter-of-fact prejudices, models for social etiquette and demeanor, certain customs and rituals suggestive of how members are to relate to colleagues, subordinates, superiors, and outsiders, and...plain "horse sense" regarding what is appropriate and "smart" behavior within the organization and what is not. (p. 1-2).

Others have opted for more succinct characterizations of organizational culture. Ouchi defines organizational culture as "a set of symbols, ceremonies, and myths that communicates the underlying values and beliefs of that organization to its employees" (1981: 41). Peters and Waterman state it is "a dominant and coherent set of shared values conveyed by such symbolic means as stories, myths, legends, slogans, anecdotes, and fairy tales" (1982: 103). Schein provides that it is "the pattern of basic assumptions that a given group has invented, discovered, or developed in learning to cope with its problems of external adaptation and internal integration" (1985: 14). Deal and Kennedy simply suggest that it is "the way we do things around here" (1982: 4).

In an attempt to provide a broader definition of organizational culture, Moorhead and Griffin (1998) examined the existing definitions and identified three comment attributes. First, definitions generally refer to the values held by individual members of an organization; these values delineate what is good and bad, right and wrong, and acceptable and unacceptable behavior within the context of the organization. Second, values comprising an organization's culture tend to be taken for granted. In other words, the values are not explicitly written; rather, they are "an implicit part of an employee's [occupational] values and beliefs" (p. 511). Finally, organizational values are typically communicated through symbolic means; they are transmitted through stories, anecdotes, myths and legends. Merging these three attributes into a single definition, Moorhead and Griffin offer that:

> Organizational culture is a set of shared values, often taken for granted, that help people in an organization understand which actions are considered acceptable and which are considered unacceptable. Often, these values are communicated through stories and other symbolic means. (1998: 513-514).

Another important element of organizational culture is its tendency to endure (Trice & Beyer, 1993). Organizational cultures tend to exist independently of individual employees; it is a tradition which transcends the duration of an individual's employment with the organization. Although employees may enter and leave an organization, its culture remains stable despite this turnover. While organizational cultures are not entirely static (they do transition in response to external pressures, changes in the law, changes in markets and industries, etc.), sweeping cultural changes are difficult to realize in short periods of time (Sparrow, 1988). This differentiates organizational culture from organizational climate.

An organization's climate refers to "current situations in an organization and the linkages among work groups, employees, and work performance" (Moorhead & Griffin, 1998: 516). Organizational climate is more analogous to individual socialization; it refers to how individuals approach their occupation and interact with others. Organizational culture refers to how work is done in an organization and how employees interact in the context of their job. Through changes in recruitment and selection, organizational climates can be altered in a short period of time, while persons seeking to change an organization's culture overnight are likely to encounter strong resistance.

TRANSMITTING ORGANIZATIONAL CULTURE

Organizational culture persists because it perpetuates itself from generation to generation. As new employees enter an organization, they are "socialized" to adopt a particular role and operational style within the context of the work environment (Goodman, Bazerman, & Conlon, 1980).

According to Van Maanen and Schein, "organizational socialization is then the process by which an individual acquires the social knowledge and skills necessary to assume an organizational role" (1977: 3). Socialization is the process by which an individual learns the customary, correct, and desirable behaviors, practices, and interactions for an organization. It is through this socialization process that organizational culture is transmitted from one generation of employees to the next. The socialization process may occur through both formal (educational and training programs) and informal (peer influences) mechanisms (Trice & Beyer, 1993).

New police officers are in no way immune to socialization as they begin their career. From the academy to their field training program to the briefing room, officers are exposed to images and ideas about what it means to be a police officer in their organization. Police academies "continue to be psychological crucibles in which occupational identities are forged" (Bahn, 1984: 392). New officers are expected to dress and behave in a uniform manner. It quickly becomes apparent that the best way to survive the experience is to maintain a low profile (i.e., avoiding any behavior which will draw attention from instructors). New officers entering "the field" are then paired with more experienced peers who serve as mentor, instructor, guidance counselor, and critic. This field training process might further reinforce a set of occupational expectations in the new employee (Van Maanen, 1974). Once the officer has completed formal training, socialization is reinforced through informal interaction with peers during pre-shift briefing, in the locker room, in the station house, on meal breaks, and outside of work (Pogrebin & Poole, 1988).

While it is necessary to train and socialize employees (to teach them "how we do things around here"), efforts to change an organizational culture may to some degree be thwarted by these processes. A manager seeking to change an organization's culture may initiate certain structural changes, such as instituting new policies or procedures, or making changes in the organization's goals, mission, or philosophy. To reinforce these structural changes, modifications might be made in the recruitment, selection, and (formal) training of new employees in an effort to bring "new blood" to the organization. Unfortunately, the success of these efforts may be tempered when this new blood mixes with the "old guard" and is taught "how we do things around here." In the context of the implementation of community policing, new officers with a college education may be open to the idea of community collaboration and problem solving endeavors. If it is easier for these new employees to fit in with their peers by utilizing traditional police practices, they may be less inclined to operate in a manner consistent with the philosophy of community policing.

ORGANIZATIONAL CULTURE AND CHANGE

Organizational culture is not always an undesirable phenomenon. Culture in the workplace has the capacity to generate a sense of solidarity among employees. It may serve to strengthen an organization's productivity and level of service. Modern management books are filled with examples of how culture has improved organizations in all sectors of employment (see generally, Moorhead & Griffin, 1998; Peters & Waterman, 1982; Trice & Beyer, 1993). When managers view the organizational culture as beneficial, an important goal would be to identify ways in which to reinforce and support the existing culture. At other times, organizational culture is viewed as something which must be altered in order to improve productivity and service.

Organizational culture can be both an aid and a barrier in the process of enacting organizational change (Moorhead & Griffin, 1998; Trice & Beyer, 1993). First, organizational change might be realized by capitalizing on the existing organizational culture. Recognizing that an organization's culture is deeply intrenched and resistant to change, a pragmatic manager might seek to work within this culture in order bring about change. The success of this strategy is contingent upon the assumption that proposed change is not contrary to the fundamental beliefs of the culture. Second, managers might bring about change by capitalizing on the informal socialization process. Once again, by recognizing that an embedded culture exists, a manager might attempt to ensure that new employees receive much of their socialization from select co-workers. An example of this in policing is the use of Field Training Officers. New officers are assigned to work with experienced officers to receive additional formal training after the completion of a police academy. The careful selection of trainers allows police managers to limit the negative socialization influences to which new employees are exposed.

It should be noted that there is not a consensus among scholars regarding resistance to organizational change. Blau (1963) examined change in the context of bureaucratic organizations. Based on his research, he concluded that "bureaucratic conditions engender favorable attitudes toward change, and not necessarily resistance to change, as is often assumed" (p. 232). While "ritualistic conformity" to traditional practices may be common, Blau found that resistance to change was not an automatic response in the organizations he observed.

At times a planned organizational change might require not only adjustments to an organization's policies, procedures, and structures, but also to its culture. If a planned change runs contrary to the existing culture, managers have no choice but to attempt to bring about a change in this culture. Successfully changing organizational culture under such circumstances may be the most difficult element in the change process. On this issue, Moorhead and Griffin note that:

> Culture resists change for all the reasons it is a powerful influence on behavior– it embodies the basic values in the firm...When managers attempt to change a culture, they are attempting to change people's basic assumptions about what is and is not appropriate behavior in the organization (1998: 530).

For these reasons and more, changing an organization's culture is a long, drawn out, slow, and difficult process (Trice & Beyer, 1993).

Culture plays a significant role in organizational change. Ott (1989) identifies several important assumptions which are frequently made in the study of organizational culture. Culture is assumed to be unique to each organization. It is a social construct which provides a framework within which members understand and interpret events and interactions within the workplace. Finally, organizational culture is highly influential in influencing the occupational behaviors exhibited by an organization's members. These assumptions, if accepted as truth, demonstrate the powerful nature of organizational culture in the change process.

Viewed in this manner, organizational change is not just about changing structure, policy, and process; it is also about changing the assumptions, beliefs, and attitudes of an organization's members. As such, culture may be one of the most significant stumbling blocks on the road to successful change. An organization's structure, policy, and process are tangible elements which can be identified, enumerated, and altered. An organization's culture is intangible and far more resistant to attempted change.

ORGANIZATIONAL CULTURE AND POLICE ORGANIZATIONS

As noted earlier, much has been written about the various dimensions of police culture, in particular the "dark side" of policing (issues of force, coercion, deviance, and corruption). It is important to distinguish between these studies of *the culture of police officers*, and this text, which in part explores *the organizational culture of police agencies*. At times it may be difficult to distinguish between these two elements as they have a reciprocal relationship and a mutual dependence.

Studies of the culture of police organizations tend to be focused on social elements which might be found in any organization. This text examines elements of organizational culture in the context of a police organization (i.e., the tension between line officers and managers, the image of policing, the way police officers perform their duties, etc.). These elements might be generally observable in all members of a specific organization. They are also not limited to police organizations and analogous elements might be observed in studying the culture of virtually any organization.

In contrast, studies of the culture of police officers typically focus on behavioral traits and qualities which tend to be more unique to police officers (i.e., rationalizing the use of force, coercion, or authority in the pursuit of specific outcomes). The culture of police officers may vary within an organization. Some "pockets" of a large police agency are often found to be accepting of deviant behavioral patterns, yet the majority of that agency's employees may view such conduct with disdain. While studies of the organizational culture of police agencies are concerned with the entire agency, studies of the culture of police officers may be concerned with only a small subset of employees.

The shared occupational culture of a set of employees can represent the greatest barrier to enacting change within an organization (Stamper, 1992; Sparrow, Moore & Kennedy, 1990). Because elements of an organizational culture can be so deeply ingrained in the basic assumptions of employees (i.e., that as a police officer I am a *law enforcer*), successful organizational change becomes very difficult to realize (Sparrow, 1988). When proposed change runs contrary to the organization's culture, it may fail in any organization (a police force, Microsoft, GM, etc.), regardless of intent, benevolence, and implementation strategies. While there is no one organizational culture common to all police agencies (Harrison, 1998), certain general observations may be made; most of these generalizations are not limited to police officers or organizations.

Police agencies, as any other organization, have a rich and complex organizational culture. A discussion of this culture could fill a book in its own right. The following is a brief discussion of the key themes in the organizational culture of police agencies. This list is not exhaustive; rather, it highlights the facets of this culture which are most important in this text. While these themes may manifest themselves in the actions and conduct of individual employees, they are (at least to some extent) a product of the organizational culture of policing.

Labor-Management Tensions

A characteristic found in many organizations is a tension between line-employees and managers (Moorhead & Griffin, 1998). Police organizations exhibit this problem as agencies struggle to deal with the tension between "street cops" and "management cops" (Reuss-Ianni, 1983). Social science research has yielded a substantial body of literature detailing the organizational culture of police agencies and how this culture plays out in the management and administration of these agencies (Manning, 1997b; Reuss-Ianni, 1983; Rubinstein, 1973; Van Maanen, 1974; Wilson, 1968). These works have demonstrated the "ease with which rank-and-file officers dismiss efforts to influence their behavior" on the part of their supervisors (Goldstein, 1990: 29).

Street cops tend to express confusion over the actions taken by "the bosses" (Reuss-Ianni, 1983). Faced with different pressures, obligations, and responsibilities, street and management cops develop different interests; in some situations, these differing interests can bring about competition (Steinman, 1986). Caught in the middle of this labor-management tension is the patrol sergeant, who becomes a *defacto* mediator between these two components of the organization (Trojanowicz, 1980). The tension and "distance" between street cops and management cops tend to be proportional with the size of the agency (Greene, Alpert, & Styles, 1992). Larger organizations tend to have larger hierarchies, more centralization, and more specialization, all of which can contribute to labor-management tensions.

Harrison (1998) notes that "...tension played out due to the management vs. street cultural characteristic can be significant. *It can become the root cause of distrust of new initiatives by the rank and file officers*" (emphasis added). Because tension can lead to distrust, the process of organizational change may be impeded by the reflexive action of line personnel. Change fails not because it is change, but because it is proposed by management and is, therefore, automatically suspect. Considering the animosity and distrust which exist between "street cops" and "management cops," the prospects for change can seem rather daunting. Within this setting, "many of the exhortations for change in policing do, indeed, look naive" (Goldstein, 1990: 29) and overly simplistic.

Changing this relationship becomes particularly problematic with programs that seek to encourage participatory management or creativity by patrol officers. Traditionally, the role of police managers has been to stifle creativity and nonconformity among line personnel (Kelling & Bratton, 1993). Community policing often requires that supervisors relax their control over the discretion and actions of the personnel they supervise. One possible way to overcome employee resistance and to loosen supervisory control is through employee participation in the management process. By integrating line personnel in the planning and decision making process, resistance due to labor-management tension may be minimized (Harrison, 1998).

Unfortunately, due to their rigid and bureaucratic nature, police organizations often do not solicit such employee involvement in the decision making process (Weisel & Eck, 1994). Traditional managers may be uncomfortable with the idea of sharing their authority and control with subordinates (Moorhead & Griffin, 1998; Swanson, Territo, & Taylor, 1998). Despite the common perception that "participatory management" is an empty concept, research has shown that this is not always the case. "When they are included, officers can emerge as motivated planners and problem solvers" (Wilkinson & Rosenbaum, 1994: 124). Although police organizations have traditionally been oriented toward strictly one-way management, it may be possible for agencies to move toward a structure in which decision making and management are shared processes.

Image

> I have repeatedly found that the greatest barrier in opening the minds of police officers to problem-oriented policing is that they continue to cling to notions of policing that have been abandoned by more progressive police agencies and officers (Goldstein, 1990: 178-179).

One of the barriers in implementing community policing is the perception by police officers that this approach is "soft" on crime and that it does not involve "real" police work (Sadd & Grinc, 1996). This concern may be especially acute where community policing is a specialized function. Members of the specialized unit may become marginalized from the department as a whole; they may be viewed as "empty holsters" or the "grin and wave squad" by their peers (Skogan & Hartnett, 1997). From this perspective, community policing only gains legitimacy among officers where it is perceived as effective in controlling and preventing crime (Sadd & Grinc, 1994)

Individuals commence a career with a set of expectations about the work they will be doing and the role they will fulfill (Bahn, 1984). These expectations are a product of their early socialization and cultural images of what that career will entail (Katz & Kahn, 1978). In the case of policing, individuals may have been acculturated, selected, and trained to fill a more traditional "crime fighting/crook catching" occupational role (Gaines, 1993; Lurigio & Rosenbaum, 1994). When their organization attempts to reorient itself toward community policing, the role expectations of the individual employee may no longer be fulfilled. Officers might rebel against programs or policies which they perceive to place them in the roll of "social worker" rather than "crime fighter."

Many of the perceptions, beliefs and expectations held by the neophyte employee are inaccurate and unrealistically high (Wanous, 1977). Policing is an occupation which is not immune to this problem. It has long been noted that the image of police officers portrayed by the media is far different from the realities of this occupation (Haney & Manzolatti, 1977). Police officers in the media spend the majority of their time investigating major cases as a vigilant "crime fighter." To the contrary, the vast majority of the work done by police officers is related to order maintenance and service provision, not crime (Reiss, 1971, Skolnick, 1994; Wilson, 1968). These distorted media images may color the perceptions and role expectations of a new police officer. Even after a new police officer has come to understand that the reality of their job is far from the images and expectations they held when they began their career, the officer may still cling to the notion that they are a "crime fighter" and nothing else. Any task which does not fall under the classification of fighting crime is viewed with disdain (Manning, 1997a).

Traditional Police Operations

Earlier sections of this chapter have discussed police operations under traditional and community policing paradigms. Nonetheless, it is necessary to briefly reiterate the tension between these two orientations in the context of the organizational culture of police agencies. Traditional police operations were reactive and call driven. When a call for service was received, police officers responded rapidly and then spent as little time as possible handling the situation so that they could be available for the next call for service. When officers were not handling a call, they were expected to patrol their assigned area in order to prevent crimes from occurring. Police officers viewed themselves as crime fighters, law enforcers, and crook catchers. As such, they were the experts on crime and had little need for input from the community they served. Because they were hired, trained, and paid to enforce the law, police officers did not need citizens telling them how to perform their duties.

Police agencies were closed systems; while some information may have flowed in from the community, very little information was ever released back out to the community. Agencies were structured in a bureaucratic and hierarchical fashion. Employees observed a strict command and control relationship between the ranks. Within the organization, communication flowed up the chain of command, but rarely back down or across divisions. Police supervisors and executives viewed their subordinates as liabilities who needed to be controlled and managed. Policies and procedures were cumbersome and detailed in order to minimize the discretion exercised by line-level employees. Front line officers were expected to follow established procedures in carrying out their duties; there was little room for creativity or innovation.

Community policing does not completely eliminate some of these characteristics of traditional police operations. By it's very nature, policing will always require a certain degree of deference to ranked officers and police agencies will always need to have the capacity to rapidly respond to emergency situations. Despite these factors, community policing alters some of the fundamental dimensions of how police officers and organizations operate. Community policing requires officers to proactively identify problems and quality of life issues in the neighborhood they patrol. Where there are numerous problems or issues, officers may turn to local residents to help them establish priorities (in effect, admitting that the police are not always the experts on crime and safety). Once problems and issues have been identified, police officers are expected to collaborate with citizens and other governmental agencies to seek out and enact permanent solutions. Enforcing the law becomes a means, not an end, toward the goals the police are pursuing.

Organizational structure must also be altered if community policing is to work. Most prominently, front-line officers need to exercise creativity and innovation in generating solutions to community problems. To do this, officers must also be given the freedom to exercise discretion and organizations must develop a capacity to accept some failure from their officer's efforts. While supervisors still maintain authority over officers, the relationship becomes more reciprocal as officers look to superiors for support and guidance in their community policing endeavors. Communication ideally travels uniformly across all levels and divisions of the organization's hierarchy. In addition, information is openly shared with community residents.

If community policing is to succeed, there must be a dramatic change in the occupational culture of police organizations. Prospective employees will need to fully understand the nature of the job they wish to enter. Selection practices must be modified to ensure that new employees possess skills which are complementary for the success of community policing. Formal training and informal socialization must be modified so that officers learn how to carry out community policing and come to accept that it is a better way for them to serve their community. Relationships with supervisors must shift from adversarial to collegial. Some of the fundamental dimensions of what it means to be a police officer must be redefined. For all of these reasons, implementing community policing requires attention to more than just the "nuts and bolts" of redesigning deployment plans and altering the wording of an agency's philosophy and mission statement.

ORGANIZATIONAL CULTURE AND COMMUNITY POLICING

As one would find in any organization, police organizations have distinct cultures which help define how employees behave, interact, and carry out their occupational responsibilities. While this culture may be a benefit in general, it can present a significant obstacle in the pursuit of organizational change. "Police organizations have been some of the most intractable of public bureaucracies, capable of resisting and ultimately thwarting change efforts" (Greene, Bergman & McLaughlin, 1994: 93). The organizational culture of police departments is one of the greatest contributors to the resistance observed by Greene and his colleagues.

Ideally, studying organizational culture as it relates to organizational change would be conducted using data from multiple agencies. This would allow the researcher to assess the culture in each agency and test if/how it impacted the subsequent success of organizational change. This text is limited because it only includes data from a single agency; this does not allow for such a comparison to be made. In the absence of data from multiple agencies it is possible, to a degree, to assess the role organizational culture plays in organizational change.

Respondents in this study answered items which indicated their perceptions of the culture in their police agency (i.e., level of participatory management, degree of positive relations between rank and file, strength of management objectives). Respondents who report a "healthy" organization culture can be contrasted with those who report an "unhealthy" organizational culture. It is then possible to determine if a respondent's assessment of the agency's organizational culture in any way predicts attitudes toward community policing. In this way, the relationship between these factors may be assessed and illuminated.

Some scholars have contended that changing organizational culture is a relatively easy process if it is simply planned and carried out in a rational manner (Deal & Kennedy, 1982; Ouchi, 1981; Peters & Waterman, 1982). Despite these claims, others have asserted that when there are abrupt changes to an organization's culture (as a result of intentional efforts or through unforseen circumstances), conflicts, firings, attrition, and power struggles often occur (Haught, 1997). These events are not adequately addressed by the "planned change" proponents.

In reality, changes in organizational culture may be more accurately attributed to attrition, rather than a "sanitary" re-socialization process. As Kilmann, et al., note (1986): "Because they are unwilling to part with their own beliefs and submit to the ideology of the new leaders– hence relinquishing their power– the old guard is more often purged than socialized to a new set of beliefs" (p. 225). Weisel and Eck (1994) quote German physicist Max Plank, who observed that: "A new scientific truth does not triumph by convincing its opponents and making them see the light, but rather because its opponents eventually die, and a new generation grows up" (p. 72). Although it is possible to modify organizational culture, sweeping changes made in an expeditious fashion may be difficult in the absence of simultaneous changes in the organization's membership.

CHAPTER 5

The Role of Organizational Planning

Individual socialization and organizational culture may be largely outside of the control of planners seeking to bring about change. There are, however, a number of issues which are within the direct control of an organization. If proper attention is given to these manageable issues, police organizations may exercise a certain degree of influence over the outcome of change efforts. Chapters 3 and 4 of this book reviewed the most salient human and behavioral factors which might impede successful organizational change. This chapter will examine those factors which are related to the way in which change is planned and structured, and which organizations have the capacity to manipulate; if not properly addressed, these factors might act as barriers to successful change.

Specifically, the chapter examines those elements of the planning and implementation process which are generally within an organization's control. If the planning process is not properly executed there is an increased risk that organizations will encounter barriers in the change process. Once an organization has resolved the key elements of a planned change, it is necessary to communicate these decisions to line level employees and provide clarity where necessary. In the process of implementing change, agencies must consider ways in which they might foster support among line-level employees. In addition, organizations must consider how broader forms of organizational change might require a reconsideration of accountability patterns, employee evaluation and reward systems, and the relationship between supervisors and subordinates. These factors have been persistent problems for police organizations seeking to implement community policing.

PLANNING FOR CHANGE

> With any sizeable programmatic or organizational change there is always the risk of serious setbacks or delays in achieving the optimum level of implementation due to poor planning, employee or community resistance, or other factors. (Wilkinson & Rosenbaum, 1994: 110).

Organizational change may be either adaptive or purposive. Adaptive change occurs in response to changes in an organization's environment (i.e., news laws, budgetary constraints, fluctuating community expectations, emerging client demands, etc.). Adaptation is a "response by an organization to its external environment" (Zhao, 1996: 14). Planned change occurs when an organization's leaders intend to alter a specific facet of policy, procedure, structure, or operation. In contrast to adaptive change, which is driven by external forces, the impetus behind purposive change is internal. Given that the stimulus originates from within the organization, purposive change efforts typically have a longer planning phase than adaptive efforts (Hudzik & Cordner, 1983). Unfortunately, a longer planning period is not always feasible and does not guarantee success.

Research literature from the past fifteen years is replete with anecdotal examples of successful planned organizational change in police agencies in major American cities such as Madison, WI (Wycoff & Skogan, 1994), Chicago (Skogan & Hartnett, 1997), Newport News, NJ (Eck & Spelman, 1987), Flint, MI (Trojanowicz, Kappeler, Gaines, & Bucqueroux, 1998), and other large communities (Skolnick & Bayley, 1986). Despite these success stories, organizational change in American policing is more accurately characterized by adaptation (Zhao, 1996). While it may be better if the impetus for organizational change is internal, purposive organizational change always runs the risk of falling into the trap laid out by Hudzik & Cordner (1983); too often, agencies may still be planning when a change has already commenced. Furthermore, police agencies exist in a very tenuous environment in which well planned purposive organizational change (or even well-formulated adaptive change) is not always possible.

Even where there is sufficient time and resources, pre-action planning may not be sufficient to ensure effective organizational change. In the 1970's the Dallas Police Department initiated a comprehensive overhaul of its organization in an attempt to improve the quality of service it provided. The project was characterized by pre-action planning, a well designed and coordinated implementation effort, strong financial backing, a panel of expert consultants, and a relatively long (five years) time line for completion. Despite these beneficial characteristics, "[t]he Dallas department encountered problems at every stage of the innovation process" (Wycoff & Kelling, 1978:76). In the final analysis, the principal investigators concluded that although the efforts had been admirable, there were still numerous human and organizational factors which had not been accounted for in the planning process.

Thus, while change may be more successful where efforts are purposively initiated from within the organization and when there is a period of pre-change planning, success is not guaranteed. Planners may believe that the efforts they have made in advance of implementation are thorough and comprehensive, yet problems may still emerge which confound and ameliorate such consideration.

PLANNING CHANGE IN POLICE AGENCIES

There are a number of general reasons why both purposive and adaptive change efforts may fail in police agencies. First, even when agencies attempt to rectify historical problems with their structures and internal relationships (i.e., by attempting to decentralize authority and empower individual officers), they often rely on traditional planning methods. By relying on existing mechanisms of centralized planning, agencies may restrict officer input, thus creating resentment and withdrawal by those most likely to be affected by the change (Wilkinson & Rosenbaum, 1994). Analogously, when management handpicks employees to be involved in the planning process, the remainder of the workforce may mistrust those involved and view management's efforts at involving employees as disingenuous (Polzin, 1997). Thus, the first challenge facing a planner is to develop a planning mechanism which will not elicit automatic resistance from employees.

Second, even where affected employees are allowed to participate in the planning process, there must be a sufficiently long implementation phase before results may reasonably be expected to materialize. Generally, the more rigid the organization and the more radical the change, the longer the implementation phase should be (Wilkinson & Rosenbaum, 1994). Seagrave (1996) surveyed police executives in Canada to assess their views toward community policing. She found that while leaders were supportive of the shift toward community policing, they argued for a gradual, slow, and incremental change process. When an organization and its personnel have a long history of operating in a specific fashion, it may take a great deal of time to change this manner of operation. The larger an organization (Greene, Alpert & Styles, 1992) and the more formal and complex its bureaucracy, the longer it may take for change to be realized (Wilkinson & Rosenbaum, 1994). In writing on the issue of change in large organizations (at times termed "organizational inertia"), Sparrow (1988: 2) makes the analogy that "...a huge ship can nevertheless be turned by a small rudder. It just takes time, and it requires the rudder to be set steadfastly for the turn throughout the whole turning period."

A third reason planned change may fail is simply because the proposed change cannot result in a realistic attainment of the desired outcomes. At times, planners overestimate the outcomes their programs might achieve (Eck, 1992) and administrators may miscalculate how much they can produce with their resources and personnel. As Merton (1936) noted, social action often yields unanticipated consequences (some good and some bad). Such unanticipated consequences may overshadow or occur in place of the results which had been intended by a planned organizational change.

The question police agencies must ask themselves is: "How do we as an organization define success in the context of our planned community policing implementation?" The answer to this question is unclear and somewhat unique in each agency. Herman Goldstein suggests that an agency making even limited efforts toward long-term problem resolution is better than an agency which does nothing, writing that: "Any movement toward increased concern with substantive problems is better than none at all" (1990:177). Perhaps the standard by which success is measured should not be the successful implementation of community policing (however an agency chooses to define this concept). It may be more realistic to be satisfied if officers carry out their duties with a greater concern for substantive community problems, and therefore determine that a community policing effort was successful.

A fourth reason change is difficult in American policing is a product of crime and justice in the 1990's. According to many police executives (Zhao, Thurman & Lovrich, 1995) and scholars (Goldstein, 1990; Kelling & Moore, 1988), organizational change is a more pressing issue now than at any other time during the history of modern policing. Unfortunately, in the current era of falling crime rates, it may be difficult to see the need for such change. Police executives may have a difficult time convincing their officers that change is necessary; why should we redefine "the way we do things around here" when we seem to be experiencing some measure of success? City leaders and community residents may be reluctant to see the need to finance proposed change requiring the allocation of additional financial resources; why allocate additional money when there is no apparent need? For those who wish to believe that the police can have such a dramatic impact on crime rates, it might appear that there is no need to modify contemporary policing practices.

Finally, community policing innovations frequently give rise to a fifth reason why organizational change fails: lack of clarity. A common complaint heard from patrol officers in agencies attempting to implement some form of community policing is that their organization has not been sufficiently clear about the nature of their new job, how they will be evaluated, to whom they are accountable, and how they are to carry out their duties (Sadd & Grinc, 1996). Police agencies need to provide their officers with a clear idea of how they are operationalizing community policing in their organization.

The operational parameters of community policing are intentionally vague in order to allow agencies sufficient latitude in determining the style most appropriate for the agencies. Unfortunately, this ambiguity often leaves line officers with an insufficient understanding of their role and responsibility under a community policing paradigm. Officers affected by the implementation of community policing need to understand this concept, both in theory and in practice. They need to understand the goals of community policing and how these goals fit into the future of the organization (Walker, S., 1993). Agency structure needs to be designed to support community policing efforts. Accountability, performance measures, and reward systems need to be fashioned to encourage officers to perform their duties in a manner which is consistent with community policing objectives.

Changing police organizations is difficult and complex. "It is complex because alteration of a department's philosophy of policing will simultaneously affects numerous other variables" (Oettmeier & Brown, 1988: 128). Change is difficult because it affects the skills employees will use in performing their duties, the leadership and management styles employed by supervisors, and the values, goals and objectives embraced by officers. Experience suggests that the process of planning for and implementing community policing is not an easy undertaking. There is no magic formula for successfully bringing about change in an organization; each agency will experience unique successes and failures (Goldstein, 1990). The key is for managers, planners, and executives to engage in as much pre-action planning as possible, to provide ample training, to communicate with affected employees, and to be prepared to encounter barriers to their efforts. They must have realistic visions of what their efforts will accomplish and be prepared to deal with unforseen challenges and opportunities.

CLARITY

> It is also frequently the case that throughout transitional periods for organizations, police at all levels lack a clear understanding of the new role called for by community policing. Departments that are adopting community policing are likely, at the outset, to be uncertain or still experimental about many aspects of what they are doing, giving officers and their sergeants, at best, mixed messages. (Skogan & Hartnett, 1997: 73)

Officers new to a community policing work environment are often critical of the lack of clarity provided by their organization in relation to the mission, goals, and objectives of such innovations. Officers consistently reflect little understanding of the goals and means associated with community policing innovations. This lack of understanding can result in resistance as officers struggle to understand exactly what they are supposed to be doing (Sadd & Grinc, 1996). Such confusion is common in the context of a changing organization (Trojanowicz, Kappeler, Gaines, & Bucqueroux, 1998); problems arise when this confusion is not clarified in a reasonably timely manner. Officers who feel discombobulated due to insufficient clarity may resist change or may simply be unable to carry out new responsibilities because they do not know how to do so.

Officers need to have a sense of clarity about a number of key points: they need to understand community policing in theory and in practice; they need to be aware of available resources and support which will enable them to operate in a community policing environment; they need to understand the nexus between their conduct and evaluations of their performance; and, they need to understand why their organization is adopting a community policing orientation (Sadd & Grinc, 1996; Skogan & Hartnett, 1997; Trojanowicz, Kappeler, Gaines, & Bucqueroux, 1998; Walker, S., 1993).

In the absence of clear objectives and sufficient training in problem-solving methods, community policing officers tend to revert to the traditional operational styles with which they are most comfortable (Sadd & Grinc, 1996). "In general, future behavior is predicted by past behavior...people will go on doing what they have always done...This picture is neither cynical nor pessimistic; it is simply reality" (Territo, 1980: 396-397). Problems arise when officers attempt to use traditional strategies (citations, arrests, etc.) to solve community problems. Such strategies may be incongruent with the philosophical underpinnings of community policing. In addition, a perceived lack of clarity may generate confusion, resentment, resistance, and/or apathy on the part of those employees affected by an organizational change. Planners, managers, and executives often believe that sufficient clarity has been provided to affected employees. Unfortunately, if employees do not share this sentiment, successful organizational change may prove to be elusive (Sadd & Grinc, 1996).

Goffman (1959) describes how individuals learn "routines," or procedures to handle complex situations. Routines are used by individuals in an effort to negotiate uncertain social encounters in a predictable manner. These routines assist the "performer" in presenting the desired image to the "audience." Through the formal and informal socialization processes, new officers learn a set of routines which will guide them in performing their duties on a daily basis. Under a traditional policing paradigm, examples of such routines might include making a traffic stop, making an arrest, handling a neighborhood or family disturbance, and taking a report (Manning, 1997a).

Problems arise when there is a shift from a traditional to a community policing paradigm within an organization. New routines must be developed in order to guide officers through salient community policing activities, such as planning and leading a neighborhood meeting, networking with employees in other government agencies, critically analyzing a situation, and, perhaps most elusive, solving a community problem. If officers are not provided with adequate training and socialization (i.e., the SARA method, best practices, leadership by example), it may be very difficult for them to develop these new routines. If these new routines are not developed, the officers might continue to use those routines with which are most familiar: crime fighting routines. Although such routines are not inherently "bad," they are not always consistent with the philosophy of community policing.

At times, police executives and planners may wish to be somewhat ambiguous in describing the full nature of their plans. This intentional ambiguity gives provides flexibility as they "feel out" the specifics of an innovation. While innovation must preserve some flexibility to allow for fine-tuning, this must not be done at the expense of those officers most affected by change. If officers are expected to produce under a new system, they must understand the goals, objectives, and mission of the innovation. Officers need to be provided with sufficient resources and training to achieve success in their efforts. Affected employees need an understanding of for what, and to whom, they will be accountable. It is unreasonable to expect employees to change their work habits if the employees do not understand the "why, what, how, & for whom" of said change.

It is a daunting task to take employees who have been selected, trained, and socialized to perform one task, and to tell them they must now perform in a manner which fundamentally changes how they will operate and the ends they are to pursue. Several authors have likened the transition to community policing to a battle for the very "hearts and minds" of the ordinary patrol officer (Lurigio & Skogan, 1994; Sadd &

Grinc, 1994). If community policing is to be successful in an organization, managers must truly win over the hearts and minds of their patrol officers. They must win their employee's hearts so that officers have the desire to pursue goals associated with community policing (problem solving, collaboration with citizens, cooperative goal determination, etc.). One way to do this may be to make sure employees understand why community policing is a better alternative to traditional policing practices and how it still allows them to be a "crime fighter" (Goldstein, 1990). Mangers must win their employee's minds so that officers understand what community policing entails and how it is going to be operationalized within their department. Agencies must make it a priority to educate their officers in the theory and practice of community policing if they expect implementation efforts to succeed. "One of the primary reasons for the lack of support for...community policing in general among patrol offices was a simple lack of adequate knowledge" (Sadd & Grinc, 1994: p. 36).

UNIONS AND KEY ACTORS

While police unionization is not universal, where unions are present, they pose a significant force with which organizations must reckon in planning for change. Police unions were originally established to address concerns over basic interests of police officers, such as wages, hours, benefits, and retirement (Guyot, 1991). In more recent years unions have become increasingly involved in issues relating to management and administration. Across the country police organizations and unions are negotiating grievance procedures and memos of understanding (More, 1998), as well as organizational policy and job bidding (Hewitt, 1978). Surprisingly, based on the limited available information, there is "little evidence of significant labor (or employee/supervisor) involvement in the design and implementation of community policing" (Polzin, 1997: 1).

Police unions can be a blessing and a curse in organizations proposing change. Police unions can have tremendous impact on the efficacy of organizational change. One way to ensure program failure is to exclude unions from the planning process and to give no attention to whether or not a proposed change is consistent with the union contract (Skogan &

Hartnett, 1997). Unions are adamantly opposed to some forms of change. For example, communities attempting to implement civilian review boards often face tough opposition from the local police union (Swanson, Territo, & Taylor, 1998). On the other hand, police unions can be a driving force to assist organizations in initiating change and securing officer support (Skogan & Hartnett, 1997).

Involving a union in planning and implementing organizational change does not guarantee that an organization's management will receive the union's support. Bypassing a union, however, may ensure resistance and opposition from both the union and the employees which it represents. If an organizational change runs contrary to the desires of the union, or appears to violate a contractual right of employees, the union may have a legitimate right to require that the change be resolved in the course of the collective bargaining process or by a third-party neutral. In police organizations with strong unions, managers must be constantly cognizant of the support (or lack there of) which their proposed change may receive from the union. Without such support, planned change may fail before it is ever implemented.

Employers must also be aware of the "key actors" within their organization. Like the "champions" discussed by Peters and Waterman (1982), key actors can help mitigate the disruption associated with the change process. Most organizations have employees who are held in high regard by their co-workers. Regardless of whether these key actors are managers or supervisors in formal positions of authority, they hold sufficient respect and admiration to lead their peers. When a change is introduced to the organization, other employees may look to these key actors in determining how to respond to the management initiative (Barker, 1999; Guyot, 1991). If an organization secures the understanding and support of key actors, it may ease any difficulty in the implementation process (Territo, 1980). If an organization's work force observes key actors accepting a new policy, program, or initiative, other workers may be more likely to follow suit.

By taking a joint labor-management approach to the development of organizational change it is possible for police agencies to achieve greater success (Polzin, 1997). Working closely with unions makes it is possible for police executives to develop good relationships, to enforce their policies, and to secure organizational change (Hewlett, 1978).

Unfortunately, labor-management relations are more often characterized by distrust and hostility (Guyot, 1991; More, 1998). This relationship does not have to be filled with animosity or tension. If police organizations accept unions as partners and involve key actors, police managers may be able to function more effectively. Polzin's assessment of labor involvement in the implementation of community policing is equally poignant for other forms of organizational change:

> Community policing is a process of organizational change that is most effective when it has the commitment and involvement of its key stakeholders. Employees are the stakeholder group most critical to the initiative's success. Unionized police departments have a unique opportunity to make the use of the workforce's knowledge and expertise through the collective voice of the union. A joint labor-management committee using a systematic approach...offers the greatest opportunity for community policing success (p. 5).

ACCOUNTABILITY, EVALUATIONS, & REWARD ALLOCATION SYSTEMS

Police officers, as public employees, have always been accountable for what they do and what they produce. Early police officers and police organizations were accountable to the political machine which they served (Fogelson, 1977; Walker, S., 1977). Evaluations were virtually nonexistent; as a general rule, as long as the elected party maintained their control, the police were doing a "good" job. The bureaucratic model of police organizations removed accountability from political influence and vested it within the police agency. Under a hierarchical structure, each employee was held accountable to their immediate supervisor; for the average patrol officer, accountability started with their sergeant. Personnel evaluations were quantitative measures which could be quickly and easily computed. Typically, officers were given numerical or Likert ratings which assessed their quantitative performance (citations, arrests, calls for service handled), their demeanor and appearance, their ability to follow orders, and their compliance with policies and procedures. These accountability patterns and personnel evaluation methods are still found in police organizations with traditional structures and orientations.

Organizations implementing community policing find that traditional accountability patterns are no longer sufficient to meet their changing needs. Accountability under community policing becomes more complex than it has been in the past because of increased concern with community expectations and needs (Trojanowicz, Kappeler, Gaines, & Bucqueroux, 1998). Under community policing, officers and organizations accept a level of accountability to the public. Greater consideration is given to incorporating the community in the process of formulating policy and action plans (More, 1998). There are few clear models for how agencies may ensure that officers remain accountable under a community policing system.

A significant challenge facing police managers and planners who seek to implement community policing is determining how they might ensure accountability that goes beyond simple rhetoric. Officers operating under a community policing philosophy attempt to achieve goals set by the residents of the neighborhood they serve. Simultaneously, these same officers also have an obligation to help their organization achieve its broader goals for the entire community. Furthermore, these officers are attempting to fulfill their own professional goals and aspirations. The challenge for managers advocating a community policing approach is to determine who individual employees are to balance these three sets of goals. How will employees resolve the inherent conflicts which will arise as they attempt to remain accountable to the needs of the community, the organization, and themselves?

One of the key ways to ensure accountability in bureaucratic organizations is through the development of accurate evaluation techniques and performance measures. Experience has proven that the actual job-performance of street-level officers can be extremely difficult to measure in a meaningful manner (Lipsky, 1980). Employee evaluation is a process by which employers are able to determine whether an individual employee is producing enough of the right "things." Police organizations have traditionally made evaluations by relying upon a set of performance measures which are easy to observe and quantify (Alpert & Moore, 1993). Police employers have focused on the quantity (the amount), rather than the quality, of policing services produced by employees. For example, employees might be evaluated based upon the number of traffic citations written, the degree of professionalism they exhibited, and their ability to follow orders. These traditional methods and measures of employee performance are insufficient in police agencies which have implemented community policing.

Under a community policing paradigm, traditional measures and techniques fail to serve as an accurate gauge of police performance. Community policing highlights the broader range of services which police officers provide. This illuminates the short comings found in traditional evaluation methods and suggests that appropriate methods should incorporate both a broader quantity of police services as well as indicators of the quality of an employee's performance. Developing well-designed evaluation procedures can be critical to the successful implementation of community policing. These procedures will help employees understand how community policing has: modified the organization's goals (Moore & Stephens, 1990); redefined acceptable means for fulfilling goals; and, altered the definition of a "good" employee. Evaluation methods aid in the implementation process by: emphasizing the importance of the relationship between the organization and the community; promoting proactive efforts to solve community problems; and, guide employees and the organization in fully embracing a community policing philosophy (Alpert & Moore, 1993).

Reward allocation systems are closely related to accountability and evaluations. Ideally constructed, such systems have the same effect on employee behavior as accountability and evaluation processes. All three serve to push employees toward a specific pattern of behavior. Accountability and evaluation achieve this end by delineating the parameters of acceptable behavior and then measuring how well an employee is doing at meeting these standards. A reward allocation system achieves this end by providing extra benefits to employees who do an exceptional job operating within the parameters of acceptable behavior as defined by their organization. For example, an officer working in an organization adopting a community policing philosophy may be recognized for a particularly innovative and successful problem solving endeavor. The reward given to the officer is not necessarily tangible; it may just be a certificate designating him or her as "problem solver of the month." The important facet of this scenario is not the tangibility of the reward, but that the organization took the time to recognize the contributions of the employee.

It is important to note that as organizations are in transitional phases, reward allocation systems may need to be redefined (Goodman, Bazerman, & Conlon, 1980). The type of behavior which the organization chooses to reward may be different from what was recognized during earlier times (i.e., from recognizing the officer who made the "bust of the month" to the officer who initiated the "problem solving activity of the month"). In addition, old rewards may no longer motivate employees to go "above and beyond the call of duty." Unlike the evaluation process, which attempts to coerce individuals to exhibit certain behavioral patterns, the reward system serves as a way to motivate and compensate officers who do more than their peers; in this way, the reward system does not have a negative stigma.

Organizations experiencing change must ensure that reward systems continue to recognize desirable behavior and provide a proper incentive. In making alterations to the reward system or in initiating organizational change, it is important to bear in mind that "changes may threaten those groups in the system that profit from the present allocation of resources and rewards" (Katz & Kahn , 1978: 715). Planners must be mindful that employees may resist a proposed change because it may redefine the behaviors which the organization will reward. Employees invest considerable time and energy attempting to be a "good" employee in the hope that they will be rewarded. When change threatens to redefine the type of behavior which will generate a reward, resistance is likely. In the context of community policing, employees may resist its implementation not because of their beliefs about this philosophy, but because it might nullify the efforts they have made to exhibit "good" behavior in the hope of being rewarded accordingly.

Organizations experiencing change must rethink accountability patterns, evaluation procedures and reward systems. In the absence of changes on these dimensions, employees have little incentive to alter their behavioral patterns to support a new program or organizational philosophy. Employees affected by a planned change must be held accountable for making the necessary changes in their conduct and behavior. When employees are not held accountable for their actions it decreases the likelihood that the change will be successful. Agencies must redefine evaluation measures and develop ways in which to reward officers who are performing in a manner consistent with the organization's new philosophy and goals. In the absence of a performance evaluation system linked to these new goals, agencies cannot expect to achieve widespread success with community policing programs.

CHANGING THE ROLE OF SUPERVISORS

Supervisors in police organizations have traditionally been concerned with the prospect that their subordinates have been engaged in some form of misconduct (Weisburd, McElroy, & Hardyman, 1988). They have focused on ensuring that subordinates were not engaged in any forms of graft, corruption, or vice, and that they were obeying organizational policy. This focus on employee wrongdoings is an outdated response to the early years of American policing when many officers were engaged in such inappropriate behavior. After more than a century of reform efforts, police supervisors must ensure that they have updated the issues upon which they are focused. In order for community policing to work, supervisors must balance concerns with the legality of their subordinate's conduct with considerations of the "workmanship" of employee performance (Bittner, 1990).

One of the primary objectives of supervisors under a community policing paradigm is to work to help their subordinates. Supervisors, especially front-line supervisors, can best serve their organization by ensuring that their subordinates are knowledgeable of, and involved with, the community they serve. In addition to focusing on whether officers have an adequate knowledge of laws and organizational policies, these supervisors might need to focus on the adequacy of the problem solving activities in which officers engage (Weisburd, McElroy, & Hardyman, 1988). As long as police officers are treated as employees who must be closely monitored and directed, they cannot be expected to develop the skills and values necessary to engage in successful community policing (Bittner, 1990). While supervisors must still be concerned with the legality of officer conduct, under community policing they must also concern themselves with the quality of the workmanship these officers exhibit. This workmanship "involves the maintenance of minimally acceptable levels of knowledgeable, skilled and judicious performance" necessary to support the organization's goals and objectives (Bittner, 1990: 350).

If police officers are going to develop and execute the skills necessary to solve community problems, their supervisors need to grant them sufficient flexibility and autonomy. Officers expected to exercise creativity and innovation in solving problems need to be provided with adequate resources (Wilkinson & Rosenbaum, 1994). The organization's internal environment will need to be structured in a manner which will facilitate autonomous and flexible policing approaches. The structure (a rigid and dense hierarchy) and supervisor-subordinate relationships (command and obey) found in traditional police organizations will be insufficient to meet these needs. In the process of planning, organizations may discover that their existing structure, internal relationships, and modes of supervision are ill-suited to support community policing. It may be necessary to redefine these elements in order to create a climate in which community policing endeavors can thrive.

Police supervisors, particularly those on the "front line" (such as patrol sergeants), can be an asset or a liability in the process of organizational change. Supervisors play a critical role in helping officers understand the "why's" and "how's" of community policing. When they understand community policing, why it is important, how it works, and how they can support the community policing endeavors of their subordinates, supervisors have the potential to mitigate some resistance in the implementation process. When supervisors do not understand community policing and how its implementation changes their role within the organization, they will tend to revert to their traditional role within the organization (Territo, 1980) rather than effectively supporting the efforts of line-level employees (Trojanowicz, 1980).

SUMMARY

> ...for community policing to become a central feature of American law enforcement, the institutional framework and organizational apparatus of police organizations must be altered if they are to accommodate the sweeping changes implied by

> community policing proponents. The success or failure of community policing, then, is in large measure affected by the organizational structures and processes that characterize modern-day policing (Greene, Bergman, & McLaughlin, 1994: 93).

The success of an organizational change may also be mediated by certain facets of the organization's existing structure, the degree of planning undertaken before the change is initiated, and the process by which the change is implemented. All else held constant, the more a proposed change departs from an organization's current structure or culture, the greater the likelihood that it will encounter resistance. When more time and energy are invested into planning for change, resistance may be minimized. This is in part because many "bugs" can be worked out of the system, providing for a smoother transition; when employees perceive that there are faults in a proposed change or a new policy/program, they may be more likely to develop an incredulous attitude. The process by which change is implemented may also play a key role in its success. When the logic behind a change is clearly explained to those it affects, when these employees are given proper training to meet new demands accompanying change, and when accountability and rewards are modified to support/encourage adaptation, it is more likely that change will succeed.

CHAPTER 6

Methodology

Innovative police executives, such as August Vollmer, attempted to apply scientific principles to policing during the early decades of the Twentieth Century (Carte & Carte, 1975). Despite their efforts, social research endeavors have a relatively short history in criminal justice, dating back to the initiatives which emerged in the wake of the President's Commission on Law Enforcement and Administration of Justice in 1965 (Walker, S., 1999). As a result of the Commission's preliminary findings, federal funding was made available to conduct evaluation research in criminal justice agencies. The subsequent policing research by innovative scholars such as Albert Reiss, Jerome Skolnick, and George Kelling, still stand as some of the seminal pieces of evaluative research in the field of criminal justice.

This text used data derived in the process of conducting an evaluation of the reorganization of a police agency. The original analysis of this data was carried out in a manner consistent with the tenets of evaluation research, which Hagan (1997: 383) categorizes as "measurement of the effects of a program in terms of its specific goals, outcomes, or particular program criteria." The research team used a number of outcome measures (in particular, attitudes and opinions of employees and citizenry, analysis of official data and documents, and field observation) to determine whether a planned reorganization yielded the expected/desired results. This text moves beyond a strictly evaluative approach in analyzing the data generated by this evaluation. Using portions of the data derived in the original study the author developed a model detailing the barriers to effective change in police organizations seeking to implement community policing.

The chapter begins by describing the evaluation research project which generated the data examined in this text. This information is provided to acquaint the reader with the context in which the data was collected. Next, the methodological considerations most salient to evaluation research in organizations are described. In particular, the discussion examines the strengths, weaknesses, and applications of qualitative research interviews, focus groups, and survey data. This discussion also considers the validity and reliability of the case study approach to social scientific inquiry is also discussed. The chapter concludes with a brief consideration of the analysis of survey data and the elaboration of specific hypotheses tested in this research.

THE ORIGINAL EVALUATION PROJECT

Motor City (a pseudonym) is a Midwestern community of approximately 100,000 residents; it is located in a metropolitan area with a population of approximately 300,000. Motor City has a mixed labor force, with many residents employed in education, government, and blue- and white-collar auto industry positions. The Motor City Police Department (MCPD) employs more than 250 sworn police officers and 100 civilian staff members. This text performs secondary analysis on existing data derived through a research partnership between the Motor City Police Department and faculty members in the School of Criminal Justice (SCJ) at Michigan State University.

This research partnership was initiated in January of 1996. The intent was for SCJ to provide insight and guidance pertaining to recent organizational changes initiated by MCPD. Specifically, MCPD was attempting to make the transition from specialized to generalized community policing. Motor City had been one of the first police departments in the country to experiment with community policing and they had continued their efforts for more than five years. Top leaders were seeking to redefine MCPD's approach by generalizing community policing and problem solving so that all road officers would be involved in these activities. To that end, the city had been divided into twenty patrol areas. Each patrol area was assigned a team of officers from the patrol, canine and traffic units. These officers were supplemented by members of the detective bureau and specialized community policing officers (CPO's), and were lead by a sergeant from the patrol division. Team members and supervisors were only assigned a single team so that their efforts could be focused upon the needs of that group. The teams were given responsibility for addressing the long-term quality of life issues in that geographic area. In addition, these officers were to be the primary providers of emergency services within that area.

On the surface, the responsibilities held by MCPD employees did not change dramatically, despite the restructuring. Patrol officers still answered routine calls for service and answered to the sergeant(s) who happened to be in charge of their shift in their precinct on any given day. The teams were, in essence, secondary responsibilities for all of the parties involved. As individuals, officers were still expected to have a short-term focus of handling incoming emergency calls for service. As a team, the members were expected to address medium and long-term neighborhood problems within their geographic area. It was believed that by bringing together members of different units (investigations, canine, traffic, CPO and patrol), neighborhood level problems could be addressed in a more efficient and effective manner.

The research team from SCJ consisted of four faculty members and a graduate assistant who would handle the day-to-day operation of the project; the author was selected to serve as the project graduate assistant. During the next two and a half years, the research team collaborated with key planners and managers from MCPD to assess how the organizational change was perceived by line officers, to study the "state of affairs" in the Department, and to determine how the community viewed the agency and its employees. A wide array of research methodologies was employed to carry out this research initiative. Initially, key leaders in the Department were interviewed about changes within the organization's structure and operational style. These officials also provided insight into the state of the Department (from a management perspective) and where the Department envisioned itself in the future. These findings were augmented by the analysis of basic call-for-service data.

This initial research effort allowed the research team to develop a loose set of issues and questions which seemed to be particularly salient to the state of affairs in MCPD. Armed with this information, the graduate assistant conducted a series of field observations/interviews with the patrol officers, CPO's and sergeants in a purposive sample of team areas. MCPD research partners selected two areas in each precinct for closer study. These areas were selected not because they represented the "best" or the "worst" adaptation to the organizational change, but because MCPD partners believed the personnel working these areas would be particularly open and honest with the graduate assistant. Efforts were made to conduct a "ride along" that encompassed at least one complete shift (ten hours) with each member of all four teams.

The SCJ research team felt that it was best to use the graduate assistant to conduct these field observations/interviews for two reasons. First, it was believed that the officers would be more open and honest with someone adopting the role of "student" as opposed to the role of "expert" (a role into which officers might automatically cast a professor). Perceiving the observer in the role of student would minimize reactivity among the research subjects. Second, it was more pragmatic to utilize a graduate assistant. In order to observe each member of the four teams for a complete patrol shift, field observations had to be made at all hours of the day. The life of a student was more conducive to working varied hours in order to conduct all of the necessary "ride along" sessions. Faculty members had less flexibility and fewer hours to devote to conducting field interviews and observations.

The field observations/interviews provided the research team with invaluable insights and information about those issues which were most salient to the research project. The observer's duties were twofold: to note how officers did their job in the context of the organizational change and to talk with officers to better understand their opinions, attitudes, and experiences as they related to the change. Using a loose set of interview questions, augmented by questions probing key issues as they emerged, the next step of the research project began to clarify itself. The field observations allowed for the collection of information about both attitudes and actions of the officers assigned to the four study teams. Once initial suspicions had subsided, officers began to open up to the graduate student. The informality of loose interview questions and casual conversation "in the field" enhanced the level of honesty by the officers being studied. In addition, by accompanying officers in the field for ten hour blocks of time, the researcher was also able to interact with countless other officers. This allowed the researchers to identify key issues based on the attitudes and actions of a far larger group of officers.

The insights gained during the field observation/interview period allowed the SCJ research team to identify those issues which required further systematic elaboration. The research team wanted to conduct a survey of those officers most affected by the organizational change to ascertain their attitudes, beliefs, opinions, and experiences[1]. Specifically, the research team wished to target those sworn police employees holding the ranks of officer, sergeant and lieutenant who were assigned to perform patrol and community policing functions. To aid in the process of developing a research instrument, two sessions of focus groups were conducted with a purposive group of patrol officers and sergeants. This purposive selection scheme was not done to exclude the "bad" or include the "good"; rather, the intent was to ensure that participants would be vocal (and constructive) about their beliefs, opinions, attitudes, and experiences.

The first focus group sessions were used to ensure that the SCJ research team had accurately assessed the "big picture" of how the implementation of team-based community policing had affected MCPD officers. With this knowledge, the SCJ team developed a self-administered survey instrument which was to be administered to members of the patrol and community policing units. Focus group participants were asked to review this instrument prior to a second meeting. During the second set of focus group sessions, participants provided feedback about wording, instrument construction, and administration procedures. It is believed that these focus group sessions greatly enhanced the validity and reliability of the officer survey. This second iteration of the survey instrument was the version which was ultimately administered.

---

[1] Strictly speaking, the original evaluation study conducted a census of community policing officers and lieutenants, sergeants and officers assigned to the patrol division and community policing unit of the Motor City Police Department in the spring of 1997. Every member of this narrowly defined population was given the opportunity to complete the questionnaire. Although this was a census in the technical sense, it will be referred to herein as a survey. The instrumentation and methodological issues used in a census and survey are largely the same; the primary difference is whether a sampling scheme is used.

The research team also conducted a series of systematic field observations using 17 undergraduate and graduate students from MSU. These students were being trained to carry out systematic social observations in conjunction with another grant held by SCJ. Observers accompanied patrol officers during the entire duration of their patrol shifts (ten hours). During the course of the shift, observers took brief field notes to record how officers spent their time, interacted with citizens, and performed their duties. After an observation session had been completed, the observers used these notes to write a detailed and structured narrative account of what they witnessed and to answer a fixed set of questions about the encounters and activities officers engaged in, and the citizens with whom officers interacted. Thus, each student produced in-depth qualitative and quantitative data for each "ride along" they performed. Because the students were still being trained to use this highly customized systematic technique, analysis of the data was limited. These findings were primarily used to assess how patrol officers in Motor City spent their time while on duty. In addition to these two major data sets (the officer survey and observation data), a community survey and a limited number of departmental records were examined to further augment the field observations.

The officer survey was ultimately administered to approximately 140 patrol officers, sergeants, lieutenants, and CPO's. Participation was voluntary and responses were anonymous; the response rate was approximately 85 percent. Despite the wealth of information collected from this survey, it was subjected to only minimal descriptive analysis (frequencies and crosstabs). The same was true for the other sources of information used by the research team. The evaluation project was primarily conducted to provide MCPD administrators and city officials with descriptive information about the state of the Department. The "consumers" of the research results were not interested with in-depth causal analysis; they were simply concerned with whether the organizational change was succeeding in terms of employee attitudes and citizen perceptions. The data sets derived through the evaluation process contain a wealth of information which has been largely untapped. This text re-analyzes portions of the data using the conceptual framework elaborated in the preceding chapters.

This text reports on the advance analysis of portions of the original data sets. The data from the officer survey have been used to test hypotheses about the relationships between variables deemed important in light of the text's conceptual framework. The author seeks to understand the relationship between organizational culture, individual socialization, and organizational planning, and attitudes toward community policing both specifically (as instituted in MCPD) and generally (as a philosophy). Qualitative findings from structured interviews, field observations/interviews and focus group sessions are used to provide supplemental information about the implementation process in MCPD and to assist in interpreting the results of the tested hypotheses. Other data sources derived in the original study have been used as need, primarily to provide further elaboration of the qualitative results and the issues related to this text's conceptual framework.

Instrument Construction

The officer survey instrument was developed in collaboration with the officers who participated in the focus group sessions. Based upon individual interviews, field observations/interviews, data analysis, and the first session of focus groups, the SCJ research team developed a draft instrument. This instrument was provided to the focus group participants prior to the second session of meetings. The second meetings allowed the participants to comment on the wording of questions and their associated response options. Participants were also able to provided feedback to ensure that the instrument addressed the most salient issues in the Department relating to the organizational change. This review by the focus group participants was very similar to a pretest and strengthened the reliability, face validity, and construct validity of the survey instrument which was ultimately administered.

Specifically, the officer survey instrument was designed to gauge a number of factors, including the respondents':

- attitude toward the philosophy of community policing
- attitude toward the process by which the organizational change was structured and implemented in MCPD

- attitude toward community policing as it was implemented in MCPD
- views on the proper role of police officers and what constitutes a "good" police officer
- opinion on citizen-police cooperation
- involvement in problem solving efforts and other endeavors supportive of a community policing philosophy
- stance on the proper role of supervisors
- opinion on the current role of supervisors in MCPD
- belief about what departmental priorities ought to be

Respondents also provided demographic information (years of service, education, gender, and race) and experiential information (rank, CPO experience).

Critical survey construction techniques were used in the process of designing all of the instruments used in the evaluation project. Among the most important survey construction techniques employed were:

1. The use of closed-ended questions (to the extent possible) and response options which were both mutually exclusive and exhaustive.
2. Utilizing common wording and terminology.
3. Ensuring that questions and their associated responses were neutral and did not "lead" the respondent.
4. Ordering questions to avoid asking questions which might affect response to subsequent questions.
5. Asking only those questions which were germane to the research objectives.
6. Limiting the amount of demographic information requested and avoiding questions which might allow for the identification of individual respondents.
7. Providing simple and sufficient instructions on how to complete and, where relevant, return the survey.
8. Ensuring that it was convenient and confidential for participants to respond and that doing so required a minimal investment of time.

These measures were employed so that the data collected would be both valid and reliable (making this data suitable for the testing of hypotheses) and to ensure an adequate response rate (thereby maintaining external validity).

Population

The officer survey was administered approximately one year after the organizational change was initiated in MCPD. During this year, it became apparent that several groups of personnel assigned to the team area were not active members of these units. Because their duties required them to work on a precinct or city level, officers assigned to the canine and traffic units were never able to focus their thinking on a smaller area. In addition, members of the detective unit had actively resisted being assigned to handle all of the investigations in their assigned team area; this required employees accustom to working as a specialist (i.e., auto theft, burglary, domestic assault, etc.) to operate as a generalist (handling all but the most serious crimes in their area). While there were isolated exceptions, members of these three units did not become integrated members of their designated teams.

As a result of these historical events, officers assigned to these three units (canine, traffic and investigations) were excluded from participating in the survey. The survey was administered to every officer, sergeant and lieutenant assigned to the Patrol Division, and also every officer currently designated as a Community Policing Officer. Therefore, the population is defined as all CPO's and all road officers, sergeants, and lieutenants assigned to the Patrol Division of the Motor City Police Department. This definition targeted the survey at those employees most affected by the organizational change initiated by MCPD. Because the population was finite and relatively small (approximately 140 individuals), a sampling protocol was not necessary. Every member of the population was given the opportunity to complete the instrument, in effect making the "survey" a "census." Because a sampling protocol was not used, the data resulting from this endeavor is free of errors associated with sampling.

Procedures

The instrument was constructed based upon the findings of earlier research efforts, on the prior experiences of the SCJ research team, and, to a small degree, drawing upon other efforts to assess similar issues in agencies experimenting with community policing. Upon completing the instrument construction and taking steps to enhance its reliability (via focus group review), data collection commenced. The officers who participated in the focus groups were given a set of survey packets and a list of officers to whom they were to deliver the packets. These lists were carefully checked to ensure that no members of the population were either omitted or listed more than once. Officers were given the names of other officers working in their precinct and on their own shift; this was done to maximize the likelihood that they would see everyone on their list without going to any extra trouble.

The packets consisted of the survey instrument (see Appendix C) and a cover sheet (see Appendix B) which: (1) explained the purpose of the study; (2) provided them with assurance that their responses were anonymous and that individual responses would not be provided to MCPD (to further protect their identity); (3) provided the name and phone number of an SCJ research team member whom they could contact if they had any questions or concerns; (4) provided instructions for completing and returning the survey. These items were in an unsealed standard manilla envelope. Upon completing the survey, the respondent was to seal it in the envelope. The sealed envelope was then returned to the officer who had given them the survey (the survey was not to be completed in the presence of this administrating officer). Completed surveys were given to a specific patrol lieutenant who was a member of the MCPD research team. Surveys (which remained sealed while in the custody of all MCPD employees) were picked up periodically from the liaison lieutenant by members of the SCJ research team.

The logic behind this unusual administration process was as follows. Members of the MCPD research team expressed concern over providing officers with their surveys via traditional departmental channels (i.e., placing them in each officer's mailbox). They preferred that each officer be given the survey in person. For this reason, it was necessary to develop a way to deliver the survey packets so that every member of the population received one and only one packet. In addition, it was believed that the focus group participants were generally respected and trusted by their peers. It was hoped that this trust would lead to an increased response rate because respondents would be receiving the survey from a respected peer who explained the purpose of the study and encouraged the respondent to participate.

The focus group participants did not keep track of who had returned the surveys. They were instructed to refrain from aggressively following-up to ensure instruments were completed and returned. Although this would have enhanced the response rate by making sure surveys were completed and returned, it would also appear that officers had to respond. Participation was voluntary and it was felt that officers should not be coerced into completing the survey. No member of MCPD was allowed to view completed surveys and they were not provided a copy of the coded data file. All subsequent reports to MCPD consisted only of aggregated responses to protect the identity of individual respondents.

METHODS OF EVALUATION RESEARCH

Evaluation research frequently involves the application of several methodological approaches to generate insights and information. Some of these approaches may be used in other forms of social research, while others are rarely used for other endeavors. This section describes three methodologies (the qualitative research interviews, focus groups, and survey research) and their application in the evaluation research process. This is followed by a discussion of the case study method of organizational research.

Qualitative Research Interviews

Because the term "interview" may be used to refer to a number of slightly different methodologies for obtaining data, it is necessary to begin this section by defining the term as it applies to this text. The type of interview approach used in social scientific research is largely dependent upon the nature of the research question to be addressed. The interview method used herein is best termed the "qualitative research interview" (King, 1994). This approach differs from other forms of interviews in that it relies on open-ended questions, probing by the administrator, and a freely-flowing interview dialogue. In the context of the original evaluation research project the qualitative research interview was deemed appropriate given the interview setting (most often an interviewer accompanying an officer on duty) and the data acquisition needs of the research team (preliminary insights into the research issues).

According to King (1993) there are a number of situations in which the qualitative research interview is most appropriate as a means of social inquiry. Chief among them is where "exploratory work is required before a quantitative study can be carried out" (p. 16). The qualitative research interview generally relies on a loose interview guide, rather than a formal schedule of questions asked verbatim in a specified order during each interview session. The interviewer has a list of questions or general issues which might be addressed during the course of the interview. As sessions are conducted, the interview guide may be modified (i.e., adding probes to address issues as they emerge, dropping or reformulating items which are poorly worded or irrelevant, etc.).

Interviewing, like any other research methodology, offers a distinctive set of advantages and disadvantages for the collection of social data. A key concern is that the interviewer maintains the ability to remain neutral (Babbie, 1973). Much like field research, the interviewer must be conscious of how his or her actions, comments, or demeanor might influence the interviewee. If the interviewer is not conscious of this possibility, the interviewee may feel compelled to provide a socially acceptable answer to a question. Interviewers must also use care to avoid unintentionally "leading" the interviewee to provide certain answers (Hagan, 1997; Maxfield and Babbie, 1998). Interviewers must make sure that their appearance and mannerisms are appropriate for the group being studied (Hagan, 1997). In addition, the interviewer must be prepared to deal with interviewees who are too talkative, not talkative enough, wander off topic, or attempt to turn every question back onto the interviewer.

There are a number of practical issues related specifically to qualitative research interviews (King, 1994). Interviewers must have the ability to operate flexibly as this is the key to the qualitative research interview process. Although interviews may begin with a few common questions, each session tends to be unique and the interviewer must be able to adapt and identify appropriate follow-up questions to probe for further information. The phrasing of the questions must be on the level of the interviewee; this may be particularly challenging when the interviewer is asking probing questions.

Interviewers must also be prepared to deal with difficult interviews with subjects who do not wish to participate, become emotionally upset over the subject of the interview, or are simply not responsive to open-ended questioning. Finally, the interviewer must make sure proper deference is shown to high-status interviewees. This final point is of particular importance in conducting evaluation research in organizations when interviews may be conducted with members of an organization's leadership. Such individuals may be accustomed to being treated with a certain degree of deference and formality in their occupational role. An interviewer whose approach is too friendly and informal may offend the interviewee, unintentionally restricting the resulting information.

Interviews, as any other form of social inquiry, must be conducted in such away to maximize reliability and validity. Reliability may be particularly problematic with the qualitative research interview. A reliable interview format would result in roughly the same interview data being obtained by any interviewer because the interview guide is consistent and the interviewer's tone, appearance, and demeanor are (hypothetically) neutral factors in the process. Because they do not have a firm interview format that is consistent across all interview sessions, qualitative research interviews can be particularly weak in terms of their reliability. Each researcher's subjective determination of exact issues to be discussed and probing questions to be asked makes it unlikely that the same interview conducted by different interviewers would yield similar findings. The best remedy for this situation is to only use data obtained in these interviews for exploratory purposes. In light of this limitation, the data may not be appropriate for theory testing or other forms of rigorous qualitative data analysis (Miles & Huberman, 1984).

In quantitative research, validity is a reflection of how well a measurement device actually measures what it claims to measure (Maxfield & Babbie, 1998); validity may be defined analogously in qualitative research (King, 1994). While quantitative research validity focuses on method, qualitative research validity focuses on interpretations.

If qualitative research is valid, a researcher's conclusions and interpretations are accurate reflections of "reality." One way to enhance validity in interpreting data obtained in a qualitative research interview is to engage participants in "feedback loops" (King, 1994). The researcher returns to interviewees with interpretations and conclusions to verify that they have correctly captured the "world" of the participants.

The qualitative research interview can be a powerful exploratory tool in the process of conducting social research. These interviews enable researchers to obtain insights into meanings which are not available through quantitative approaches or other forms of qualitative investigation. Researchers may sort out complex patterns and develop full understandings of contextual issues surrounding organizations and relationships between individuals. In an organizational setting, the qualitative research interview has an additional advantage because research participants might be open to engaging a researcher in such a dialogue because "most people like talking about their work– whether to share enthusiasm or to air complaints– but rarely have the opportunity to do so with interested outsiders" (King, 1994: 33-34).

Focus Groups

Focus groups have been used for years to assist in marketing research and political planning. More recently, they have gained increasing attention as a method to aid in social research. Conventional focus groups were designed to assess public reactions to a new product or a dimension of a political campaign by "testing" them before a group of people who were felt to represent the target audience of a product or issue (Hagan, 1997). A focus group is similar to a group interview where a researcher's questions alternate with responses from the participants (Morgan, 1997). Organizers of focus groups bring together a purposively selected group of volunteers or participants (Kruger, 1994). These individuals are selected for a variety of reasons, including their demographic attributes, personality and personal beliefs, and willingness to share their ideas and opinions. A group moderator meets with the participants in an informal setting and guides them through a semi-structured discussion/interview about a designated topic (Carey, 1994).

The defining characteristic of focus groups as a research tool is the use of group interaction to produce ideas and information which would be inaccessible in the absence of the interaction (Morgan, 1997). Focus groups are not intended to be a more efficient way of interviewing large numbers of people (although they may be). Rather, researchers use them as a way to both collect data from a large number of people and to elicit ideas and information which might not emerge in a one-on-one interview. Carey (1994) provides one of the best descriptions of the underlying rationale of focus groups, describing it as the belief that:

> ...with proper guidance from the focus group leader, group members can describe the rich details of complex experiences and the reasoning behind their actions, beliefs, perceptions, and attitudes. The impact of the group setting can enhance the quality of the data elicited. (p. 226)

Although focus group administrators may seek to direct the general flow of the dialogue, they are also concerned with studying the interactions of the group members as respondents address particular questions. In other words, the focus group is intended to simulate a real life "bull-session" (Babbie, 1992) which a group of citizens might have with one another about a given topic.

Focus groups serve a variety of important functions in the evaluation research process. Informal and semi-structured interviews can be used to generate early insights into the topic under examination. These preliminary individual interviews can generate ideas and information which are invaluable in structuring subsequent focus group sessions. It is also common for individual interviews to produce seemingly contradictory information and insights which will require resolution (Carey, 1994). The focus group gives the researcher an opportunity to present contradictions for clarification and to delve deeper into matters of interest which might have emerged during preliminary individual interviews (Morgan, 1997). In addition, the focus group might be used as a self-check by a researcher; participants can verify that the researcher has "gotten to the root" of the social phenomena under consideration.

Focus groups may be used to develop and/or refine interview or survey instruments. At times, researchers may not be able to interview all of the members of a study population. Interviewing a (presumably) representative sample of the entire population allows the researchers to develop insights into the most salient issues and concerns affecting the population. Researchers can use the knowledge they obtain in focus group sessions to develop a survey instrument which will allow the entire population (or a larger sample) to voice their opinions. Focus groups can be reconvened to review survey instruments before this broader administration begins. Group members may ensure that the instrument's vocabulary is culturally appropriate for the target population and that questions will "effectively convey the researcher's intent to the survey respondent" (Morgan, 1997: 25). Participants may review the issues an instrument addresses to ensure that the researchers are targeting the appropriate matters for further inquiry (in the appropriate fashion).

In this way, the focus group can be used as a check on both the validity and reliability of an interview or survey instrument. As a result, the integrity of subsequent data may be improved before the time and energy are devoted to an instrument's full-scale administration. Instrument validity is enhanced (particularly in organizational research) because the researcher can be assured that the key issues are being addressed by the instrument. Instrument reliability is enhanced because the group review process helps the researcher ensure that "differences in how the respondents interpret the questions" have been minimized (Morgan, 1997: 26).

According to Kruger (1994), focus groups are appropriate tools in social science research when: the researchers are interested in developing preliminary or exploratory information about a subject; researchers are seeking information about complex behavior or motivations; the ideas generated by a group cannot be achieved by individuals alone (i.e., groups offer a unique synergy); capturing open-ended comments is of great value; and, researchers need information and insights in preparation for a large-scale study.

Despite the strengths and merits of focus groups, they are not always appropriate. Kruger (1994) also stipulates that there are many circumstances under which focus group interviews should not be used, including: when research is being carried out in an emotionally charged environment (especially when conflict may be intensified through the interview process); when a researcher loses the ability to control critical aspects of the study (i.e., participant selection, question development, analysis protocol, data interpretation, etc.); where a study requires strong statistical projections (focus groups usually do not involve sufficient numbers of participants and their purposive nature makes their generalizability highly questionable); and where other methodological approaches would produce information which is either of a better quality and/or more economical.

Focus groups are not without their limitations. The purposive nature of participant selection in focus group interviews may preclude generalizing their findings (Kruger, 1994). The intent of this research approach is to provide exploratory knowledge which may illuminate the appropriate direction to be taken during further analysis. In addition, while group dynamics may be synergistic, they also limit the researcher's ability to control the flow of the interview as compared to the control offered in individual interviews. Data derived from focus group interviews may be difficult to analyze, creating the risk of comments being taken out of context and/or interpreted incorrectly. Focus groups may also present logistical problems, as it may be difficult to assemble a desired group of participants in an environment which is conducive to open conversation.

In summary, focus group interviews may be a valuable research tool in certain situations and this methodology may offer advantages which outweigh potential limitations and weaknesses. Focus groups may be an efficient and economical way in which to gather information which can serve as a foundation for further exploration. The social dynamics of the interview process may also result in important findings which might be difficult to obtain via other research methodologies. In this text, the use of focus groups was particularly appropriate because it allowed the researchers to confirm the findings of preliminary individual interviews. Focus groups were also used to develop, refine and test survey instruments before they were administered to the entire study population. It is expected that this enhanced the overall validity and reliability of the survey data.

Survey Research

The objective in using a survey in social inquiry is very basic. Moser and Kalton write that "[t]he purpose of many surveys is simply to provide someone with information" (1972: 2). Survey research allows for "systematic measurements [to be] made over a series of cases yielding a rectangle of data" (Marsh, 1982: 6). Babbie notes that although survey research is not an appropriate means to study many topics, survey methods "can be especially effective when combined with other methods" (1973: 45). In examining survey research, it is important to remember that "surveys record either expressed attitude or claimed behavior and seldom the behavior itself" (Hagan, 1997: 141).

According to Babbie (1973) there are a number of characteristics which define survey research. Survey research is logical– it is aimed "at the rational understanding of social behavior" (p. 28). Through the use of logic and rationale, it is believed that complex propositions may be effectively tested through empirical means. Survey research is deterministic; researchers attempt to use survey results "to explain the reasons for and sources of observed events, characteristics, and correlations" (p. 46). When a survey is used to elaborate a logical model, cause and effect may be determined in order to explain the observed phenomena. Survey methods are especially useful in the "academic quest for knowledge and understanding" because they allow for the collection and analysis of data of "immediate policy relevance" (p. 359).

Survey research is general. Coupled with rigorous sampling techniques, researchers hope to draw conclusions about an entire population, while only dealing with a portion of its members. Survey research is parsimonious; unlike other research methods, a survey researcher can "construct a variety of explanatory models and then select the one best suited to his aims" (Babbie, 1973: 47). Finally, survey research is specific. By their very nature, research results are very explicit and generally quantitative, lending themselves to highly detailed results and great specificity in analysis.

Surveys may be administered in a number of different fashions (generally either face-to-face, via telephone, or self-administration). For the purposes of this text it is necessary to give extra attention to self-administration, as this approach is most relevant. Self-report surveys gather data by asking respondents to disclose their attitudes, opinions, and behavior. Self-report surveys have the advantage of being efficient (requiring far less personnel than telephone or face-to-face surveys), cost effective, and less sensitive to biases introduced through survey administration (Salant & Dillman, 1994). An additional advantage of this approach is that "respondents make critical comments and report the less socially acceptable responses somewhat more readily" than they might in responding to other forms of surveys (Moser & Kalton, 1972: 258).

Despite these merits, there are disadvantages to using self-administered surveys; this text may be most affected by two specific categories of disadvantages. First, because respondents generally complete the survey instrument without any assistance (although this might not always be the case), reliability of the responses may be weakened. In the absence of qualified assistance, respondents encountering a question they do not understand are forced to guess as to the question's meaning (Maxfield & Babbie, 1998; Reynolds & Sponaugle, 1982). Consequently, different respondents may interpret a question in differing manners, resulting in answers which are not entirely congruent with one another (Hagan, 1997). Second, validity is always a problem with any form of survey research. People may not provide correct responses due to blatant lying, subtle exaggeration, a faulty memory, or the desire to provide socially acceptable answers to sensitive or controversial inquiries (Hagan, 1997; Reynolds & Sponaugle, 1982).

Although a researcher may never completely overcome these threats to validity and reliability, steps may be taken to minimize their impact. The reliability of an instrument may be enhanced through the use of focus groups (Carey, 1994; Morgan 1997; Salant & Dillman, 1994) and/or the pretesting of an instrument (Babbie, 1973). The merits of focus groups as a means to enhance reliability were discussed previously in this chapter. Pretesting an instrument allows a researcher to work the "bugs" out of the survey and its planned administration before full-scale administration is initiated. Different drafts of a question may be used to see which version is the most "readable" to the target population. Contradictory or confusing questions may be identified and corrected. Ambiguous terms may be properly defined to ensure consistent interpretation by respondents. In general, pretesting allows the researcher to maximize the reliability of their survey by ensuring that it is both written in a manner which will allow for maximum consistency in interpretation and administered in a manner which will maximize the response rate.

The validity of an instrument can be improved when that instrument is administered through some form of self-completion. When a survey is in some way administered by someone other than the respondent, undesirable reactions may occur, particularly when the survey relates to sensitive or controversial material. Respondents may provide the answer they think the administrator wants to hear or the answer they think they ought to provide in order to be socially correct. In addition, administrators may unintentionally offend the respondent or in some other way bias their answers (Reynolds & Sponaugle, 1982). Self-administration may overcome this potential validity threat by ameliorating the respondent's self-imposed desire to alter how they present themselves to the administrator. The respondent is less likely to believe that there is a need to embellish or lie, particularly when anonymity has been assured.

Basic social research ethics might have the unintended consequences of bolstering survey validity. One of the most basic principles of ethical research is protecting the interests of research participants (Babbie, 1992). If revealing survey responses may result in harm or injury to participants, anonymity or confidentiality ought to be offered to participants. This is certainly true when conducting research in organizations, where a participant might face negative repercussions if they speak out against certain ideals, beliefs, programs or people (King, 1994). Survey responses are anonymous where the researcher is unable to match a particular response with a particular respondent; responses are confidential when a researcher is able to match a respondent with a response, but promises not to do so (Babbie, 1992; Hagan, 1997). When respondents know that their identity is being protected by the researcher, they may be more likely to provide truthful answers, thus enhancing validity. While respondents may still choose to lie in answering a question or may still make a human error, self-administered surveys using either confidentiality or anonymity offer the greatest protection against other threats to the validity of survey responses.

The Case Study Approach to Organizational Research: Merging Qualitative and Quantitative Approaches to Social Inquiry

Case study research is a valid form of social inquiry "when the phenomenon under study is not readily distinguishable from its context" (Yin, 1993: 3). Examples of such phenomena might include projects or programs being examined in an evaluation study. Yin contends that using the case study method under such circumstances has advantages, including the ability to have a broader focus, the capacity to include contextual conditions related to the phenomena in question, and the capacity to use multiple sources of evidence. He also notes that these advantages may become a proverbial double-edged sword for the researcher. The broad focus of such studies may result in an overload of data, making it difficult to extract the contextually relevant information. The richness of the findings may necessitate the use of multiple sources of evidence, making a simple data collection protocol out of the question. It is worth noting, however, that the case study technique allows the researcher to blend qualitative and quantitative forms of data collection, which may enhance the validity and reliability of the research findings.

Case study research, like qualitative research, may be subject to criticism because data collection may be undertaken prior to the development of the study questions and hypotheses (Yin, 1993). Some view this approach as sloppy, unstructured, and unscientific. Unfortunately, there are times when not enough is known about the phenomena researchers seek to study. When this is the case, "qualitative methods can be used to uncover and understand what lies behind any phenomenon about which little is yet known" (Strauss & Corbin, 1990: 19). Thus, an exploratory case study may use flexible approaches in order to obtain further descriptive information about a phenomenon; this information may then be used to structure a more rigorous research project (Ogawa & Malen, 1991).

Strong similarities may be noted between exploratory case study research and the "grounded theory" (Glaser & Strauss, 1967) approach to social scientific inquiry. Both approaches allow a researcher to generate hypotheses using a flexible strategy, loosely structured methodologies, and descriptive accounts. Both may also rely on qualitative findings to aid in the generation of knowledge which may then be used to develop controlled, structured techniques through which assumptions may be systematically tested. These initial qualitative methods may not yield findings with the objective precision of quantitative methods. These qualitative approaches, however, may provide significant insights into a phenomenon and may serve as the foundation for the identification of critical variables, the generation of hypotheses, and the construction of theory (Dey, 1993; Miles & Huberman, 1984; Strauss & Corbin, 1990). Advocates of grounded theory warn that researchers must avoid using existing theoretical or conceptual models in approaching a new study (Glaser & Strauss, 1967). Although it is helpful to have a working knowledge of the literature relating to the area of study, this knowledge should not cloud the researcher from seeing emergent issues as the study at hand progresses.

When it is properly designed, exploratory case study research may lend itself to the inductive construction of knowledge. An initial broad exploratory approach to a social phenomenon allows for the emergence of important research questions. This approach is much like grounded theory, which Strauss and Corbin (1990) describe as follows:

> A grounded theory is one that is inductively derived from the study of the phenomenon it represents. That is, it is discovered, developed, and provisionally verified through the systematic data collection and analysis of data pertaining to that phenomenon. Therefore, data collection, analysis and theory stand in reciprocal relationship to each other. One does not begin with a theory, then prove it. Rather one begins with an area of study and what is relevant to that area is allowed to emerge. (p. 23)

A similar approach was used to develop the data under consideration in this text. A research project was initiated to explore a very broad topic (how well is a planned organizational change working in the Motor City Police Department?). Initial research efforts were exploratory and descriptive in nature (field observations, informal and formal interviews, analysis of official records, etc.). This allowed for the emergence of the most relevant issues. Once identified, these issues could be clarified (through the use of focus groups) and then addressed in a more systematic manner (self-administered surveys) to allow for quantitative analysis in order to further understand the phenomena. As this illustrates, when done properly, the case study method may be a valid scientific approach to understanding a social phenomenon.

One of the reasons the case study method has such a high degree of utility is because it allows for improved reliability through the use of multiple modes in inquiry (Blau, 1963). Individual modes of inquiry each have their own strengths and weaknesses (Hagan, 1997); the use of an assortment of research methods in examining a social phenomenon allows a researcher to maximize the overall integrity of their research findings (Babbie, 1973). While survey methodologies allow for the quick and easy collection of data, they tend to be rather one-dimensional; where possible, such approaches should be used with other methods to provide greater depth to research findings. As Babbie wistfully notes "few researchers employ a variety of methods in their inquiries" (p. 361). By it's very nature, the case study approach encourages the use of multiple methods and provides an overall picture of a social phenomenon which has greater depth and, perhaps, greater accuracy.

Because case study research may utilize both qualitative and quantitative methods and because it is a scientific approach to understanding a social phenomenon, reliability and validity are issues which must be addressed by those employing this method. Reliability can be preserved by using standardized protocols whenever possible; for example, interviewers might be required to ask the same questions every time. Validity can be strengthened by using multiple indicators to assess specific issues (thereby compensating for weaknesses in individual approaches to collecting data) and by ensuring that instruments are properly constructed. Because case study research may be based upon findings in only one setting, the generalizability of the findings may still be an issue; it is difficult to know if the findings would be the same in a similar environment. It should be noted that proponents of the case study method do not view generalizability as a limiting characteristic of this methodology (Yin, 1993).

ANALYZING SURVEY DATA

The survey data collection process can produce either open-ended or close-ended responses (Maxfield & Babbie, 1998). For the purposes of data analysis, closed-ended responses allow for more efficient analysis as the range of responses is finite in nature. Even where researchers use open-ended responses, it is usually necessary to go through the data and classify responses into a finite number of categories. The categorical nature of survey results lends these data to a wide range of statistical analysis. One of the most basic ways in which to analyze a single variable is through examining its frequency distribution. Through the use of contingency tables (or "crosstabs") it is possible to examine the basic relationship between two or more variables. This relationship may be elaborated upon through the use of tests of significance and measures of association "to verify the existence and strength of any apparent relationship between variables" (Rea & Parker, 1997: 166).

This text makes use of a number of descriptive and inferential techniques for quantitative data analysis. Descriptive techniques include frequency analysis and contingency tables. Frequency analysis provides a simple count of individuals in each response category for a given variable. Although this information may seem simplistic, it provides important insights about the distribution of responses for the given variable, which can then be used as a guide for conducing further analysis. Contingency tables order the frequency distribution of two or more variables. For example, we might want to know how many survey respondents had served as a community policing officer cross-tabulated with the respondent's rank. The cells of the contingency table would reflect how many respondents had expressed a co-occurrence of these two variables (i.e., how many sergeants had never served as a community policing officer).

In addition to these descriptive measures, this text will also employ a number of inferential statistical measures. In most cases involving survey data, the variables are measured at the nominal or ordinal level (Rea & Parker, 1997). In cases where a survey variable is measured at the ordinal level, the Independent Samples Test may be used to compare responses between two groups of respondents (Bachman & Paternoster, 1997). The Independent Samples Test determines if the "mean of a single variable for subjects in one group differs from that in another" (SPSS, 1997: 103). For example, the mean evaluation respondents gave their supervisors may be compared based upon the respondents' gender. This test allows a researcher to determine if observed variation in responses between different groups is statistically significant.

One limitation of survey data is that it may not measure the full range of concepts of interest to a researcher. For a variety of reasons, some important concepts may not be measured either because they do not lend themselves to assessment through a survey instrument or the authors of a survey instrument were not concerned with such concepts. There may be situations, however, when elements of such concepts have been estimated through survey questions. Factor analysis allows such elements to be merged.

Factor analysis is a "combination of a group of variables (items) combined to represent a scale measure of a concept" (Walker, J.T., 1999: 234). This scale measure may then be examined through other statistical tests to examine the relationship between the concept and other salient variables. Factor analysis is a form of data reduction which allows a researcher to create a single variable to reflect a number of other theoretically and/or mathematically related items. Where necessary, factors are developed in this text to measure social phenomena which were not directly measured by the existing variables.

Where data are measured at the ordinal, interval or ratio level, analysis of variance may be used to measure the amount of variability of the dependent variable that can be attributed to differences among categories of the independent variable (Rea & Parker, 1997; SPSS Inc., 1997). In this text, analysis of variance is used in conjunction with regression analysis to determine to what extent (if any) the independent variable(s) values of a particular case might be used to predict the value of the dependent variable (Vito & Latessa, 1989). In this way, relationships between multiple variables may be better understood by determining the extent to which one or more independent variables predict the value of a dependent variable (while controlling for the effects of other variables).

This text will employ a variety of statistical measures to test for relationships between data derived through a survey instrument. In examining complex relationships between multiple variables it is necessary to employ a variety of statistical tests. Analyzing data through a variety of statistical means (some basic and descriptive, others complex and inferential) balances the risk of committing either a Type I or Type II error (Bachman & Paternoster, 1997).

Coupling this discussion of methodological and analytical issues with the materials derived from the literature review allows for the identification and elaboration of specific research hypotheses. Testing these hypotheses provides insight into the veracity of the text's conceptual model in the context of the research setting. The following sections articulate key hypotheses and their associated variables which will test the relationships between individual socialization, organizational culture, and organizational planning, and various attitudes toward community policing (as a philosophy, as implemented in MCPD, etc.).

Hypotheses

Preceding chapters reviewed previous research to identify a number of critical issues relating to organizational change in police agencies. Based this review, the following hypotheses (presented in the null form) have been identified and tested in this text:

Ho_1: Measures of individual socialization will not significantly affect the respondents' attitude about community policing as a philosophy.

Ho_2: Measures of individual socialization will not significantly affect the respondents' evaluation of community policing as it was instituted in the Motor City Police Department.

Ho_3: Measures of individual socialization will not significantly affect the respondents' belief about how the Motor City Police Department should organize community policing in the future.

Ho_4: Respondent demographics will not significantly affect perceptions of the organizational culture in the Motor City Police Department.

Ho_5: Perceptions of the organizational culture of the Motor City Police Department do not have a significant effect on the respondents' evaluation of community policing as it was instituted in the Motor City Police Department.

Ho_6: Perceptions of the organizational culture of the Motor City Police Department do not have a significant effect on the respondents' beliefs about how MCPD should organize community policing in the future.

Ho_7: Perceptions of the organizational culture of the Motor City Police Department do not have a significant effect on the respondents' attitude about community policing as a philosophy.

Ho_8: Attitude about community policing as a philosophy does not have a significant effect on the respondents' evaluation of community policing it was instituted in the Motor City Police Department.

Ho_9: Attitude about community policing as a philosophy does not have a significant effect on beliefs about how the Motor City Police Department should organize community policing in the future.

Ho_{10}: Evaluations of community policing as instituted in the Motor City Police Department Perceptions do not have a significant effect on the belief of how MCPD should organize community policing in the future.

In addition, these and other salient issues illuminated by the literature review will be considered in the context of descriptive statistical analysis and qualitative research findings.

Data Analysis & Key Variables

The original evaluation research project which generated the data used in this text was evaluative/descriptive in nature. This text has subjected the original survey research data to inferential testing in order to determine if the results might be generalized to other settings. Data analysis consists of both descriptive and inferential statistics. Frequency distributions and contingency tables are used to provide descriptive information about select variables. In addition, the Independent Samples Test was used to compare mean responses between categories of respondents. Predictive relationships have been tested using regression analysis. Because some conceptually relevant variables were not directly measured in the survey instrument, factor analysis has been used to construct appropriate scales.

In addition to the quantitative analysis, qualitative research findings are discussed within the conceptual framework established in the literature review. Descriptive results of other quantitative methodologies (described in Appendix A) are employed throughout the text to illuminate salient points. Critical variables have been identified for each of the hypotheses proffered above. These independent variables (IV) and dependent variables (DV) have been derived based upon the review of prior research literature. Control variables (CV) are included where relevant. The following list identifies the salient variable for each hypothesis:

Ho_1: IV- Attitude about community policing as a philosophy
DV- CPO experience, rank, gender, years of service, education, race/ethnicity
CV- Precinct

Ho_2: IV- Evaluation of community policing as instituted in MCPD
DV- CPO experience, rank, gender, years of service, education, race/ethnicity
CV- Precinct

Ho_3: IV- Belief about how MCPD should organize community policing
DV- CPO experience, rank, gender, years of service, education, race/ethnicity
CV- Precinct

Ho_4: IV- Perceptions of the organizational culture in MCPD
DV- CPO experience, rank, gender, years of service, education, race/ethnicity
CV- Precinct

Ho_5: IV- Evaluation of community policing as instituted in MCPD
DV- Perceptions of organizational culture in MCPD, CPO experience, rank, gender
CV- Precinct, years of service, education, race/ethnicity

Ho_6: IV- Belief about how MCPD should organize community policing
DV- Perceptions of organizational culture in MCPD, CPO experience, rank, gender
CV- Precinct, years of service, education, race/ethnicity

Ho_7: IV- Attitude about community policing as a philosophy
DV- Perceptions of organizational culture in MCPD, CPO experience, rank, gender
CV- Precinct, years of service, education, race/ethnicity

Ho_8: IV- Evaluation of community policing as instituted in MCPD
DV- Attitude about community policing as a philosophy, CPO experience, rank, gender
CV- Precinct, years of service, education, race/ethnicity

Ho_9: IV- Belief about how MCPD should organize community policing
DV- Attitude about community policing as a philosophy, CPO experience, rank, gender
CV- Precinct, years of service, education, race/ethnicity

Ho_{10}: IV- Belief about how MCPD should organize community policing
IV- Evaluation of community policing as instituted in MCPD, CPO experience, rank, gender
CV- Precinct, years of service, education, race/ethnicity

SUMMARY

The literature review provided justification for the various methodologies employed to gather data in the original evaluation research project. This chapter described the methodology (description of the original evaluation project, instrument construction, survey procedures, etc.) used to develop the data analyzed in this text. These data are the focus of the most rigorous quantitative analysis undertaken in this text. Data obtained through alternative means are used as needed to provide a descriptive and contextual setting for the study findings. The following chapters will provide the results of the analysis of this data and the hypotheses testing. In keeping with the case study method, the text draws upon data gathered through a number of different means to reach its conclusions.

The literature on community policing has largely overlooked the implementation process as it relates to contemporary change in American police organizations. Consequently, the research literature has a "tendency to focus on 'successful' programs...rather than acquire important knowledge about the process of COP implementation" (Zhao, Thurman, & Lovrich, 1995: 12). If community policing is going to become an innovation which redefines American policing, planners and executives need to have a better understanding of the various issues which must be addressed in the implementation process.

While existing literature may be correct in suggesting that community policing has tremendous potential, it has often been misleading by not portraying this simple reality: implementing community policing is very difficult. This text examines the implementation process in order to develop a more full understanding of associated challenges as they relate to three key concepts: individual socialization, organizational culture, and organization planning. This conceptual framework provides robust insights into the change process by examining the dynamics behind change and resistance on multiple levels (such as planning, socialization, and demographics).

Individual socialization is the "baggage" an employee brings with them to their job. It is a complex web of demographics, life experiences, education, upbringing, and prior socialization. It impacts upon how employees view their job, their peers, their supervisors, and their organization. Organizational culture consists of the traditions, values, beliefs and attitudes collectively held by an organization's employees. It is distinct from individual socialization because it generally endures with few alterations across generations of employees. Together, these concepts form the "human" issues which must be dealt with during the change process. The biases, perceptions, opinions, attitudes, and fears of employees must be confronted and addressed, regardless of how irrational they may seem to an organization's planners and executives. These factors lead to some of the most challenging dimensions which planners must confront in the implementation process. Of all the issues which planners must confront in bringing about change, these factors may be most difficult to deal with because they are intangible and often seem outside of an organization's control.

Other elements that make change a daunting process are controllable. Issues of training, clarity, policy, procedure, structure, accountability, and evaluation are clearly within a planner's control. These are the "bread and butter" of the police planner's world. Hypothetically, if a planner pays enough attention to these controllable elements, they should not serve as a barrier to successful organizational change. What makes these elements difficult is that they are linked to more human elements. For example, involving select employees in the planning process may help produce important ideas and insights; at the same time, it may make management's efforts to instill participatory management seem ingenious and hollow to those employees who are not given a voice.

Thus, while these three core ideas are conceptually distinct, they are all analytically interrelated. The goal of this text is to merge qualitative and quantitative measures to develop a more holistic understanding of the challenges to effective organizational change. The author uses data derived through a variety of methodologies to better understand these experiences in the context of the conceptual framework derived in the literature review. Specifically, examining how individual socialization (demographics, the psychological contract, distrust of management, perceptions of change as a threat, and employee attitudes), organizational culture (tensions between labor and management, the image of traditional and community-oriented policing, and attitudes toward change), and organization planning (clarity, accountability, evaluations, rewards, unions, key actors, and the changing role of supervisors) may intersect to create barriers to effective organizational change in police agencies.

In the context of this text it is important to remember that an officer's attitudes toward community policing may be distinct from their evaluation of how community policing was instituted in the Motor City Police Department. Much of the resistance encountered in the MCPD may not have been because officers resist the principals of community policing, but that officers tend to resist any change which deviates from traditional policing practices and operations. The change process forces employees to "relearn" how to do their job, how to interact with their superiors and peers, and how they will be evaluated and rewarded. This relearning may generate feelings of uncertainty and also requires extra work on the part of employees.

Perhaps one of the greatest challenges in studying issues of police practice and operation is created by the very nature of the occupation. Although this challenge will not be directly addressed in this text, its impact should be recognized. In an occupation in which uncertainty, ambiguity, confrontation, and animosity are daily staples, many endeavors designed to enhance police services and modify occupational practices seem horribly "academic" in nature. Herman Goldstein best described the dilemma when he noted that: "One takes on a heavy burden in exploring theories, principles, and organizing concepts in a field in which there is an ever-present, urgent need to provide immediate relief from threatening problems" (1990: xi-xii).

The following chapters will report on the analysis of the survey data as specified in this chapter. The analysis incorporates both quantitative and qualitative data to provide a more thorough understanding of barriers to effective change in police organizations. Chapter 7 establishes the context in which this data was collected by providing the reader with a history of community policing in Motor City. This is followed in Chapter 8 by a presentation of relevant univariate and bivariate survey results, along with key qualitative study findings. Chapter 9 provides the final portion of the analysis by detailing the development of factors and testing the hypotheses proffered above[2].

---

[2] Although these chapters may seem very critical, it is not the author's intent to besmirch the image or reputation of the Motor City Police Department. It is an agency with dedicated leaders and planners, and a high-quality front-line. The organization's experiences with the challenges of implementing successful organizational change were nearly universal. The problems encountered by MCPD were due to causes other than poor quality employees, inept planning, or aimless leadership. The Department serves as an example of the problems which arise when planners and managers do not learn from the lessons of the past.

CHAPTER 7

Community Policing in Motor City

This text considers the implementation of a team-based, generalized community policing system in a medium-sized police agency. Prior to considering data which describe this implementation experience, it is necessary to provide the reader with an appreciation for the context in which the data were gathered. This chapter will acquaint the reader with Motor City and its history with community policing efforts. It elaborates upon the nature of an organizational change initiated by the Motor City Police Department in 1995. The chapter also describes the officer survey response rate and respondent characteristics. Finally, it examines the level of community policing and problem solving which was actually occurring within the Motor City Police Department at the time of data collection. This information will acquaint the reader with the research setting and the historical circumstances which preceded and directed Motor City's experience with generalized community policing.

A HISTORY OF COMMUNITY POLICING IN MOTOR CITY

This study is focused upon an organizational change initiated by the Motor City Police Department in the mid-1990's. Prior to undertaking an analysis of data relating to the effects of this change, it is important that the reader have a basic understanding of certain preceding events. The following history was developed using Annual Reports published by the Motor City Police Department for the years 1990-1996. Additional information was also obtained through interviews with (current and former) MCPD executives and patrol officers who had been given early community policing responsibilities in the Department.

Early Community Policing Efforts

The Motor City Police Department began its community policing initiative in the fall of 1990. At that time, a number of inner city neighborhoods were experiencing problems with "crack" cocaine. The sale of crack was frequently taking place from open air markets, which had a disruptive and disturbing effect on community residents and the integrity of the affected neighborhoods. The Department determined that they would deploy officers to work directly with community residents in developing and implementing solutions to this rapidly emerging crime problem. Initially, two small areas were chosen in which to test the impact these "community policing officers" (CPO's) would have in the community.

The original CPO's were embraced by the residents of the neighborhoods in which they worked. Although the drug problem persisted, it improved a great deal in a short period of time. Over the course of the next few years, one CPO working on the westside of Motor City was able to "shut down" (have residents evicted or otherwise forced from a rented property) more than 150 suspected drug houses. While the crack cocaine problem still existed, it had been disrupted and displaced. As it became clear that the efforts of the CPO's were successful, the Department began to expand the community policing program by adding more officers in new areas throughout the community. Each community policing officer was assigned to a specific area (usually a fraction of a square mile) where they were given sole responsibility for improving the quality of life for that neighborhood and its residents.

By the end of 1990, the Community Policing Program (CPP) consisted of five officers and one sergeant. In 1991, the CPP added two more officers and established its first "network center" (a facility which brought various police, government, and social services under one roof to facilitate communication and cooperation). The CPP became the Community Policing Unit (CPU) in 1992. The CPU was led by a lieutenant and a sergeant, who directed the activities of twelve officers; a member of the investigations division (who was still under the control of investigations division supervisors) was given the designation of "community policing detective" with the responsibility of handling investigations within the community policing areas.

In 1993, the CPO's were once again moved within the organization. The CPU merged with the former Community Services Unit (responsible for school education programs, neighborhood watch, and senior citizen programs) to create the Community Bureau (CB). The CB contained more than ten percent of MCPD's sworn personnel, with 23 officers (13 designated as community policing officers), three sergeants, and a lieutenant. The 1994 Annual Report contains no record of how many officers held a community policing officer designation, nor does it reflect where they were located within the structure of the Department.

Both the Department and the community believed that community policing was making a difference. Neighborhoods that received CPO's generally welcomed them with open arms. It was very common for strong ties to develop between neighborhood residents and their CPO. One neighborhood was so enamored with their CPO that he became the namesake for their neighborhood association. By the mid-1990's, all of the early CPO's had moved on to other responsibilities within the Department. Despite this, even a decade later, some maintained ties with residents and organizations in the neighborhoods they once served (often volunteering their free time to work with after-school programs, neighborhood cleanups, and neighborhood association meetings).

Almost from the outset, those officers given community policing assignments were granted flexibility in scheduling their hours and determining which tasks they would address on a given day. This was done to enable officers to adjust their availability in order to best serve the needs of their neighborhood. Officers in the Patrol Division, while assigned to a specific beat, handled emergency situations, responded to routine calls for service, and provided back up for other officers throughout the city. In contrast, the CPO's rarely responded to any incident occurring outside of their assigned neighborhood. This specialist approach to community policing was one that was adopted by many law enforcement agencies around the county. Although it kept the CPO's in a fixed area during most of their working hours (which served the ends of community policing), specialization tended to create tension between these "specialists" (CPO's) and "generalists" (road officers).

There was little stability in where these CPO's were located within the organizational structure. From 1990-1995, CPO's were housed in no less than four units/bureaus/programs within MCPD. This continual shifting only contributed to the perception that the community policing initiative was in chaos. Regardless of the reason for these changes, the informal message sent to patrol officers was that the Department did not know what it was doing with community policing. Although there was logic behind each shift, to road officers it appeared that upper management did not know what it was doing with community policing. To officers working as CPO's, the continual shifting did not have an impact on day-to-day operations, but made their duties less certain.

The Team-Based System

In late 1994, after pursuing this specialist approach to community policing for approximately four years, it became apparent to the Department that many changes needed to be made. The Department was organized in a manner which was typical for police agencies in cities of Motor City's size. There was a dense organizational hierarchy in a central police headquarters; all officers and activities originated from this central facility. Communication patterns were up and down the chain of command; request for information "went through the channels." Decision making was highly centralized and it was felt that the Department was too far removed from the community which it served.

During this same time period (1994-1995), three significant events were taking place. First, after a period of introspective evaluation, upper management was coming to the realization that MCPD was operating in a very inefficient fashion. There was a great deal of redundancy as officers in various branches of the organization attempted to address the same problems without any cooperation. The cliché description of the "right hand not knowing what the left hand was doing" aptly described the state of affairs within the Department. For example, the crack cocaine problem was being targeted by a multi-jurisdictional task force, a Departmental drug enforcement unit, the Patrol Division, and Community

Policing Officers. All of these groups were working on the same problem at the same time, but with little or no communication and coordination of their efforts.

Second, community policing had evolved to a point where the bulk of the Department viewed it as a "bastard child." Given the nature of their duties, the CPO's had little direct supervision or accountability. In addition, they had been granted considerable flexibility in making their own schedule and deciding how they would spend their work hours. These issues were a source of contention for patrol officers, supervisors, and the union. Many officers resented having to spend eight hours "running from call to call" and writing multiple incident reports in order to allow CPO's to spend eight hours "planting flowers" or taking a group of children to watch a professional sporting event.

The third significant event was a shift in the City's leadership. A new mayor was elected in 1992 and the City leadership was shifting from conservative to liberal tendencies. Many officers saw the new mayor as the proverbial "bleeding heart liberal." He was perceived by many as a micro-manager who wanted to approve everything done by all City departments. This was contrary to a long-standing tradition of allowing the police chief to be the "king of his castle." Persons employed by the city or active in city government began to sense that there was a strong underlying tension between the Chief of Police and the Mayor. The common perception in certain sectors was that community support was the only thing which was keeping the Chief, an "at-will" employee, from being fired by the new Mayor.

The Department was highly committed to their community policing strategy. The Chief of Police and other top executives wanted to see all of the organization's personnel actively engaged in community policing endeavors. The Department believed that the CPO's were effective and efficient in "cleaning up" their assigned neighborhoods and improving police-citizen relations. Unfortunately, it was also becoming apparent that much of what the CPO's were accomplishing was achieved through displacement. Problems were migrating out of CPO neighborhoods and into neighborhoods that had previously been safe and quiet. MCPD administrators began to realize that if community policing was ever going to be effective on a broader scale (i.e., throughout Motor City), it could not just be delegated to specialists operating in select areas of the city.

Such an effect would only be realized through the collective efforts of every officer in the Department.

A Reorganization Committee (consisting of officers and supervisors below the rank of lieutenant) was formed to develop possible means by which the Department could be realigned so that all officers were working together to target community problems. The Committee was told that its recommendations would be reviewed by the Mayor and the Department's administration, who would ultimately decide upon the future structure and operation of the Department. The Mayor gave his endorsement to the Committee and promised to do his best to ensure that their recommendations would become a reality. Efforts were made to keep the Committee's activities "in the light" as much as possible by publishing meeting minutes. The patrol officers' union (a lodge of the Fraternal Order of Police) and civilian staff representatives also sat on the Committee so that all voices in the organization would be heard. After several months of research and debate the Committee submitted three proposals to the administration for consideration.

In the end, the Department's administration selected a plan that required them to give patrol officers temporal and geographic responsibilities within the beat they policed. This plan was also designed to strengthen the traditionally weak ties between the Detectives Bureau and the Patrol Division. It was a large leap from where the Department was at the time the Committee issued its report to where it would have to go to make the selected plan a reality. MCPD administrators formed another committee to facilitate this transformation process. This Implementation Committee was not allowed to change the theme of the reorganization. Instead, their task was to move the department from organizational structure A (community policing as a specialized responsibility) to organizational structure B (community policing as a generalized responsibility). Members from the lower ranks of the Department made up the bulk of this Implementation Committee, with seats for civilian and union representatives.

The Department instituted plans to adopt a strategy in which all officers would have responsibilities as problem solving generalists (while keeping the designation of Community Police Officer for some individuals). Patrol officers would still have responsibilities for handling incoming calls for service in an assigned geographic area during the course of their shift. At the same time, the officers were expected to develop collaborative ways in which they could solve long-term neighborhood problems within this same area. Every officer would be assigned to a "permanent" area which they would patrol each time they came to work. Officers would respond to routine calls for service, while also seeking out more informal and proactive ways to come into contact with the public.

One way in which officers would build ties with area residents was through attending meetings of "neighborhood associations." One by-product of the early community policing efforts was an explosion in neighborhood associations– coalitions of area residents who would meet periodically to discuss neighborhood events and issues. These neighborhood associations were concerned not only with crime, but also with quality of life and fostering a sense of community in their neighborhood. While meeting topics might include drug dealing and wayward youth, they could also involve neighborhood beautification and social activities. A high priority under the team-based system would be to ensure that team officers routinely attended the meetings of the various neighborhood associations within their area to facilitate improved communication and relations between the Department and the community.

Thus, in addition to patrolling their area, officers would also work closely with area residents to identify and solve neighborhood problems (both criminal and non-criminal). These solutions would be the collective effort of a "team" of patrol officers and detectives who were responsible for policing a given area around the clock. In other words, officers had responsibilities to handle the immediate problems which occurred on their shift (temporal responsibilities), as well as the long-term problems which might occur in their assigned area at any time of the day (geographic responsibilities). This was the basis of, and impetus behind, the reorganization plan that was placed into effect in March of 1995.

The purpose of the reorganization was to remove structural obstacles to the effective and complete implementation of a community policing philosophy. This approach would make community policing a generalized (something done by every employee), rather than a specialized (something done by a select few) function within the Department. The reorganization plan was based upon this new strategy of taking a team approach to community policing. The plan specified that the Department was to be divided into two precincts, North and South (each covering approximately ½ of the city). Rather than working out of a centralized facility located in downtown Motor City, team members would be relocated into new facilities located more centrally within each precinct. For deployment purposes, each of the precincts was further subdivided into ten patrol districts, or team areas, for a total of 20 team areas city wide.

This new configuration was a departure from the Department's traditional way of organizing and deploying personnel. Previously, the Department had deployed officers into 14 patrol districts. Generally, senior officers were assigned to a specific patrol district on an ongoing basis; every shift they worked would be in the same district. Officers with less experience would work a different district every day, covering for co-workers who had the day off. While there were informal and voluntary mechanisms through which officers covering a patrol district could share information across shifts, such collaboration was not the norm. The new organizational structure would improve upon this existing deployment method (in which only senior officers policed the same area every time they worked), while also requiring collaboration across shifts. In addition, communication would be improved between patrol, investigative, traffic, canine, and community policing personnel.

The number of sergeant positions in the Patrol Division was increased to twenty so that each sergeant could oversee the operations of one team area. The sergeants oversaw a "team" of four to six officers from the Patrol Division, one or two officers from the traffic unit, one or two detectives, and, in some instances, an officer from the canine unit. If a team encompassed an area which had historically been serviced by a Community Policing Officer, this situation was not modified. Although there was originally discussion of removing all CPO's from the neighborhoods, this idea met quick opposition from the community and was abandoned. While team members outside of the Patrol Division (i.e., canine, traffic, detectives and CPO's) still "answered" to the supervisors within their unit, they were expected to work with their team sergeant to address long-term neighborhood issues.

Patrol officers were responsible for providing primary policing services in their team area during their hours of duty. Unfortunately, personnel limitations precluded having a team officer actually working in each team area around the clock. This meant that officers would still handle calls for service and provide back up in team areas other than their own. For example, three adjacent team areas (A, B, and C) might each have an officer assigned to the day shift. During any given shift, the officer assigned to team A might have the day off and the officer assigned to team B might be in training, testifying in court, or handling a call for service. This left the officer assigned to team area C with the responsibility of handling incoming calls for service in not only her own team area, but also in team areas A and B. This increase in the workload of officer C made it difficult for her to find the time to engage in long-term problem solving efforts. Despite this restriction, MCPD administrators hoped that officers would be able to spend much of their shift in their assigned team area or at least a smaller sector of their precinct (3-4 team areas).

Under the supervision of the team sergeant, each team identified and targeted team-specific problems which needed to be solved. Teams also worked closely with neighborhood associations and a concerted effort was made to send officers to the meetings these associations held. Each officer had a voice mailbox to facilitate communication within the team, and between officers and citizens. These voice mailbox numbers were widely advertised within the team areas. This was done to encourage residents to bring persistent neighborhood problems directly to the attention of a member from the team which policed their area.

Initially, teams also included detectives. Detectives in Motor City, as in most police organizations, had historically been specialists, focusing most of their time on the investigation of a specific category of offenses (i.e., robbery, auto theft, sex crimes, etc.). Under the new organizational plan, investigators would be assigned to a team area where they would work as generalists, providing all investigative services needed in that area (although homicides were still investigated on a city wide basis by a small group of detectives). Even before the reorganization was officially implemented tension emerged between the Detective Bureau and the Department's administration.

Investigative personnel felt that it reduced the Bureau's overall effectiveness to have each detective focus their energy on a geographic area rather than a specific category of offenses. The original logic for having one or two investigators handle the investigation of incidents of a specific offense was twofold. First, to allowed investigators develop a degree of specialization in the investigation and case formulation necessary to successfully arrest and prosecute a specific category of offender. Second, it allowed the investigators to track serial offenders who were committing crimes throughout Motor City. By having investigators focused on handling all the investigations in a specific geographic area, these elements were lost. Although the detectives may have simply disliked being involved in community policing, there was a logical rationale behind their argument.

The detectives were worried that offending patterns (which rarely limit themselves to a specific beat) would be lost because investigators handling different team areas would not know that they were tracking the same offender. In addition, detectives assigned to "slow" team areas had little to do, while detectives assigned to "hot" team areas were forced to select which cases would receive more of their attention. Although having the detectives working closely with the teams improved communication between investigators and patrol officers, it was believed that this was occurring at the expense of communication within the Detective Bureau. This loss of communication allegedly compromised the overall integrity and quality of criminal investigations within the agency. After a 12-month trial period, it was decided that this generalist approach to investigations was not yielding the expected results. The detectives were relieved of team-based duties and were once again given crime-specific investigative responsibilities.

Officers from the canine and traffic units were also assigned to teams. Even after detectives were removed from the teams, this practice persisted, although these officers generally had little involvement with team matters. Members of both units had duties that required them to devote their efforts on a scale larger than a standard police beat. Although at times members of the canine unit would spend a shift assigned to a particular beat, the nature of their function necessitated that they travel throughout the precinct (and at times, the City). Members of the traffic unit often had daily obligations which resulted in them traveling throughout the entire City. Although these officers had some "free" time in which they could engage in targeted traffic enforcement, many of their efforts were devoted to special events and directing traffic. Consequently, most members of both of these units never developed any type of psychological attachment to their assigned team area. Their involvement was primarily on paper and team sergeants were generally reluctant to push them to become more active in their assigned team area.

When the reorganization was implemented in 1995, there were twelve CPO's in Motor City. Seven were assigned to areas in the newly created North Precinct and the remaining five served areas in the newly created South Precinct. The CPO's were no longer a part of the Community Bureau (which was moved from the Patrol Division to the Central Services Division), but they were not fully integrated into the precincts. Throughout the course of the original evaluation study there was confusion over how CPO's "fit" with the remained of the Department. While not a completely separate unit, CPO's were never fully integrated into the team system. Each CPO served a neighborhood within a larger team area. They worked with the supervisor and officers who policed this area, but, outside of their assigned neighborhood, had few formal obligations to the team. In addition, because they were granted a limited ability to "flex" their schedule, CPO's were not accountable to a particular shift. Given this arrangement, CPO's were still on the fringe of the Department. They were perhaps less integrated within the Department after the team system was implemented because they were not formally a part of any larger unit within the organization.

The Role of the Union

MCPD administrators made several efforts to work cooperatively with the police officer's union in negotiating changes in the process by which officers selected the precinct and shift they wished to work. Traditionally, every third scheduling cycle (every twelve weeks) officers were allowed to "bid" (based on seniority) for the shift they wished to work. By splitting the Department into two precincts, it became necessary to allow officers to also select the precinct in which they wished to work. This created a troubling situation in that an officer could now switch both her shift and precinct every three months, which might seriously erode the cohesion and integrity of the teams.

The union agreed to allow officers to continue to choose their shift on a quarterly basis and consented to limit officers to one precinct change per year. In other words, once an officer selected a precinct, she or he had to remain there for at least one year. The only exceptions would occur if the officer were transferred to another unit within the Department or if the Department needed to reassign him/her to balance the distribution of officers. In exchange for this agreement, the Department consented to deploy officers on a "four & ten" (four ten-hour shifts per week) schedule. Although the annual hours worked by an officer were not significantly impacted, officers could now enjoy an extra fifty-two days off every year (something which they found very desirable).

This agreement was reached in order to maintain stable team assignments. Allowing officers to change shifts and precincts every three months would force the Department to continually shuffle team assignments. This shuffling would be necessary to accommodate the movements of senior officers. To compensate for the movements of senior personnel, new officers, because of their low seniority, would also have to be displaced to balance out personnel deployment. It was recognized that this quarterly movement would make it much more difficult for officers to get to know the area in which they worked. In addition, the active citizens in a neighborhood would be continually learning the new names and faces of the officers policing their area.

By keeping officers in a precinct for a year, a certain amount of movement across shifts could occur without disrupting team assignments. It meant that two officers from a given shift might be assigned to the same team, while another team might have no one from that shift. The Department weighed the advantages and disadvantages of this approach and felt that it was the best possible compromise. Although this agreement occasionally resulted in a team which was rather "lopsided" for a few months, it seemed to be the best way to balance the demands of the union with the needs of the Department. If the team deployment plan was going to work, mechanisms had to be in place so that officers would be working within the same geographic area on an ongoing basis.

Concerns With Continuity

Community policing is based upon the idea that an officer will work in the same neighborhood on a daily basis. This allows the officer to get to know the "in's and out's" of that section of the community. By attending the meetings of neighborhood associations and working with community leaders, officers can build alliances with the citizens, while citizens put a name and a face with their police department. Although they recognized the contractual and pragmatic limitations which necessitated the shift/precinct selection compromise, some team sergeants still felt the arrangement detracted from team accomplishments. Every time officers bid for the shift they wanted to work, a small percentage would be reassigned to a new team or precinct. This had to be done to balance where and when officers were working. While efforts were made to keep changes to a minimum, shifting personnel was always necessary.

This concern over continuity emerged repeatedly in interviews with command officers and during focus group sessions with patrol sergeants. A patrol lieutenant remarked that the turn over of officers (and, to a lesser extent, sergeants) hampered the progress of the teams. Each time someone rotated out of a team, it was a small step backward. When the turn over issue came up during the focus groups, sergeants expressed great concern. They indicated that the rapid turn over eroded team stability and made it difficult to foster a sense of continuity. Every time the teams shifted (typically every third month) community residents had to develop a relationship with a new officer (and vice versa).

Just when things were beginning to work well within the team and within the area, one or two officers would be shifted out and new replacements would arrive. Sergeants felt that the situation forced them and their officers to continually devote time and energy into developing relationships with the community. One sergeant reported that in the first year of the reorganization he had eight officers rotate out of his team (in addition to several officers who were permanent fixtures). Consequently, this sergeant was constantly introducing new officers to neighborhood associations and community leaders, a task which he found embarrassing. Concerns with stability were also expressed by officers. Some feared that turn over allowed some officers to escape from team responsibilities. By shifting teams every three months, officers could avoid becoming integrated into team efforts and sharing in any of the extra work created by the team-based system.

Resocialization

The process of changing from a traditional to a team-based community policing organizational structure and policing style involved two key elements. First, the organizational structure of MCPD had to change. Deployment, training, and supervision structures would need to be modified in order to allow officers to function as a team to solve ongoing problems in their assigned geographic area. Second, there would need to be a resocialization process within the organization. Officers would have to learn how to "do" community policing and why it was important to do so. While organizational structure can "push" officers to do community policing, resocialization can "pull" them to do so. The structural elements can force officers to do their duties in a certain manner, while resocialization can make officers want to perform their duties in this fashion. Both elements are important.

Officers needed to have a structure which supported team-based operations; at the same time, they needed to have the desire to succeed in carrying out problem solving in a team-based setting. Unfortunately, MCPD made only half-hearted attempts at changing their structure in support of team-based community policing; resocialization efforts, on the other hand, were almost nonexistent. Examples of resocialization in support of the team-based system might have included many elements; most important, changing the organizational culture to place a collective value on successful problem solving and embracing a community policing orientation in policing Motor City.

This resocialization could have occurred through a variety of mechanisms. The Department might have solicited union support for efforts to bringing about organizational change. This support could have served as one "seal of approval" to encourage officers to accept the restructuring. Key actors could have been involved; if the organization had taken the time and initiative to bring central employees "on board" with the changes, other employees might have followed suit. Mid-level supervisors could also have played a key role in the resocialization process. Sergeants and lieutenants could have become leaders within the Department and within their own teams. Seeing their team sergeant embracing a community policing orientation might have encouraged officers to take the reorganization seriously.

In the process of bringing about successful organizational change, police planners need to give due considerations to resocialization. Too often, police planners may focus their energies on the structure of a change. While this structure can help "push" officers toward new patterns of occupational behavior, it is only half of the change equation. Tactics aimed at modifying officer behavior and attitude need to account for those elements which can "pull" officers to exhibit desired occupational conduct.

The Effects of Community Policing on Officers

The reorganization plan represented a major shift in the approach the Department was taking toward community policing. Problem solving activities were no longer limited to those officers holding CPO assignments and the small geographic areas that they policed. Instead, problem solving activities were expanded to the entire Department and the whole city. The Department hoped that the "team" approach would capitalize on the benefits of task specialization (e.g., developing strong skills in "bonding" with the community, instilling officers with a sense of ownership) without incurring the usual costs such specialization brings (e.g., alienation of generalists from specialists and the marginalization of specialists from the core functions of policing).

MCPD's prior history with specialization issues in community policing was typical of many departments where such problems have arisen. Community policing had traditionally been a specialized assignment which was not taken seriously by most line officers. The constant shifting of community policing within the organization in the early 1990's contributed to this situation. To line employees, the constant shifting was an indication that community policing should not be taken seriously. Community policing was not viewed as "real" police work and officers actively avoided CPO assignments. By the mid-1990's, few officers were willing to volunteer for a CPO position. Instead, the Department had to "draft" rookie officers to work as CPO's.

CPO's reported that their peers often treated them differently (which was one reason officers were reluctant to volunteer for the position). CPO's were perceived as "glorified babysitters" who planted flowers and took kids to amusement parks while "real cops arrested dopers." One newly appointed CPO remarked that her co-workers treated her differently as soon as she began her CPO assignment (even though she had been "drafted" into the position). According to this officer, it was not that her peers disliked her as a person, they just disliked her current position within the organization. Her co-workers were not treating her in an overtly hostile fashion– they simply ignored her.

The team approach was an attempt to create a community policing design which would overcome these common, but persistent, problems with how community policing had been organized. The Department hoped that the team approach would better serve the community, while making the work experience for all police officers better than (or at least as good as) the previous community policing system. The Department also recognized that the full potential of community policing would only be realized by integrating community policing into the organizational philosophy. It was felt that MCPD's success in integrating specialists (CPO's) with generalists (patrol officers) depended upon the ability to convince personnel in all units of the interrelatedness and interdependency of specialized and generalized operations.

The evaluation project which produced the data used in this text was initiated by MCPD administrators in order to better understand whether the change process was working. The administrators were also seeking input on what they might do in order to successfully make community policing a function of every employee of the organization. The reorganization took place in stages over the course of a year. The SCJ research team first began to study the change process near the end of this year when the final transitions were being made. The project continued for approximately two and a half years. At that time, a new Chief of Police entered the scene and altered the organizational structure (in a fashion inconsistent with the research team's recommendations).

The analysis that follows is based upon interviews, surveys, and observations made by the SCJ research team during their two and a half year involvement with the Motor City Police Department. The author will focus on data which relates to those barriers which prevented the organization from successfully adopting a community policing philosophy. Many of the issues addressed in this study were addressed in project reports that were collaboratively prepared by the author and SCJ faculty members. However, the following analysis is set in a conceptual framework independently developed by the author. Any errors, conceptual short comings, or analytical faults are the sole responsibility of the author and should not be imputed on the SCJ researchers involved in the original project.

RESPONSE RATE & RESPONDENT CHARACTERISTICS

During the spring of 1997, the survey instrument (Appendix C) was administered to all patrol officers, Community Policing Officers, patrol sergeants and patrol lieutenants in the Motor City Police Department. Administration was carried out by those officers and sergeants who had participated in the initial focus groups. At the time of the survey administration there still appeared to be a degree of paranoia in the relationship between line officers and upper management. It was unclear how officers would respond to a survey administered by SCJ staff. External administration could have been viewed as a way to identify officers who were not "on the band wagon" with the new organizational structure. The personnel who participated in the focus groups had been selected because they were respected by their co-workers. By utilizing these internal personnel to administer the survey, it was hoped that officers would be open in their responses and that the response rate would be improved.

One hundred and forty-three officers were eligible to complete the survey at the time of its administration. Participation was voluntary. Officers who administered the survey were instructed not to pressure their co-workers into completing the survey. Respondents were supposed to be given the opportunity to complete the survey in private. Officers not wishing to complete the survey were told to simply seal the blank instrument in an envelope (provided with the survey) and return it to the administering officer. Using this protocol allowed officers to "save face" by appearing compliant in the eyes of their co-worker (if that was their desire).

The SCJ research team received 128 surveys from MCPD officers; eight blank surveys were returned. One hundred and twenty (120) of these surveys were usable, yielding a response rate of 84 percent. In recent years there has been considerable debate among criminal justice scholars about the adequacy of survey research response rates (Hagan, 1997; Neuman & Wiegand, 2000). Hagan (2000) describes how response rates for survey research have declined in the second half of the Twentieth Century, making the determination of adequacy more complicated. Despite this growing uncertainty, most scholars categorize response rates above 70 percent as "very good" (Babbie, 1992: 267) and those approaching 90 percent as "excellent" (Neuman & Wiegand, 2000: 239). The response rate in this study appears to be well within the normal range for this approach to survey research (Hagan, 2000), particularly in light of the limited amount of follow-up by the research team.

The characteristics of the survey respondents (years of service, gender, race/ethnicity, assigned shift, assigned precinct) were generally in proportion with the characteristics of the eligible population. There is not an identifiable subsection of the population who declined to participate in the survey process. Therefore, the author assumes the survey data is a general reflection of the attitudes, beliefs, and characteristics of the eligible study population.

This section provides a brief description of the characteristics of the survey respondents. This information also provides the best indicator of the overall individual socialization in the Motor City Police Department. Although the conceptual framework presented in the literature review presented a broader view of individual socialization, more thorough information about employee backgrounds and experiences were not available. Given this limitation, this research has relied on those measures (demographics, education, years of service, etc.) more readily accessible through the survey data.

Univariate descriptions of the survey respondents are provided in Table 2. While many survey respondents had been employed with the Motor City Police Department for over a decade, 40 percent had less than five years of experience with the agency. Almost one quarter (22.6%) had less than two years of experience. This verified the concern many officers expressed about the relative youth of the Department. In particular, officers with more seniority indicated concern that newer officers did not have the training and experiences to be effective problem solvers without extra supervision and direction from their peers and command officers.

Table 2.
Characteristics of Survey Respondents. †

Years with MCPD (n=115)	
less than 1 year	4.3%
1-2 years	17.5%
3-5 years	16.7%
6-10 years	19.2%
11-15 years	17.5%
16 or more years	20.8%
Ever been a Community Policing Officer (n=120)	
Yes	17.5%
No	82.5%
Level of Education (n=115)	
Some college (>bachelors)	35.7%
Bachelors	53.0%
Some graduate/law school	2.6%
Graduate/law degree	8.7%
Rank (n=113)	
Officer	80.5%
Supervisor (sgt/lt)	19.5%
Race/ethnicity (n=99)	
White	86.9%
Black	7.1%
Hispanic	3.0%
Asian	1.0%
Other	2.0%
Gender (n=106)	
Female	10.4%
Male	89.6%

† Figures in parentheses indicate the number of valid responses for each item. Percentages are based upon the number of valid responses for the respective item. Percentages for some items may not total 100.0 due to rounding.

The majority of all officers reported having worked for more than six months in the area to which they were currently assigned. Approximately two-thirds (65.7%) of all patrol officers and supervisors indicated that they had routinely worked in their present geographic assignment for over a year. About one in six respondents had experience as a Community Policing Officer (past or present assignment).

Respondents were well-educated. Consistent with the Department's minimum hiring standards, all respondents had some level of college education. Over one-third (35.7%) had a college education which had not (yet) resulted in being awarded a bachelor's degree. Over half (53%) had a bachelor's degree. Approximately one in ten respondents had taken courses in law school or a graduate program; most of those with graduate/law school experience had been awarded an advanced degree.

It is interesting to note that newer officers were more likely to have a bachelor's degree, while older officers tended to have less college experience. Although the Department only required the completion of 60 credit hours (the equivalent of an associate degree), newer employees often had twice this level of education. It is not clear if this is due to a high level of education among applicants or if the Department favored hiring those candidates who surpassed this minimum standard. In addition, most officers with advanced degrees were in the mid-career range (6-15 years with MCPD). This would suggest that many officers were entering the Department with a bachelor's degree and then pursuing graduate education (if they were so inclined) after they had obtained some experience.

The race/ethnicity, gender, and rank of the respondents were all approximately proportional with the Department as a whole. As is common in American policing, the Department was predominantly white and male. According to the 1990 census, Motor City was approximately 75 percent white and 20 percent black. Although the Department was not entirely homogeneous with the City, these demographic figures reflect a certain degree of racial/ethnic diversity. Census data also indicate that only 47.4 percent of Motor City residents were males. Few American police agencies reflect the race/ethnicity and gender distribution of the community they serve (Walker, S., 1999), therefore, these observed disparities do not necessarily reflect poor recruitment, selection, or retention practices on the part of the Department.

Although not reflected in Table 2, respondents appeared to be distributed across the precincts and shifts in the same proportions found in the population. These similarities suggest that the survey respondents were representative of the eligible population in terms of these demographic and experiential characteristics. Survey findings may be safely generalized to represent the attitudes, beliefs and opinions of the entire population (patrol officers, sergeants, and lieutenants, and community policing officers in the Motor City Police Department).

LEVEL OF COMMUNITY POLICING AND PROBLEM SOLVING

An important question researchers must confront (but often ignore) in investigating community policing is the extent to which study agencies actually "do" community policing. In other words, are officers operating in the spirit of a community policing philosophy, or is community policing just rhetoric? This study is focused upon attitudes more than action. Therefore, the level of community policing and problem solving in the Motor City Police Department does not necessarily enhance or diminish subsequent research findings. Nonetheless, the degree to which officers were involved in community policing and problem solving efforts sets the context within which data were collected.

Patrol officers and sergeants issued frequent complaints about the difficulty of engaging in problem solving activities. By it's very nature, police work has an inherent reactive element– police officers will always have to be prepared to respond to certain emergency situations in a rapid fashion. While community policing may reduce this necessity, it cannot be eliminated. Even in a police department attempting to focus on proactive problem solving efforts, it is difficult to overcome this reactive, call-driven orientation. When an agency is oriented toward call-driven policing, officers may find it difficult to create time to engage in problem solving efforts during the course of their normal working hours (especially when faced with staffing shortages, as discussed below).

Consequently, one of the greatest frustrations MCPD officers and sergeants expressed was their inability to set aside time for problem solving efforts. The Patrol Division had a strong orientation toward the notion that "the radio has to come first." As long as the public was calling upon the police to perform certain services, other efforts should be secondary considerations[1]. Even when officers were attempting to engage in problem solving activities, they often had to set aside their efforts to handle calls for service. Because they did not feel that officers had been given the resources (sufficient personnel and time) to carry out problem solving, sergeants did not seem to expect their officers to produce much in this area. The common sentiment expressed throughout the evaluation project was that a team had to produce sufficient problem solving efforts to avoid drawing scrutiny from Department administrators. Sergeants did not push officers to produce any more than this "subsistence" level.

Elements of the officer survey attempted to determine whether MCPD officers were really "doing" community policing. Survey respondents were asked a series of questions about their recent problem solving efforts and other activities which might indicate whether officers were operating in a fashion consistent with a community policing philosophy. Because community policing is uniquely operationalized in each organization, it is difficult to interpret the following results. Rather than providing a firm indication of whether MCPD officers were operationally committed to community policing, these findings simply set the context within which data were collected.

The Motor City Police Department did not have predetermined quantitative goals which would allow them to determine the effectiveness and success of the reorganization. In addition, there are not absolute thresholds which indicate whether an agency and its employees are "doing" community policing. Activity which might be viewed as "success" by one organization may be viewed as "failure" by another. Rather than reflecting success or failure, these results must be considered as a whole to indicate if community policing and problem solving were actually integrated into the activities of patrol officers in the Motor City Police Department.

A central tenet of community policing is the belief that the police should work with citizens to identify and resolve neighborhood problems.

---

[1] The author does not wish to imply that a call-driven approach is inappropriate. Rather, it is suggested that such an approach may create certain tensions when an organization is also attempting more proactive policing strategies.

Where community policing is highly influential in directing the efforts and attentions of officers, it might be expected that officers would rely on input from community members in identifying neighborhood problems. Table 3 presents sources of information which respondents used "often" or "sometimes" to find out about public safety problems in their assigned beat. Caution must be used interpreting this table. Because the data were collected at a "snapshot" point in time, there is no way to know how these frequencies differ (if at all) with officer behavior before the reorganization. In addition, as previously mentioned, these findings are neutral. There is no baseline for determining how appropriate it is for patrol officers to rely on various information sources.

Table 3.
Frequency with which officers used various sources to obtain information about problems in their assigned area. †

Source...	Often	Some-times	Rarely	Never
Respondent's supervisor	30.6%	50.9%	15.7%	2.8%
Citizens living in beat	48.1%	40.7%	10.2%	0.9%
Co-workers	66.7%	31.5%	1.9%	0.0%
Crime statistics & other data	13.9%	43.5%	28.7%	13.9%
Community meetings	25.9%	35.2%	30.6%	8.3%

† Each item had an identical number (n=108) of valid responses. The table reflects row percentages based upon the number of valid responses for the respective item. Percentages for some items may not total 100.0 due to rounding.

Table 3 suggests that officers tended to rely more on their co-workers and informal contact with citizens to obtain information about problems in their beat. Less emphasis was placed on using crime data and formal contact with community groups as a means to find out about neighborhood problems. Analyzing the answers by respondents' rank and experience yields expected patterns. Respondents who were current or former CPO's were more likely to "often" use citizens and community groups as sources of information. Respondents holding supervisory positions were less likely to obtain information from their own supervisors and were far more likely to rely on crime data.

Respondents were asked how long it had been since they had completed a problem solving effort. The distribution of results for this response yielded surprisingly polar responses. Over one-quarter (27.9%) of the respondents reported that they had not completed a problem solving effort. Alternatively, more than 40 percent reported completing such an effort within the month preceding the administration of the survey. When these rates are broken down between the two precincts, unexpected differences emerge. As Table 4 indicates, respondents working in MCPD's North Precinct were much more likely to report having completed a problem solving effort within the month before the survey than were their counterparts in the South Precinct (51.8% versus 33.4%, respectively). South Precinct respondents were more likely to report having completed no problem solving efforts.

The explanation for this disparity is not readily evident. Based on informal interviews and focus groups, there was no indication of a significant disparity between the problem solving activities in the two precincts. One possible explanation might lie in how "problem solving" was defined in the survey instrument. Respondents were told that problem solving meant "doing something to reduce the frequency or seriousness of an ongoing problem in a given area" (see Appendix C, text between items 63 and 64). It is possible that officers in the two precincts interpreted this definition in different fashions, resulting in their reporting analogous behavior in disparate fashions.

Officers who had recently completed a problem solving effort were asked to provide additional information about such endeavors. Respondents reported that their most recent problem solving efforts were aimed at a variety of different problems, the most common of which was drugs (35.7% of completed problem solving efforts). Respondents spent anywhere from one to forty hours working on these most recent problems during the average work week (the mean reported time was eight hours per week). Most problem solving efforts involved the respondents doing much of the work independently. Respondents indicated that on average they only spent about one third of their time working closely with one or more officers. On average, four other officers made significant contributions to this most recent problem solving effort. These latter indicators suggest officers were working independently on an operational level, while coordinating their overall efforts to address problems; tasks were presumably divided to address issues in the most efficient manner.

Table 4.
Length of time since completion of last problem solving effort; all respondents and by respondent's precinct. †

Length of time...	All respondents (n=111)	North Precinct (n=58)	South Precinct (n=45)
Completed no problem solving efforts	27.9%	20.7%	35.6%
Within the last week	18.0%	19.0%	15.6%
Within the last month	24.3%	32.8%	17.8%
Within the last two months	9.9%	10.3%	6.7%
Within the last four months	3.6%	5.2%	0.0%
Within the last six months	9.0%	3.4%	17.8%
Within the last twelve months	7.2%	8.6%	6.7%

† The table reflects column percentages based upon the number of valid responses (figures in parentheses) for the respective item. Percentages for some items may not total 100.0 due to rounding.

Survey respondents overwhelmingly indicated that their most recent problem solving endeavor was a success, with 48.8 percent classifying it as "somewhat successful" and 46.3 percent classifying it as "very successful." The basis for these assessments was largely informal. Almost half of the respondents (45.1 %) made the assessment based on their personal impressions; other common sources included feedback from citizens (32.4%) and feedback from supervisors (14.1%). Supervisors were far more likely to make "success" assessments based on data or a study than were non-supervisors (30.8% versus 2.1%, respectively). Although many respondents (39.7%) felt their project was as successful as possible, one third (32.1%) believed it would have been more successful if additional time and/or resources had been devoted to the problem. Among supervisors, there was a noticeable perception that greater success would have been achieved if there had been more participation from other government agencies.

As previously discussed, implicit in the reorganization plan developed by MCPD was the notion that officers would spend a good portion of their time patrolling and solving problems in their designated team area. Despite assumption, the reality of how officers spent their time was very much to the contrary. The student observers (see Appendix A) recorded approximately how long officers spent in and out of their team area during the course of the observation period. Table 5 displays the percent of shift time officers spent within their assigned team area. The reader is reminded that the observation periods were not random, that observer-officer assignments were not randomized, and that students might not have always known the boundaries of an officer's beat (see Appendix A for a through discussion of the observation data and its limitations).

Table 5.
Percent of shift time officers spent in assigned team area by shift.

Shift	Percent
Day Shift (6:30 am - 4:30 pm)	64%
Special Shift (11:00 am to 9:00 pm)	33%
Afternoon Shift (4:30 pm to 2:30 am)	40%
Night Shift (9:00 pm to 7:00 am)	37%

Source: Mastrofski, Schafer, DeJong & Bynum, 1997.

With the exception of officers on the Day Shift, officers were spending very little time in their assigned team area. It cannot be stated for certain that officers were spending time outside of their shift for official reasons, rather than personal choice. There are, however, two indicators which would suggest that the former, rather than the latter, was the case. The observational data suggest that officers had only a small amount of free time during the course of their shift. The average officer spent about 20 percent of their shift engaged in "general patrol" (Mastrofski, Schafer, DeJong & Bynum, 1997). Within the operational parameters of the coding system used by the student observers, general patrol would be a close analogy to "free time"; this was time when an officer was not handling a call for service, engaged in directed activity, or handling administrative manners. It must be noted that this time would occur intermittently throughout an officer's shift.

The second indicator was the daily staffing level for the two precincts. The SCJ research team reviewed all of the staffing records from 1997 for both precincts. Useable data was obtained for 727 of the 730 "staffing days" in the department (365 days per precinct). These records were used to compute the average number of personnel hours worked in each precinct by officers in the patrol division. It must be remembered that MCPD executives never claimed that each team area would be staffed 24 hours a day. Ideally, each precinct would staff 240 personnel hours each day (24 hours for each of the ten team areas in each precinct) to ensure that most calls for service could be handled by the officer assigned to that beat. The staffing analysis indicated this was rarely the case.

The precincts were only staffed with 240 (or more) personnel hours on 12.9 percent of the days in 1997. One-quarter (25.9%) of the time they were staffing less than 200 personnel hours, meaning that during most of the day at least two team areas were not staffed. While this analysis may be somewhat convoluted, the implications are simple. Because it was rare for each beat to be staffed at any given time, officers were frequently directed to handle calls for service outside of their own team area. As a result, officers were spending less time in their team area and had less discretionary time to devote to solving problems within their beat. This staffing study does not take into account the time officers might spend involved in on-duty court time or training, which would further diminish the number of officers working.

One final element indicates the degree to which community policing and problem solving efforts were being carried out in the Motor City Police Department. In coding data from their observations, student observers answered several questions relating to the degree to which officers engaged in problem solving activities in encounters with the public. Although there is not a baseline for "acceptable" levels of problem-oriented actions, Table 6 suggests that few encounters with the public reflected a long-term orientation on the part of the police. This table only accounts for encounters with citizens and not those actions officers took outside of the presence of a community member. In addition, some encounters may have fit one or more of the following criteria without the observer being aware of that fact (i.e., no obvious cues of that fact).

In the absence of a clear baseline defining high and low levels of problem solving approaches, it is difficult to fully assess the results in Table 6. These percentages may seem to be rather low. It cannot, however, be assumed that every contact the police have with the public relates to a long-term issue requiring a more complex police response. It is not clear whether police officers could attempt a problem-oriented approach in a larger proportion of their contacts with citizens. What this table does suggest is that the overwhelming majority of encounters between the police and the public occur without apparent consideration for underlying problems (assuming such conditions exist in most encounters).

Table 6.
Percent of encounters in which officers exhibited problem-oriented approach.

Action taken by officer	Percent of encounters in which action was observed
Indicated situation was part of a larger problem	7%
Tried to determine nature, extent or causes of the larger problem	1%
Tried to prevent a recurrence of the problem	11%
Encounter was part of a long-term plan or project	7%

Source: Mastrofski, Schafer, DeJong & Bynum, 1997.

The rub of this section on problem solving and community policing in the Motor City Police Department is this: a) although many survey respondents were engaged in problem solving, a sizeable number were not involved in this process; b) most officers developed information about neighborhood problems through informal means; c) when officers were involved in problem solving, they usually worked independently, but in coordination with others; d) officers had a limited amount of free time and spent a good portion of their committed time outside of their assigned beat; e) an overwhelming proportion of police-citizen encounters did not seem to involve any consideration of broader problems.

As indicated in the beginning of this section, it is difficult to truly determine when an organization or an employee is "doing" community policing or problem solving. Expected outcomes are unique to individual organizations and few agencies give any forethought to such desired outcomes in organizing for community policing. Taken as a whole, however, these data do suggest that only a limited amount of problem solving activities were occurring in the Motor City Police Department at the time these data were collected. Although many officers were involved in these problem solving activities with some frequency, such considerations were only reflected in a very small proportion of the calls for service they handled. Furthermore, even those officers wishing to engage in community policing and/or problem solving activities would have to face very real restrictions on their ability to do so vis-a-vis a low amount of free time in their beat.

Chapter 8

Barriers to Change in Motor City

A key focus of this text is to explore the attitudes and beliefs of Motor City police officers. Prior to doing so, it is necessary to examine the responses to specific survey items within the context of the study's conceptual framework. Responses and findings are organized into two categories: individual socialization and organizational culture, and organizational planning. As addressed earlier in this text, although individual socialization and organizational culture are conceptually distinct, the author contends that they are analytically interrelated (especially in the context of this study's data). As such, they are considered concurrently. In this chapter, survey results will be presented with relevant qualitative findings. This discussion highlights the key barriers which Motor City experienced in its efforts to implement generalized community policing.

INDIVIDUAL SOCIALIZATION/ORGANIZATIONAL CULTURE

The sample characteristics provide the best quantitative indicators of the overall background and experiences of the survey respondents. Although the available measures only offer a limited picture of individual socialization as conceptualized in the literature review, no other measures are readily available. The author has attempted to use qualitative findings to provide additional insights into the possible role of individual socialization in the change process.

Ideally, in studying the effects of organizational culture on planned change, data would be collected from multiple agencies. Using this procedure, organizations with different cultures could be compared and contrasted to determine if such variances were associated with divergent experiences in the change process. The use of a single agency in this study precludes such comparative analysis; however, an alternative approach still allows for the assessment of organizational culture as a factor in the change process. By evaluating each respondent's perceptions of the culture in the organization being studied (i.e., whether it was a "healthy" organization with open communication and little distrust between labor and management), the attitudes, opinions and beliefs of respondents can be examined to determine if they are affected by cultural perceptions. This latter approach is used to account for the role of organizational culture in the change process in this analysis.

To reiterate the sample characteristics, respondents were mostly white males. Most respondents had a Bachelors degree, although there were a variety of reported levels of education. The length of time respondents had been employed with MCPD ranged from a few months to several decades. Overall, their years of service were (approximately) evenly distributed, indicating a range of survey respondents from very new, to mid-career, to veteran employees. Although years of service are not analogous with age, it may serve as an approximate measure; presumably respondents ranged in age from officers in their early twenties to officers in their late fifties.

Many of the salient issues and concerns mentioned by the officers during ride alongs, informal meetings and focus group sessions appeared to transcend their demographic characteristics. Reactions to the attempted reorganization of the Motor City Police Department seemed to be consistent across demographic attributes. Officers reported highly consistent attitudes, opinions and reactions, regardless of their race/ethnicity, age (approximated by their years of service), and level of education. It is less certain if other elements of individual socialization may have played a role in mollifying an employee's response to organizational change.

Select survey items and qualitative findings relate to the organizational culture which existed in the Motor City Police Department at the time of the original evaluation study. Dimensions of organizational culture can be divided into two categories. The first category consists of the degree to which the organizational culture (as reflected by the survey respondents) was oriented toward either a community policing or traditional policing philosophy. The second category consists of elements which indicate the overall culture and climate of the organization (i.e., relationship between labor and management, nature of supervision, degree of communication).

Elements of individual socialization and organizational culture are discussed in the following sections. Consideration will be given to the psychological contract, distrust of management, perceptions of change as a threat, the contrast between community policing and traditional policing, employee attitudes toward community policing, organizational climate, communication and changing relationships with supervisors, supervisors as change agents, and unions and key actors. All of these discussions relate to individual socialization and organizational culture as they pertain to change in the Motor City Police Department.

Psychological Contract

As described in the literature review, an employee's psychological contract specifies what he/she expects to contribute to, and receive from, their employer. While monetary considerations are important, many non-monetary elements are also crucial. These elements might include an employee's need for recognition, job security, respect, and involvement. The officers in the present study were never directly asked to identify the elements of their psychological contract with the Department; however, based upon existing literature it is possible to impute common elements onto these employees. Such an exercise suggests that numerous incidents of psychological contract violations may be identified in the course of this change effort in MCPD.

The structural processes of the reorganization resulted in numerous violations of the psychological contracts existing between MCPD and its line employees. Many employees felt that the Department had never clarified what it expected to achieve through the reorganization or specified how officers were supposed to do their job under the team-based system. To some officers, this lack of clarity (discussed more fully later) was translated as reflecting a lack of respect by the organization. The Department was not respecting their employees' need to understand the expectations being placed upon them. Officers felt that the Department's administration was out of touch with the pressures and challenges confronting patrol officers. They believed administrators did not understand what tools, resources, and training the officers needed in order to effectively operate under the team-based community policing system.

Employees felt that their voices were not being heard. Although the Department made pretenses of involving employees in the change process, most officers felt that their needs and opinions were being overlooked. Officers were not recognized for efforts which contributed to the team-based system. There were no incentives in place which might encourage employees to perform any extra duties in order to further the success of problem solving or team-based community policing. Overall, reported employee morale was very low. Although every organization has problems, longtime employees felt that morale had rarely been as low as it was during the time of the evaluation study. Officers believed that they were not being supported in the aftermath of several sensitive situations which had resulted in public/media scrutiny of the Department.

At the onset of the reorganization, many officers were led to believe that they would have the time to engage in the problem solving called for by the team-based system. Some felt that the Department had implicitly promised to provide the necessary resources so that officers could make a positive difference in their team area. These implicit promises (whether real or falsely perceived) had failed to materialize, resulting in the officers' disillusionment with the team-based system. The organization had implied that the changes would make the Department a better place to work, but the reality (at least initially) was far more harsh. Some also questioned whether the Department was misleading the public about its efforts and outcomes within the community. They believed that the Department and City were misrepresenting their capacity to enhance community service and improve public safety within Motor City.

Employees were also disappointed with community policing as a whole. They saw that the Department had spent more than five years attempting to improve the quality of its service within the community, while the rest of the City's government had remained indifferent. The police had become the *de facto* caretakers of Motor City's social ills, while support from the rest of the City was never forthcoming. The fact that other branches of municipal government had not "jumped on the bandwagon" left officers feeling alone in their struggle. While they indicated support for the overall idea of community policing, they were disappointed that other service providers had not taken a more active role in improving the quality of life in Motor City. Officers also questioned whether the police (armed with simplistic "band aid" solutions) could address massive social ills (which could only be resolved through more extensive "surgery"). While the Department could generate the perception that officers were getting to the root of crime problems, some believed the best officers could do was displace crime problems.

Cumulatively, these violations of the psychological contract had left employees feeling cynical about community policing, the Department, the agency's role in the community, and their job. They questioned whether the police had the capacity to do more than simply displace crime. In looking at MCPD's organizational efforts over time, many veteran officers felt that structure followed money; the Department would claim to support the philosophy or program currently being funded by the federal government. When money for one initiative dried up, the Department's philosophy would change to support the next "cash cow." They felt the agency was being run without a clear direction of where it was heading and what role it would play in the community's future.

In keeping with the belief that front-line officers had no voice in how the Department was run, it was questioned whether anything would come of the research and reports prepared by the SCJ team. Within the Department, some saw a historical pattern of ignoring feedback from officers and questioned if anything would be done in response to the findings of the evaluation project. Unfortunately, to some extent, their concerns that the feedback would be ignored were well founded (although this was more a matter of a transition in MCPD leadership, rather than a product of systematically ignoring the concerns of line employees).

Distrust of Management

The literature review described the distrust of management that is commonly exhibited by line level employees in many types of organizations. There seemed to be no shortage of such distrust in Motor City. It was very common for officers to indicate that top leaders were out of touch with line employees. These patrol officers felt that top leaders did not understand the general challenges and concerns which confronted them as police officers. In the context of the team-based system, they believed administrators did not appreciate how difficult it was for officers to create time for problem solving efforts. They also felt top management did not appreciate the training, resources, and support that would be required for the team-based system to be successful and effective.

Decentralization enhanced the perceived divide between management and line employees. MCPD had historically experienced the tensions between "street cops" and "management cops" found in many police organizations. As a result of their newfound physical separation, this sense of isolation was especially profound for officers working in the South Precinct[1]. Officers felt distant from top leaders under the old system, but they had engaged in casual interactions with one another (the offices of top leaders were on the same floor as the "briefing" room where officers began their shifts). With the move to the South Precinct, half of the employees were no longer experiencing these informal contacts. For officers in the South Precinct, the divide with top management became even more pronounced; the only "contact" was in the form of one-sided orders and written memos which would periodically "trickle down" from headquarters. Top leaders rarely appeared in the South Precinct, enhancing this sense of isolation and neglect, and reinforcing the notion that management was indifferent and could not be trusted.

Recent hiring, assignment, and promotion patterns also gave officers another reason to distrust the actions and decisions of management. Officers questioned whether merit mattered anymore within the organization. There was a perception that the Department was so concerned with increasing diversity, that more qualified candidates were being overlooked. Some felt that top administrators favored their "golden people" over the person best suited for a position. It should be noted that although some officers felt the best candidates were not always selected for promotion, officers rarely expressed dissatisfaction with their supervisors.

---

[1] Patrol and investigative operations for the South Precinct were moved out of police headquarters in early 1996. North Precinct operations were housed in police headquarters until the fall of 1999.

Two final examples reflect the degree to which some officers distrusted the actions and intents of management. During the initial observational interviews conducted by the author, officers frequently questioned if the author was a "spy sent by the Chief." Although these comments were invariably made in a joking tone, they reflected a legitimate underlying concern. Officers feared being singled out as someone who was not a "team player" in the team-based system. This was reinforced during the administration of the patrol officer survey. Several respondents did not provide answers to demographic questions, noting on the survey that they wondered if management was seeking to link officers with responses (presumably to identify officers who were not team players for punishment or "re-indoctrination"). For those it afflicted, this fear of "Big Brother" (in the form of top management) seemed very real.

Perceiving Change as a Threat

Officers reflected traditional sentiments and perceptions that change was threatening, although their comments were not so overt. Clearly, the intended structure of MCPD under the team-based system was a significant departure from the Department's conventional way of operating. Historically, MCPD had operated with a traditional police organizational structure. Evaluation measures were quantitative, the organization was physically and mentally separated from the community, and a merit-based system was used to make promotion and special-assignment decisions. The team-based system, if fully adopted, would have challenged and disrupted this *status quo*.

Employees no longer knew what mattered within the organization. Traditionally, employees were evaluated using quantitative assessments; under the team-based system it was unclear how employee conduct would be measured. Employees seeking to be a "good officer" were frustrated when they interpreted the motivation for promotions as having been based upon demographic traits rather than merit. Employees who exhibited the traits which traditionally were valued in making decisions about promotions and specialized assignments were fearful when such decisions were apparently made based upon other considerations. Officers were left wondering what mattered to top leaders and whether or not members of non-protected groups (white males) could compete in the promotional process.

Officers indicated a belief that the general trends in the Department in recent years had adversely affected the quality of the organization. Officers felt that the increased desire to work closely with the community had forced the Department to become too political. They felt that the City (in particular, the Mayor) was too concerned with micro-managing the Department and second-guessing the actions and decisions of MCPD officers. Some indicated that certain community policing specialists were working in neighborhoods that did not need a dedicated officer, while more deserving neighborhoods were denied CPO's. When the Department tried to reassign CPO's out of certain neighborhoods, the residents would complain so much that the Department often simply left an officer in their area. The proverbial squeaky wheel (the vocal and politically active neighborhood) was given the grease (a CPO), while other areas were left unserved, regardless of their relative need.

Although there was no indication of intentional sabotage aimed at the team-based system (as was observed with "team policing" in the 1970's), sergeants seemed to dislike how the reorganization had modified the command structure. The rank of lieutenant had traditionally been a position sought by many officers in the Department. In the Patrol Division, a lieutenant helped run a shift and had a great deal of freedom and autonomy (in other words, the proper balance of fun and work). The team-based system drastically modified the roles and responsibilities of this position. Lieutenants held a great deal of administrative responsibilities and enjoyed fewer "perks" than they had in the past.

When promotional opportunities arose during the course of the SCJ evaluation project, every lieutenant applied for a promotion to the rank of captain, while less than one-quarter of the sergeants applied for a promotion to the rank of lieutenant. To many officers, this signified that the rank of lieutenant was no longer desirable. The restructuring and reallocation of responsibilities had diminished the luster of the lieutenants' position within the organizations. There was no indication of intentional sabotage on the part of the supervisors, yet it was clear that many sergeants and lieutenants were upset that this position had lost so much of its original appeal within the Department.

A few supervisors reported developing innovative ways of mollifying employee resistance in response to these perceptions of the change process and community policing,. One lieutenant believed that his officers had come to distrust anything labeled as community policing. In order to get his officers to engage in problem solving, he believed that alternative labels had to be applied to such activities. In developing a new program for dealing with residences which were chronic problems in their precinct, a very traditional acronym was developed for the program ("C.O.P.P.E.R".). This lieutenant attempted to portray the program as "fun" out of fear that it would be rejected by officers if it was in any way associated with community policing or problem solving.

Community Policing versus Traditional Policing

Respondents rated their level of agreement with a series of statements which addressed a variety of general topics related to police work. The distribution of these responses suggests that the organizational culture found in MCPD had traditional elements, but also reflected attitudes which might support a community policing philosophy (see Table 7). Although officers indicated support for enforcing the law and active patrol tactics, these elements are not necessarily incompatible with a community policing philosophy. Furthermore, officers showed high levels of support for assisting citizens and finding out what neighborhood problems concern community residents. Officers also indicated modest levels of distrust for citizens and low (but perhaps not low enough) support for overlooking the law in the pursuit of just ends.

Reflections of the organizational culture can be seen in the goals respondents identified as important for patrol officers and precinct managers. Respondents were provided with a list of seven goals which sometimes are considered to be important requisites for police officers and organizations to accomplish. The respondents were first asked to choose the two goals which they believed were most important for patrol officers. From the remaining five goals, the respondents then chose the two which they believed were the least important for patrol officers.

Table 7.
Level of agreement with statements about police work. [†]

	Agree Strongly	Agree Somewhat	Disagree Somewhat	Disagree Strongly
Enforcing the law if by far a patrol officer's most important responsibility (n=119)	42.0%	42.0%	15.1%	0.8%
Police officers have reason to be distrustful of most citizens (n=118)	7.6%	28.8%	54.2%	9.3%
A good patrol officers is one who patrols aggressively by stopping cars, checking out people, running license checks, etc. (n=119)	29.4%	57.1%	12.6%	0.8%
Assisting citizens is just as important as enforcing the law (n=118)	59.3%	37.3%	3.4%	0.0%
A good patrol officer will try to find out what residents think the neighborhood problems are (n=119)	54.6%	41.2%	4.2%	0.0%
In order to do their jobs, patrol officers must sometimes overlook search and seizure laws and other legal guidelines (n=118)	5.1%	10.2%	40.7%	44.1%

[†] The table reflects row percentages based upon the number of valid responses (figures in parentheses) for the respective item. Percentages for some items may not total 100.0 due to rounding.

The goal identified as most important by the majority of officers was handling calls for service in their assigned area. An overwhelming 71.8 percent of the respondents indicated that this was one of the two most important goals for patrol officers. Tying for second in importance were the goals of making arrests and issuing citations, and seizing drugs, guns, and other contraband. These two goals were each identified as important for patrol officers by 32.5 percent of the respondents. Respondents tended to identify three goals as the least important for patrol officers. Almost two-thirds (60.7%) identified reducing the public's fear of crime as one of the two least important goals. Similar rankings were given to involving the public in improving neighborhoods (specified by 46.2% of the respondents as one of the two least important goals) and reducing the level of public disorder (identified by 29.9% of the respondents as one of the two least important goals).

Officers were also asked to consider these seven goals and how important they were to their precinct's managers. Once again, respondents identified the two most important and least important goals for patrol officers, this time from the perspective of their precinct's management. While the magnitude of individual items was slightly variable, officers in both precincts tended to identify the same items as most/least important (see Table 8). Respondents felt that managers in both precincts believed that important goals included stimulating public involvement in improving neighborhoods, reducing the fear of crime, and having officers handling calls in their beat. Less important goals included making arrests and issuing citations, and seizing guns, drugs, and contraband.

Clearly these rankings indicate a disparity between the goals which were considered important by patrol officers and the goals patrol officers thought were important to their precinct's managers. Officers identified with goals more traditionally associated with police work, such as making arrests, issuing citations, seizing contraband, and handling the calls in their beat. Officers believed their managers wanted them to identify with goals which were more consistent with a community policing philosophy, such as reducing fear of crime and involving the public in improving neighborhood conditions. The survey data does not indicate which of the listed goals, if any, officers actually pursued in performing their job-related duties.

Table 8.
Perception of management's goals for patrol officers by respondent's precinct.

	North Precinct		South Precinct	
	Most	Least	Most	Least
Handling the calls for their assigned area	36.2%	24.1%	32.7%	14.3%
Making arrests and issuing citations	13.8%	46.6%	16.3%	42.9%
Reducing the number of repeat calls to the same address	20.7%	8.6%	12.2%	16.3%
Seizing drugs, guns, and other contraband	12.1%	25.9%	2.0%	30.6%
Reducing the level of public disorders	5.2%	27.6%	10.2%	28.6%
Getting the public involved in improving the neighborhood	51.7%	12.1%	71.4%	6.1%
Reducing the public's fear of crime	60.3%	19.0%	46.9%	28.6%

Employee Attitudes Toward Community Policing

One of the greatest barriers which may have prevented the successful development and implementation of generalized community policing in the Motor City Police Department was employee attitude. Officers expressed all of the stereotypical beliefs and perceptions about community policing: it was a waste of personnel, police officers are not social workers, the police should not be doing the job of other governmental agencies, community policing is not "real" police work. While some officers saw the value and potential of community policing, the

Department was never fully able to win over the "hearts and minds" of its employees. Even those who were not opposed to community policing as an idea questioned whether MCPD's approach was truly effective or merely "lip service."

Officer survey respondents were invited to write any comments or concerns they had at the end of the instrument. Several officers took this opportunity to voice concerns about community policing and problem solving. On the subject of community policing in general, respondents wrote (unedited comments):

> "Community policing is a good idea, but most of the function is the 'feel good' not to effectively use your manpower."

> "Community Policing in this City is a joke. Has never been done right. Taking kids to pro sporting events is not the answer."

> "These problems are usually not police related and should be handled by other departments in the city."

Comments of this nature were common throughout the course of the evaluation project. Many officers believed that community policing was not an effective way for the police to allocate their resources. They believed that at best community policing displaced crime, rather than enabling officers to resolve crime's root causes.

On the subject of community policing as implemented in MCPD, different respondents commented that (unedited comments):

> "The Department has pushed upon the public the perception of being safe, instead of making the public really safe."

> "I sometimes think that the Administration thinks that public perception of the department, and the politicians, and our effect on crime, is <u>more</u> important than the reality." (emphasis in the original)

Even officers who supported the notion of community policing were critical of the way it was being generalized in MCPD. It was believed that the main objective of the team-based system was to create an image of a safe community, even though this may not have been a reality in Motor City. The City/Department were viewed as selling the public on the idea of proactive, problem solving police officers; however, the City/Department was not willing to "put its money where its mouth is" by providing the resources to make this image a reality.

Sergeants were especially critical of the team-based system. Their criticism was of particular interest because many of them were, in fact, among the original CPO's in Motor City. They understood how community policing worked, how to solve community problems, and what community policing could achieve. At the same time, they saw inherent limitations in MCPD's approach to organizing generalized community policing. These sergeants also questioned why other government and social service agencies were not more active in providing community services. One sergeant pointedly asked "why must we do everything for everyone?"

Sergeants were also acutely aware of the complex nature of crime and the displacement problem. They tended to believe that the problems they were confronting could not be easily resolved with the resources at their disposal. Deep-rooted social ills could not be addressed through a few hours of intervention by the police. As a result, all the teams could really do was displace problems. This "get 'em out" tactic became their key goal, even when it created a new problem for another team of officers. As one sergeant remarked during a focus group session: "we're shitting on one another– we aren't making Motor City any better." Despite its inherent limitations, sergeants expressed that displacement was perhaps the only achievable goal they could pursue.

Officers had deeply ingrained attitudes toward community policing in general and the team-based system in particular. These attitudes were important in determining perceptions of community policing and its future role in the Department. These attitudes were readily apparent, yet they were overlooked in the process of implementing the team-based system. It is possible that if the Department had confronted these attitudes more directly and worked to educate officers about community policing, some of the resistance resulting from this barrier would have been assuaged.

The officer survey asked respondents a variety of questions pertaining to their attitudes toward community policing as a general philosophy.

These questions were in addition to the items discussed below, which were measures of opinions specific to community policing as it was instituted in the Motor City Police Department. It was unclear to what degree these opinions were distinct from one another (if at all). Conceptually, it is possible that an officer's views of community policing could be distinct from their views of community policing as operationalized in MCPD. An officer could support the basic philosophy of community policing, while disliking the way in which MCPD attempted to generalize it in the Department.

Interesting disparities were found in the perceived workload of CPO's based upon whether the respondent had ever held a CPO assignment. Officers who had experience as a CPO (either currently or formerly) tended to view the CPO workload as higher than other officers. More than one-third (35.0%) of the (current and former) CPO's felt that the workload of CPO's was greater than it should be; only 11.9 percent of non-CPO's held such perceptions about the CPO workload. In contrast, half (52.7%) of the non-CPO's felt that the CPO workload was lower than it should be; only one-quarter of the CPO's shared this perception.

Respondents were asked how they would feel if they received a CPO assignment at some point in the following year. One-quarter of both the CPO's and non-CPO's expressed neutral feelings about such a prospect (23.8% and 22.4%, respectively). Most (57.1%) respondents who currently were or had been a CPO indicated that they would feel positive about receiving a similar assignment (versus 5.1% of non-CPO's). In contrast, a majority (72.4%) of non-CPO's indicated that they would feel negative about receiving a CPO assignment (versus 19.0% of CPO's). This finding is consistent with other research which suggests employees are more favorable toward community policing after having personal involvement in its administration.

Respondents were given a list of possible advantages and disadvantages of being a CPO in order to provide insights into specifically why they developed certain feelings about these assignments. The lists were based upon prior research into perceptions of community policing and the findings from the interviews and focus group discussions. For each list, respondents were asked to indicate which items they believed applied to having a CPO assignment. Tables 9 and 10 display the perceived advantages and disadvantages, respectively, of working as a

CPO. Responses are separated based upon the respondent's experience as a CPO. The tables present the percentage of respondents in each category (CPO or non-CPO) who indicated that a specific item was an advantage or disadvantage of receiving a CPO assignment.

Table 9 indicates that non-CPO's believed some advantages of a CPO assignment included having a good work schedule, independence on the job, and leeway to try new methods of policing. CPO's also cited independence and leeway as advantages of a CPO assignment, along with having time to work on long-term projects and the opportunity to work closely with the public. The greatest disadvantages cited by non-CPO's included spending too much time on duties that are not traditionally associated with police work, low job status, having to pay too much attention to keeping the public happy, and inadequate training to fulfill job expectations. CPO's indicated that they felt low job status, insufficient department directions about expectations, and inadequate training were all disadvantages of their assignment.

Statistically significant differences were found on six of the nine items presented in Table 9 based upon CPO experience. Current and former CPO's tended to perceive these items as greater advantages of holding a CPO assignment. Respondents with CPO experience were more likely to believe that advantages included: independence, time to work on long-term projects, the opportunity to work closely with the public, leeway to try new things, and receiving positive feedback from the public. Those with CPO experience were also far more likely to perceive that the diversity of tasks and skills required by community policing were an advantage of being a CPO.

Table 10 presents the percentage of respondents who perceived of select items as disadvantages of being a CPO (presented by CPO experience). Respondents with CPO experience viewed many of the disadvantages of a CPO assignment as more profound than their non-CPO counterparts. While both groups perceived that unclear expectations and inadequate training were disadvantages, a significantly larger proportion of CPO's expressed this belief. In addition, significantly fewer CPO's felt that working closely with the public and trying to keep the public happy were disadvantages of a CPO assignment.

Table 9.
Perceived advantages of a CPO assignment
by respondent's CPO experience. [†]

Advantages of working as a CPO:	Non-CPO's (n=99)	CPO's (n=21)
Independence to do the job as you see fit *	63.6%	81.0%
Good work schedule	74.7%	57.1%
Enough time to work on long-term projects **	39.4%	66.7%
Opportunity to work closely with the public **	41.4%	66.7%
Leeway to try new things to get the job done **	46.5%	71.4%
Getting positive feedback from the public **	27.3%	52.4%
High status of the job among other police	3.0%	0.0%
Diversity in the kinds of tasks and skills required ***	22.2%	61.9%
Opportunities for promotion and career advancement	35.4%	19.0%

[†] The value in each cell represents the percent of the category of respondents (CPO's or non-CPO's) who indicated that the respective item was an advantage of being a CPO. Differences between the categories were significant at * $p<.10$, ** $p<.05$, and *** $p<.01$ using the Independent Samples Test.

As Tables 9 and 10 indicate, there was little agreement between CPO's and non-CPO's, perhaps reflecting the tension between perceptions and reality. The responses of non-CPO's paints an image of community policing far different from the image portrayed by CPO's. Non-CPO's felt that such an assignment provided a good work schedule and independence, but also involved having to keep the public happy and spending too much time on tasks other than police work. CPO's liked working with the public, addressing long term problems, and the independence and leeway of being a CPO, but disliked their low status (among peers), lack of

Table 10.
Perceived disadvantages of a CPO assignment by respondent's CPO experience. †

Disadvantages of working as a CPO:	Non-CPO's (n=99)	CPO's (n=21)
Insufficient department direction about expectations ***	41.4%	76.2%
Poor work schedule *	7.1%	28.6%
Not enough time to get the work done	8.1%	19.0%
Having to work closely with members of the public *	24.2%	9.5%
Inadequate training to do the job expected *	41.4%	61.9%
Not enough leeway to get the job done	8.1%	19.0%
Having to pay too much attention to keeping public happy ***	70.7%	33.3%
Low status of the job among other police	75.8%	81.0%
Spending too much time on work that isn't police work	74.7%	57.1%
Poor prospects for promotion or career advancement	4.0%	9.5%

† The value in each cell represents the percent of the category of respondents (CPO's or non-CPO's) who indicated that the respective item was a disadvantage of being a CPO. Differences between the categories were significant at * $p<.10$ and *** $p<.01$ using the Independent Samples Test.

training, and insufficient direction. Non-CPO's reflected beliefs which are consistent with many of the stereotypes police officers tend to hold about community policing. The beliefs and attitudes reported by the CPO's reflected common themes found in prior studies assessing how community policing officers feel about their job (both the advantages and frustrations it entails).

The respondents assessed various dimensions of the efficacy of community policing and citizen involvement in the problem solving process. As exhibited earlier, respondents with experience as a CPO tended to be more confident in the outcomes of the community policing process. Table 11 indicates both CPO's and non-CPO's believed that community policing made important contributions. Those with community policing experience, however, did so to a significantly greater magnitude. It is interesting to note that those with CPO experience were also significantly more critical of the willingness of citizens to involve themselves in improving their neighborhoods. Because CPO's are more intimately involved in problem solving and attempts to improve the quality of life on the neighborhood level, they may have also experienced more frustrations in attempting to work in collaboration with citizens.

An important question which emerged during the initial stages of the research project was whether members of neighborhood associations accurately reflected the concerns of the area they represented. Some officers had misgivings that associations were dominated by only the most active and vocal residents of the community; some likened associations to a "clique" where only the privileged few were allowed any power. In part, this perception may have emerged because there was not an established criterion for defining associations. As such, a group of friends living in close proximity could create their own association and define its geographic parameters. The Department (and the City) attempted to work with these self-identified groups without ever questioning whether they actually represented the concerns of their area.

Despite these misgivings, both CPO's and non-CPO's felt that associations accurately represented the views of most of their neighborhood in terms of the priorities that the police should set in that area (see Table 11). CPO's indicated a higher level of agreement on this item (71.4%) than did non-CPO's (55.4%), although the difference did not achieve statistical significance. This higher rating by CPO's may indicate that this concern is generally unsubstantiated in most associations. CPO's would have a more intimate knowledge of both neighborhood associations and neighborhood residents (including those who were not active in the association). This knowledge could help them determine if association goals were accurately reflected the goals of the entire neighborhood.

Table 11.
Agreement with statements about
community policing by respondent's CPO experience. †

	CPO's	Non-CPO's
CPO's make an important contribution toward reducing crime and disorder in the neighborhoods where they are assigned ***	85.7% (n=21)	52.0% (n=98)
CPO's make an important contribution toward improving attitudes of neighborhood residents toward the police department ***	90.5% (n=21)	71.4% (n=98)
The neighborhoods that complain the loudest are the ones most likely to receive a CPO ***	52.4% (n=21)	74.5% (n=98)
There are not enough citizens in my district who are willing to exercise the necessary initiative to make their neighborhood a nicer place to live **	85.7% (n=21)	60.2% (n=98)
Citizens in my district do not call upon the police nearly as much as they should to solve neighborhood problems ***	52.4% (n=21)	23.7% (n=97)
Neighborhood associations accurately reflect the views of the majority of citizens in my district have about police priorities	71.4% (n=21)	55.4% (n=92)
Doing community policing means officers will be unable to do more important tasks ***	10.0% (n=20)	66.3% (n=92)

† The value in each cell represents the percent of the category of respondents (CPO's or non-CPO's) who indicated that they "agree strongly" or "agree somewhat" with the respective item. Differences between the categories were significant at ** $p<.05$ and *** $p<.01$ using the Independent Samples Test.

The final item in Table 11 indicates a substantial (and significant) disparity in how CPO's and non-CPO's prioritize their tasks and responsibilities. Despite the fact that they believe community policing may make positive contributions in the community, non-CPO's indicate that there are more important things which officers could be doing. Respondents with CPO experience expressed a very different view on this item. Only a small minority (10%) of current and former CPO's believed that "doing" community policing meant that an officer could not engage in more important tasks.

A final item of importance in this section summed up the respondents' overall attitudes toward community policing and how it ought to be carried out in MCPD. Officers were asked what would be the best way to organize community policing in the Motor City Police Department in the future. Table 12 presents the distribution of their responses by CPO experience. While approximately equal proportions of both groups agreed that community policing should be the responsibility of specialists or general patrol officers, strong disagreement emerged in the last two categories. The majority of CPO's (52.6%) believed community policing

Table 12.
The best way for MCPD to organize community policing by respondent's CPO experience. †

"What would be the best way for the Motor City Police Department to organize community policing?"	CPO's (n=19)	Non-CPO's (n=96)
Make it the responsibility of specialists	21.1%	28.1%
Make it the responsibility of all patrol officers	21.1%	21.9%
Make it the responsibility of both specialists and patrol officers	52.6%	14.6%
Do not do community policing at all	5.3%	35.4%

† The table reflects column percentages based upon the number of valid responses (figures in parentheses) for the respective item. Percentages for some items may not total 100.0 due to rounding.

was being properly organized, with responsibilities being shared by specialists and general patrol officers. Only 5.3 percent of the CPO's felt that in the future MCPD should not do community policing. Alternatively, over one-third of the non-CPO's felt that MCPD should not do community policing at all. Only 14.6 percent of the non-CPO's felt that the existing system was the most appropriate way to organize community policing in the Department.

Organizational Culture and Climate

A substantial portion of the survey was devoted to asking respondents about their perceptions and beliefs relating to supervision and leadership within the Motor City Police Department. These items provide insight into the relationship between front line officers and immediate supervisors, as well as the relationship between front line officers and upper management. For the purpose of analysis, these questions can be divided into three categories[2]: items about the respondent's relationship with their shift supervisor, items about the respondent's relationship with their team supervisor, and items about the respondent's perceptions of upper management. Each category will be considered in turn.

Relations with Shift Supervisors

The first group of questions probed the respondents' assessment of the supervisors with whom they had the most contact. For patrol officers, this was the shift sergeant with whom they interacted most frequently. For sergeants and lieutenants, this was the immediate supervisor with whom they interacted most frequently. Respondents were asked to rate their supervisor on a number of criteria relevant to the typical relationship

---

[2] Extensive bivariate testing was conducted to determine if perceptions of the organizational culture differed based upon officer characteristics. Although significant disparities were found on some specific items, consistent patterns were not evident. Findings of these bivariate tests are not included in this text in the interest of space. The relationship between officer demographics and their overall perception of organizational culture are considered more fully in the hypotheses section of this chapter.

Table 13.
Ratings of supervisor by respondent's rank. †

How good a job is your supervisor doing on each of the following criteria?	Non-Supervisors	Supervisors
Being present at the scene when a subordinate is involved in a potentially dangerous or difficult situation ***	87.8% (n=90)	60.0% (n=20)
Reviewing subordinates' written reports ***	90.0% (n=90)	40.0% (n=20)
Dealing directly with citizens who are complaining about problems in their neighborhood	80.0% (n=90)	59.1% (n=20)
Dealing with personnel matters (paperwork, discipline, counseling)	82.0% (n=89)	81.8% (n=22)
Attending meetings with the public and giving talks to the public	64.4% (n=87)	68.2% (n=22)
Coordinating & scheduling the work of team members ***	72.4% (n=87)	42.9% (n=21)
Getting other public and private organizations to cooperate with the police to solve community problems	54.0% (n=87)	54.5% (n=22)
Identifying projects for subordinates and monitoring their progress with those projects	62.5% (n=88)	54.5% (n=22)
Evaluating performance of individual officers and giving them feedback	53.4% (n=88)	68.2% (n=22)

† The value in each cell represents the percent of the category of respondents (supervisors or non-supervisors) who indicated that their supervisor was "good" or "very good" at the respective item. Differences between the categories were significant at *** $p<.01$ using the Independent Samples Test.

between a patrol officer and his/her shift sergeant. Several items also reflect issues salient under the Department's reorganized structure. For comparison purposes, Table 13 presents these responses based upon the rank status (supervisor or non-supervisor) of the respondent.

Some of the differences between the ranks may be explained by the nature of what various police supervisors do and how different members of police organizations relate to one another. The relationship between patrol officers and sergeants may be more formal and distant than the relationship between various supervisors. Table 13 does reveal some surprising differences between the rankings patrol officers and patrol supervisors gave their supervisors. Patrol officers gave their shift sergeants highest marks for working with the public and coordinating team-based initiatives. Supervisors gave their own supervisors higher ratings for providing feedback on performance.

Relations with Team Sergeants

The second labor-management area examined in the survey dealt with the relationship between officers and the sergeants who supervised their team. The respondents were asked to assess their team sergeant[3] on six criteria by indicating their level of agreement to evaluative statements using a four-point scale. Table 14 presents the distribution of responses to these items. As a whole, these results indicate that most respondents thought favorably of their team sergeant. On the team level, officers felt that they knew their sergeants expected from them. Most reported favorable perceptions of the management approach taken by this supervisor and provided positive ratings for their supervisors' level of experience and professionalism.

Two other survey items related to the evaluations patrol officers gave to their team sergeants. An overwhelming majority (88.1%) stated that when they tried a new approach to doing their job that resulted in failure, their team sergeant treated this as an honest effort and did not discipline

---

[3] A set of eight questions asked patrol officers to evaluate their team sergeant. Because sergeants and lieutenants do not have an analogous supervisor, they were asked to assess the immediate supervisor with whom they had the most contact. As these latter ratings do not pertain to this section, only the responses of patrol officers are included in Table 14.

them. Respondents were also asked the following question: "When your team has a problem that higher-ups could straighten out, how often is your supervisor able to get those higher-ups to actually do something about the problem?" Responses indicated that this was the case "much of the time" (40.5%) or "some of the time" (42.9%), but that it "never" happened with some frequency (16.7%).

Table 14.
Respondents' assessments of their team sergeant. †

	Agree	Disagree
The decisions or judgements I make are seldom criticized or modified by my supervisor (n=88).	95.4%	4.5%
My supervisor lets officers know what is expected of them (n=88).	87.5%	12.5%
My supervisor's approach tends to discourage me from giving extra effort (n=89).	10.%	89.9%
My supervisor has a lot of professional experience to help officers do their jobs (n=88).	89.8%	10.2%
My supervisor looks out for the personal welfare of his/her subordinates (n=89).	92.2%	7.8%
I have complete faith in my supervisor (n=87).	87.3%	12.6%

† Table presents only the responses of non-supervisors. The table reflects row percentages based upon the number of valid responses (figures in parentheses) for the respective item. Percentages for some items may not total 100.0 due to rounding.

In considering the efficiency and efficacy of team sergeants, it is also important to closely examine issues related to the day-to-day management of a team. One issue frequently raised during interviews and the focus groups was the challenge team sergeants faced in coordinating, scheduling, and communicating with a team of officers working in a variety of duty assignments around the clock. In considering their own team, two-thirds (67.8%) of non-supervisors agreed with the statement that activities and projects were well coordinated across shifts; over half (54.6%) of supervisors gave a similar rating to the team they supervised. Alternatively, when asked how often their team sergeant provided adequate guidance in problem-solving projects, most non-supervisors responded that this was usually (32.9%) or always (38.8%) the case.

Respondents were asked if they felt that, in general, sergeants were unable to effectively supervise officers on another shift. Most non-supervisors (58.9%) and a majority of supervisors (77.3%) agreed with this statement. These findings present an interesting contradiction. On the one hand, officers indicated that there was adequate guidance and coordination in their team. Alternatively, they felt that sergeants were not able to effectively supervise their employees across shifts.

To assess the level of communication between team sergeants and team members, respondents were asked how often their team sergeant communicated with them about team projects. Almost half (44.7%) of the non-supervisors reported such communication occurred on at least a weekly basis; an additional 41.2 percent reported it occurred at least one or two times a month. Although it is difficult to determine if such levels are adequate, these findings suggest that there was a moderate amount of communication between team officers and sergeants.

Perceptions of Upper Management

The final organizational climate area addressed in the officer survey were items which reflected how officers viewed upper management in the Motor City Police Department. The percentage of respondents agreeing with statements relating to upper management are presented by rank in Table 15. As would be expected, while the general direction of the responses is similar, differences in magnitude were found based upon rank. In general, responses suggest that rank-and-file officers felt detached from top management and upper-level decision making in MCPD. Respondents also reported that expected outcomes of the reorganization were unrealistically high and that priorities under the new structure had not been made sufficiently clear.

Table 15.
Perceptions of departmental leaders by respondent's rank. †

	Non-Supervisors	Supervisors
Top department management has a good understanding of what the work of the rank-and-file police officer is like	27.5% (n=91)	22.7% (n=22)
Rank-and-file officers do not have enough opportunity to participate in developing policies and planning strategies **	86.5% (n=89)	68.2% (n=22)
Rank and file officers are kept well-informed of management's policies and plans	18.9% (n=90)	36.4% (n=22)
Top department leadership has unrealistically high expectations about how much the current organizational strategies will reduce crime and disorder in the neighborhoods	89.0% (n=91)	77.3% (n=22)
Top leaders have made the department's priorities clear	41.1% (n=90)	50.0% (n=22)

† The value in each cell represents the percent of the category of respondents (supervisors or non-supervisors) who indicated that they "agree strongly" or "agree somewhat" with the respective item. Differences between the categories were significant at ** $p<.05$ using the Independent Samples Test.

Communication and Relationships with Supervisors

The interviews and observations indicated that communication and changing relationships with supervisors were a significant problem in the aftermath of the reorganization. The transition to two precincts created tremendous communication problems for the Department. Because officers were not routinely interacting with their peers in the opposite precinct (in the locker room and at pre-shift briefings) there was a sense of separation. As one officer noted on the officer survey: "Communication between officers of the north and south precinct is practically non-existent." Some officers "affectionately" referred to the major east-west roadway which divided the precincts as the "Great Wall of Motor City" because it effectively eliminated north-south communication within the Department. It was common for officers to remark that they learned about major crimes in the opposite precinct through the local news media.

Employees were also ill-prepared to deal with the dual supervision structure used in the team-based system. This structure created "ghost supervisors" for many officers. Unless an officer happened to work the same shift as their team sergeant, the two would rarely have face-to-face contact with one another. Instead, sergeants had to supervise their employees using voice-mail. For officers, this meant that on a daily basis their team supervisor was less a person and more a disembodied voice on the telephone giving them orders "from the beyond." Sergeants were equally frustrated by their inability to have regular interactions with their team members.

The loss of the "human" element of supervision presented a situation to which many officers were not accustomed. This was compounded by the confusion associated with the dual supervision system. An officer's team sergeant was not someone with whom they had routine contact. Consequently, officers worked harder to satisfy the sergeant(s) who supervised their shift; they were more focused on the traditional orientation of pleasing their shift supervisors than on pleasing their team supervisor. This limited what a supervisor could accomplish within her/his own team, but enhanced what the productivity on the shift which they supervised. Paradoxically, supervisors benefitted from the dedication of the officers on their shift, yet this occurred at the expense of efficacy within their team.

Supervisors as Change Agents

Despite the general perception that the team-based system did not work, the story of Motor City's reorganization efforts does contain some successes. There were teams which appeared to function very well and seemed to be improving the quality of life for the residents of the area they served. Anecdotally, the original SCJ research team observed that the degree to which a team exhibited behavior consistent with the team-based system seemed to be dependent upon the attitude and actions of its sergeant. This matter was a general observation, not a definite rule. Some teams exhibited problem solving productivity despite the apparent apathy or indifference of their sergeant. Additionally, even productive teams tended to have members who were not "team players" and who did little to contribute to the team's accomplishments. It must also be conceded that although these teams produced outputs which were consistent with the team-based approach, the attitudes of individual members were not necessarily pro-community policing.

The observation that team sergeants played a key role in setting the tone for their team of officers has crucial implications. It appeared that team sergeants had the ability to pacify some of the resistance exhibited by their team officers. In the case of Motor City, this pacification did not appear to involve threats of undesirable consequences for road officers who did not work with their team. Rather, these select sergeants set a tone of acceptance within their team; they led by example. They did not spend a great deal of time bemoaning the implementation problems or questioning the utility of a community policing philosophy. Instead, they simply tried to "make do" with the little direction they were given and the resources which were at hand.

Unfortunately, top leaders overlooked the key position team sergeants (and, to a lesser extent, lieutenants) might have played in resocializing the road officers. These supervisors were in a unique position given the routine contact they had with the officers charged with carrying out generalized community policing. They had the capacity to "push" officers to work within the team-based system. In addition, they could have opened channels of communication between road officers and top leaders. Such communication could have given top leaders feedback on the resources, structural changes, and clarification which might have been needed for the reorganization to be a success.

There was little evidence that MCPD leaders attempted to capitalize on the potential benefits mid-level supervisors might have offered in the implementation process. If these supervisors had been "brought on board" to understand the logic behind the reorganization and the merits of taking a team-based approach to community policing, their support might have "trickled down" into the front line of the organization. Mid-level supervisors were in a unique position to help make the Department's efforts more successful. While they did not appear to impede the change process in Motor City, the potential benefits of using sergeants and lieutenants as change agents was clearly overlooked.

The Union and Key Actors

As the literature review suggested, organizations may sometimes ameliorate resistance to change through the involvement of key actors and, where applicable, unions. In this case study, the Motor City Police Department did involve representatives from the patrol officers' union throughout the planning phase. Representatives sat on both the Planning Committee and the Reorganization Committee, providing the union with a voice in the change process. The researchers, however, found no other evidence of substantial union involvement in either the formal implementation efforts or the informal resocialization process.

Although merely speculation, it might have been possible for the MCPD to use the union as a means to encourage road officers to embrace team-based community policing. Had the union been vocal in its support of the reorganization effort, officers might have perceived of the implementation of generalize community policing as a good idea. The union's neutrality did not prevent success in the implementation process. However, by not coming out in support of the change (or even against the change) the union sent a silent message to its members. To some, the silence might have indicated that the union felt the change was not even worth commenting upon; the transition to team-based community policing was just a fad which would go away with time.

The union's apparent indifference implied that the restructuring was not a serious and enduring issue in the Department. If the union felt that the reorganization would affect the long-term occupational environment for its members, it likely would have been more visible in the aftermath of the reorganization. The union's inactivity implied that it did not view the change as an enduring issue. Therefore, union members may have been more likely to not take the reorganization as a serious mandate for them to change how they performed their duties. While union members had to do enough to avoid attracting attention, they did not have to take the change effort seriously. Officers could simply "ride out" the restructuring until the next "paradigm of the month" emerged to replace the team-based system.

Top MCPD managers also failed to capitalize on the potential benefits key actors might have offered in the implementation and resocialization process. Key actors are those employees who are informal leaders within an organization. Although they might not hold formal rank, their peers respect them and look to them for direction. In the context of the MCPD experience, key actors might have helped to mollify some of the resistance to change and community policing in general.

The Department could have taken the time and initiative to meet with key employees and to explain why the team-based community policing system would allow the Department to better serve the community. The employees could have been given a chance to express concerns, provide ideas, and ask questions. Although not every actor might have been "brought on board" in accepting community policing and the restructuring, it is possible that many might have come to support the efforts of management. The support of such key employees could have translated into broader support within the organization. Other employees would see that these key actors endorsed the changes and believed that community policing was a better way to serve Motor City. Although not every officer would follow the lead of the key actors, it is possible that many might have done so, thus aiding the resocialization process.

The idea of using key actors emerged during the field observations and interviews. One mid-career female officer reflected the common sentiment about this issue. She indicated that if the Department had taken the time to meet with key officers (she named several specific officers) the reorganization might have been accepted by a larger segment of the Department. She felt that the majority of her peers looked up to a small number of their co-workers. If the importance of the team-based structure and the utility of community policing was proven to the key actors, she believed most other officers would have come to embrace the changes. Because the key actors were not involved, restructuring and resocialization was seen as coming from the top of the organization rather than from within the front line.

In the case of the Motor City Police Department's efforts, the informal resocialization of patrol officers could have been aided through both visible union support and the involvement of key actors. It must be conceded that the impact such support and involvement might have had is open to speculation. The absence of such forces in the MCPD experience makes their true impact uncertain; however, prior research and comments from officers suggest that the resistance to change might have been mollified through these resocialization mechanisms. Because these sources of direction where silent, the reorganization was seen as coming from the top of the Department. Had these sources been involved in the resocialization process, officers might have perceived that support for the change was coming from within their own ranks, making them less likely to reject community policing simply because it was being pushed on them from above.

ORGANIZATIONAL PLANNING

A strong theme which emerged throughout the course of the study was frustration and uncertainty with the organizational structure put in place by top MCPD leaders. There was a perception that the Department's management had not been sufficiently clear in explaining how officers were supposed to operationalize community policing under the team-based system. Officers felt that community policing and problem solving training were largely inadequate or non-existent. Accountability, evaluation procedures, and the reward system were not altered to encourage officers to adopt an occupational style consistent with the expectations of MCPD executives. The role of mid-level supervisors was not modified to support the non-traditional policing practices which the team-based system would have involved.

Officers indicated that the organization seemed to be floundering–that it had "lost its rudder." Even former CPO's did not seem to completely understand the nexus between the Department's previous community policing approaches and community policing/problem solving under the team-based system. Although Department leaders believed sufficient direction had been provided, line officers and mid-level supervisors did not share this perception. Criticism was primarily focused on several key issues, including: general implementation and reorganization issues, staffing, clarity, team integrity and guidance in problem solving activities, and accountability, evaluations, and rewards. Each issue is considered individually.

General Implementation and Reorganization Issues

A number of issues addressed in the officer survey assessed the efficacy of problem solving and supervision in the team-based organizational structure. The responses to these items are presented in Table 16. Responses are reported by rank because prior research suggests that an employee's position within an organization may determine how that employee views the organization and its management. Employees who hold supervisory positions may tend to be more supportive of management strategies and practices than non-supervisory employees.

A critical concern which was frequently expressed during the focus groups and informal interviews was that, regardless of the merits or promises of the team system, there were not enough officers to staff such an endeavor at a level which would result in success. The logic was that if there were not enough officers in the Patrol Division, there would be no time for problem solving. Those officers assigned to the Patrol Division would spend most of their time answering calls for service throughout their precinct. There would be little free time (and it would come intermittently throughout the course of their shift), so devoting several hours to a specific problem would not be feasible. The first item on Table 16 demonstrates that the overwhelming majority of respondents felt there were not enough officers to handle calls for service. Presumably, if staffing levels are not sufficient to handle incoming calls for service, then they are too low to routinely allocate officers to problem solving projects.

Although there were some differences in the magnitude of agreement expressed by supervisors and non-supervisors, the direction of their attitudes was similar. The two groups only differed significantly on one of the items reported in Table 16. Supervisors were significantly more likely to think that decentralization had improved communication between patrol officers and detectives (although both groups indicated relatively low levels of agreement). Overall, supervisors were slightly more likely

Table 16.
Issues relating to community policing as organized in MCPD; agreement with items by respondent's rank. †

	Non-Supervisor	Supervisor
There are not enough officers assigned to the patrol functions to handle the demands for calls for service (n=112)	88.8%	86.4%
It is rare for the activities and projects of my team to be well coordinated across shifts (n=112)	67.8%	54.6%
Sergeants working on another shift are unable to effectively supervise officers who work on this shift (n=112)	58.9%	77.3%
Decentralization to the precincts has improved communication between patrol officers and detectives (n=112) **	11.1%	36.4%
Top leaders have made the department's priorities clear (n=112)	41.2%	50.0%

† Figures in parentheses indicate the number of valid responses for each item. The value in each cell represents the percent of the category of respondents (supervisors or non-supervisors) who indicated they "agree strongly" or "agree somewhat" with the respective item. Difference between the categories was significant at ** $p<.05$ using the Independent Samples Test.

to view these issues relating to community policing in MCPD in a more positive fashion. One exception was that supervisors were more likely to agree that it was difficult for sergeants to effectively supervise officers working on another shift.

The dual supervision system (where officers were accountable to two sergeants and sergeants supervised two sets of officers) led to a great deal of tension within the Department. Both supervisors and non-supervisors believed that the dual supervision system was flawed because sergeants could not effectively supervise officers working on other shifts. Supervisors agreed with this issue at a rate nearly twenty percentage points higher than non-supervisors, although this difference was not statistically significant. In addition, both groups also agreed that it was rare for team activities to be well coordinated across shifts.

Respondents rated MCPD's efforts to implement generalized community policing using a 4-point Likert scale (Table 17). The

Table 17.
Views on efforts to implement generalized community policing. †

How well has MCPD done in...	Excel-lent	Good	Fair	Poor
clarifying the role of regular patrol officers in problem solving? (n=118)	2.5%	19.5%	43.2%	34.7%
distributing the workload fairly between problem solving specialists and officers who are responsible for taking calls? (n=116)	1.7%	17.2%	44.0%	37.1%
giving officers enough time for problem solving? (n=117)	3.4%	22.2%	31.6%	42.7%
providing the information officers need on the problems in their assigned areas? (n=116)	11.2%	31.0%	37.9%	19.8%
rewarding officers who do a good job with problem solving? (n=116)	2.6%	7.8%	27.6%	62.1%

† The table reflects row percentages based upon the number of valid responses (figures in parentheses) for the respective item. Percentages for some items may not total 100.0 due to rounding.

distribution of responses suggests that officers generally ranked implementation efforts as having been "fair" or "poor." On average, only about 20 percent of the officers rated the various implementation efforts as having been "excellent" or "good." Respondents gave higher ratings to how well MCPD had done providing officers the information they needed to engage in problem solving (over 40% providing a rating of "excellent" or "good"). Lower ratings were given to how well management had done in rewarding officers who engaged in problem solving (just over 10% providing a rating of "excellent" or "good").

Staffing

As previously indicated (see Table 16), a common complaint heard from officers and sergeants was that the Patrol Division was insufficiently staffed to support the team-based system. At the time of the reorganization, the Patrol Division was, on paper, allocated approximately 110 patrol officers; this was a decrease from earlier years. The authorized size of the Division had been slowly eroding during the 1980's and 1990's. Veteran officers reported that personnel were pulled from the Patrol Division to staff new units created within the Department. For example, as the community policing program was expanded many of the CPO positions were filled with positions allocated to the Patrol Division. As a result, the overall number of officers working in the Patrol Division had diminished in the decades leading up to the reorganization.

Officers also estimated that the Patrol Division was understaffed by approximately twenty-five officers. On paper, the Patrol Division was allocated more than one hundred and ten officers, however only eighty to ninety were typically available to work the road during any scheduling cycle. Some of this shortage was a result of officers who were on light duty (due to injury or pregnancy). In addition, the Department experienced a large number of retirements during the 1990's and had trouble training and replacing officers to fill these positions. Also, when an officer retired from a specialized unit or command position, they were immediately replaced from within the organization. This eventually resulted in officers from the Patrol Division being shifted into other parts of the organization. Consequently, while other units were always at or near a 100 percent staffing level (with an actual officer working in every allocated position), the Patrol Division was continually at a staffing level of 70 to 80 percent.

The net result of these diminished staffing levels was a shortage of officers available to share in handling calls for service and problem solving initiatives. As discussed earlier in the text, officers spent only a small portion of their shift working in their team area and typically had only a small amount of free time during the course of their shift. It was common for officers to complain that there were not enough "bodies" to handle all of the calls for service. Based upon the available data sources, this complaint seemed to be well founded.

Although the Department had created a structure in which officers would collaboratively address neighborhood problems, officers did not believe that they were being provided with sufficient resources. There is not an absolute standard which dictates appropriate staffing for a team-based system, making it difficult to firmly evaluate whether MCPD had provided officers with sufficient personnel resources to succeed. What is clear, however, is that officers believed these resources were inadequate. The Department provided only limited overtime budgets for teams to engage in problem solving outside of their regular working hours. In addition, observational and deployment data support the fact that officers were spending much of their shift outside of their team area. These findings strengthen the argument that it was difficult for officers to find time for problem solving during the course of their regular shift.

Clarity

A final issue of importance contained in Table 16 is the clarity of the department's goals. If an organization expects a reorganization to be successful, it is important that employees understand why the changes are being made, what the organization's new priorities are, and what outcomes will be achieved through the reorganization. These issues needed to be clarified at the beginning of the change process and elaborated upon (as needed) with the passage of time. Only half of the respondents (41.2% of non-supervisors and 50.0% of supervisors) agreed that priorities had been made clear by MCPD leaders. The fact that only half of the respondents reported that sufficient clarity had been provided could serve as a "red flag" for MCPD management. A persistent complaint throughout the course of the evaluation study was that top leaders had provided insufficient direction on the specifics of the team-based system. In bringing about organizational change, it is common for planners to be intentionally vague in certain aspects of their design and implementation. This leaves planners with a certain amount of flexibility to define issues and confront emerging challenges. In this case study, officers indicated that the lack of clarity was a tremendous stumbling block in the implementation process.

Officers felt that the team system had created a high degree of ambiguity within the Department. There seemed to be no consensus on several key issues, including: what is community policing? What is successful problem solving? How are neighborhood problems defined and identified? How should problems be resolved? Officers lacked a coherent understanding of what the Department was trying to achieve through the generalized community policing approach. Veteran officers were confused by the "team" label. For them, calling the new structure a "team-based" system invoked memories earlier failures with "team policing." The distinction was never made clear by the organization.

Officers did not fully understand what they were expected to achieve, how they were to do so, or what management wanted from them. They had not been consistently trained in the philosophy or methods of community policing or problem solving. Many officers indicated they did not know how to recognize a successful problem solving effort or a properly functioning team of officers. Officers were never told how to balance the temporal and geographic responsibilities and demands created by the team-based system. They did not understand for whom they ultimately worked under a system of dual supervision.

Sergeants had not been told how to operate under the dual supervision system. They did not know whether the wishes of a team sergeant came before the wishes of a shift sergeant. They were never informed how to supervise officers with whom they had very limited human contact. They were never told how to evaluate officer performance on non-traditional measures, nor were they given the tools to do so. There were dramatic inconsistencies in team-based problem solving efforts based upon the actions of sergeants.

This lack of clarity was a tremendous barrier preventing the success of the team-based system. Even if all other barriers (attitudes, culture, resources, etc.) were eliminated, this matter was so pronounced in MCPD that it is uncertain if the reorganization could still have succeeded. This issue was persistently visible throughout the SCJ research team's involvement with the Department. The problem emerged during the first interviews and was still evident when the team was making its final reports. Although readily evident, the matter was never directly resolved by Department leaders.

Team Integrity and Guidance in Problem Solving Activities

Despite criticisms of the team system, the problem seemed to lie outside of the individual teams. While officers were occasionally critical of a particular team member or (in rare cases) their team sergeant, most survey respondents provided positive feedback about their team and its members. The majority of both non-supervisors (85.7%) and supervisors (82.3%) stated that they could depend on all or most of their team members to contribute to problem solving efforts. Nearly three-quarters (71.7%) of non-supervisors stated that their team sergeant always or usually provided adequate guidance for problem solving projects. Supervisors (sergeants and lieutenants) rated their supervisors (lieutenants and captains) slightly lower on this item, with 56.3 percent providing an analogous evaluation.

A number of survey items asked officers to report the degree to which various factors had contributed to the development of their problem solving skills. This is an important issue as it reflects whether officers felt that their problem solving skills were being developed through formal means (training) or informal means (through interaction with peers). The distribution of responses speaks to how well the Department was doing in providing formal instruction in problem solving to members of the Patrol Division. As reflected in Table 18, most officers felt that they had developed their problem solving skills through informal, peer-based mechanisms. It should be noted that only those officers who reported completing a problem solving effort answered these items.

Table 18.
Factors contributing to the development of problem solving skills. †

Factor	Very Helpful	Some-what Helpful	Not Helpful	Not Received
Formal training in department (n=82)	9.8%	35.4%	6.1%	48.8%
Formal training outside department (n=82)	14.6%	22.0%	8.5%	54.9%
College course work (n=81)	3.7%	43.2%	32.1%	21.0%
Field Training Officer (n=80)	20.0%	38.8%	10.0%	31.3%
Supervisor (n=82)	22.0%	58.5%	6.1%	13.4%
Informal from other officers (n=81)	23.5%	55.6%	6.2%	14.8%
Personal experience (n=82)	63.4%	34.1%	2.4%	0.0%

† The table reflects row percentages based upon the number of valid responses (figures in parentheses) for the respective item. Percentages for some items may not total 100.0 due to rounding.

Personal experience, and informal contact with co-workers, supervisors and Field Training Officers all appeared to contribute to the development of problem solving skills. More formal means, such as training and college course work, were either not very helpful or never received. In other words, officers felt that their problem solving skills had been developed through various informal mechanisms, rather than through structured training programs. Because the officers were relying on these informal means to develop their skills, it is less certain if they were using consistent and successful means to address community problems.

Table 18 also holds important implications which relate to how community policing was operationalized in Motor City. The SCJ research team often heard protestations by some administrators that officers had received sufficient training in problem solving and community policing issues. Based on the interviews and focus groups, as well as the survey responses, those officers who had received problem solving training felt that it was at least somewhat helpful in the development of their skills. Unfortunately, around half of the survey respondents reported that they had not received training relevant to the development of their problem solving skills. These responses indicated a lack of training in problem solving methods, contradicting the management contention that sufficient formal training had been provided.

Accountability, Evaluations and Rewards

In the process of bringing about change, organizations need to provide employees with feedback about performance. Such assessments benefit both the employer and the employee. They allow the employer to assess the status of a transition and provide insights into areas requiring improvement on the part of management. They also benefit employees because they aid in understanding what is expected under the new organizational structure. The processes of ensuring accountability and providing evaluations can be enhanced through the use of rewards. While evaluations serve as a warning to those employees whose work performance needs to be adjusted, rewards are a way to recognize exemplary service.

Accountability patterns were complicated by the transition to the team-based organizational structure. Police officers are generally held accountable only within their organization, with responsibility vested in their immediate supervisor. Traditionally, officers have focused their energies on producing the outputs demanded by their organization (arrests, citations, field contacts, parking tickets); little consideration has been given to the outputs desired by others. Officers had a responsibility to follow the orders of their immediate supervisor. While an officer must ultimately answer to any superior officer, on a daily basis they strive to please those supervisors directly above them in the organization.

As discussed in the literature review, community policing complicates traditional accountability patterns in police organizations; this complication was even more pronounced in MCPD. Under a community policing philosophy, officers are accountable not only within their organization (to their superiors) but also within a broader context (to the community they serve). Officers must work to satisfy the demands of a variety of individuals; complications may arise as these various demands may be in conflict with one another. The team-based structure developed by MCPD made accountability even more problematic. As discussed elsewhere, officers (and supervisors) had trouble with the dual supervision created by the team-based system because it bifurcated accountability. The challenge of this bifurcation was made even more complicated by the organization's failure to delineate whether the directives of one supervisor (shift or team) superceded that of the other.

The Motor City Police Department had historically used quantitative means to evaluate their employees. The traditional outputs demanded of employees (arrests, citation, field contacts) allowed supervisors to make simple assessments of officer productivity. Unfortunately, these traditional quantitative measures are insufficient for evaluating employees operating under a community policing philosophy. Such a philosophy makes it far more difficult for agencies to evaluate their employees; qualitative measures must often be incorporated with quantitative indicators.

Faced with a need to restructure their evaluation mechanisms, leaders in the Motor City Police Department simply ceased providing officers with regular evaluations. One survey respondent noted that they "haven't had an evaluation in <u>years</u>" (emphasis in original). In the summer of 1999 one mid-career officer informed the author that she had not been evaluated since before the initial stages of the reorganization (in early 1995). She indicated that she believed this was the norm among most of her veteran peers. For reasons which were never clear to the SCJ research team, personnel evaluations were no longer systematically used in MCPD after the mid-1990's.

In implementing the team-based system, MCPD did not attempt to devise a reward system that would recognize officers for exemplary service. Several respondents made note of this on the officer survey. Unedited comments pertaining to rewards included:

> "Officers are not formally recognized for doing a good job on some incidents as much as they should be."
>
> "They want to reward their 'golden children' and do not recognize others."
>
> "There is no reward."
>
> "Few rewards can be provided except informally through supervisors on shift."

Public sector organizations have a limited ability to provide formal rewards (awards, monetary prizes, etc.) to their employees. Agencies can, however, do a great deal at virtually no cost by taking the time and initiative to recognize officers for their contributions.

In the context of this case study, the Department could have published periodic "best practices" bulletins which might have highlighted innovative problem solving strategies employed by officers. Such bulletins would have served a twofold purpose. First, they would have provided a mechanism by which the Department could have recognized commendable behavior by employees. Second, they would have demonstrated successful problem solving. Given the difficulty the Department was facing in these areas, such demonstrations would have been an important learning tool and training resource for employees.

Supervisors were especially frustrated that top leaders were not doing more to recognize those officers who were diligently trying to make the team-based system a success. In focus groups and interviews they indicated the Department needed to be doing more to recognize employees who were innovative in their problem solving initiatives. Lacking evaluation protocols and in the absence of a reward system, mid-level supervisors had little leverage in trying to modify the behavior of the officers on their team. As one lieutenant observed, officers were paid the same amount regardless of the diligence with which they performed their duties. Without an impetus (evaluations) or incentive (rewards), what reason would there be for an officer to put forth additional effort in an attempt to reduce problems within the community?

SUMMARY

Quantitative findings were developed from a survey administered to a large group of Motor City police officers; this group was demographically representative of the Department as a whole. The survey respondents were mostly white males. Most respondents had a Bachelors degree, although the reported level of education varied from some college through graduate degrees. The respondents had been employed with MCPD for anywhere from a few months to several decades. Approximately one in five was a supervisor (sergeant or lieutenant) and nearly one in six had been or was a CPO.

Officers indicated dissatisfaction with their general work environment and their relationship with their supervisors. Employees reported violations of their psychological contracts through the Department's failure to clarify goals/objectives, to give employees a voice, and to provide employees with the training, resources, and support required for generalized community policing to succeed. The dual supervision system had created confusion and uncertainty for both line officers and supervisors. Many officers seemed to distrust the Department's management. The transition to a two-precinct department had increased the psychological (and physical) distance between line officers and top leaders. A few officers demonstrated clear suspicion of the SCJ research team, suggesting that they were the Chief's spies.

The reorganization left officers uncertain about the Department's values and beliefs. They felt that they no longer knew "what mattered" within the organization and were not clear what behaviors were valued by the organization. Officers were uncertain how the transition to generalized community policing would alter the criteria upon which promotion and special assignment were allocated. Beyond the transition to team-based community policing, some respondents were worried that the Department was becoming too political in general. They were specifically concerned that the agency was catering too much to the demands of the community and that decisions relating to promotions and specialized assignments were being made based on diversification, rather than merit. Supervisors recognized that structural changes had modified the responsibilities and roles of some management positions, making them less desirable.

Both quantitative and qualitative data were concerned with assessing respondents' attitudes toward community policing, both as a general philosophy and as implemented in the Motor City Police Department. Some officers questioned whether community policing was a valid function for the police. Others believed community policing was a valid police function, but that it was not being done "right" in MCPD. There were also concerns relating to the capacity of community policing to truly alter entrenched social problems. Many officers, including former CPO's, felt that the Department was attempting to address serious community ills (which required "surgery") with overly simplistic responses ("band-aid" solutions).

Disparities were observed between the attitudes of respondents based upon their experience as a CPO. Although both CPO's and non-CPO's believed that community policing officers made an important contribution in the neighborhoods they served, non-CPO's indicated that an officer could be spending their time engaged in more important tasks. CPO's and non-CPO's also indicated diverse perspectives on the advantages and disadvantages of having a CPO assignment. Non-CPO's held perspectives which seemed to be more "stereotypical" than those reported by officers with CPO experience. Non-CPO's characterized the job as a "fluff" assignment which was primarily a public relations tool. Officers with CPO experience felt that the assignment involved a great deal of uncertainty, but that it served a vital role in enhancing police services. Overall, officers felt that CPO's were not being given sufficient direction or training, but did have the advantage of working independently, addressing long-term problems, and working closely with the public.

One of the most significant items from the officer survey asked respondents how the Motor City Police Department should organize community policing in the future. This provided one of the most pointed assessments of community policing obtained in the evaluation project. One in three respondents felt that the Department should not engage in any form of community policing in the future. This item provides a blunt assessment of how those affected by the implementation of community policing felt about this philosophy and its appropriate role in the future of the Department. Those respondents with CPO experience were much less likely to hold this sentiment, instead feeling that the Department's current generalized strategy was the best approach for the future.

Respondents were critical, and at times contradictory, in their perceptions of the organizational culture and climate in the Motor City Police Department at the time of the officer survey. When asked to rate their immediate supervisors, respondents provided positive evaluations on both traditional and community policing criteria, including criteria which were specific to the team-based system. On the other hand, both supervisors and non-supervisors felt that the dual supervision system had rendered sergeants unable to effectively supervise officers on another shift. Respondents were satisfied with the specific supervision they were receiving, but were critical of the general ability of supervisors to be effective under the Department's contemporary structure.

Respondents were less positive in their perceptions of top MCPD leaders. Their responses to several items present an image of a Department which did not seem to exhibit strong organizational "health." Respondents felt that top management did not understand rank and file employees. They believed that officers were denied the chance to participate in making decisions and were not kept informed of the rationale behind such decisions. In addition, respondents indicated that the department's priorities had not been made clear by top leaders. Consequently, respondents were unsure of the direction in which the organization was heading.

Communication, both within teams and between precincts, generally received low ratings. Respondents felt that there was poor communication between precincts and among units (i.e., patrol and detectives) within the Department. Many respondents felt there was insufficient communication within their team. The communication which was occurring took place through impersonal mechanisms, such as voice mail, rather than via face-to-face interaction. Communication between front-line employees and top leaders was a consistent source of contention throughout the evaluation project. Officers continually reported that key problems were not being addressed, clarified and resolved by Department administrators, generating uncertainty, confusion, apathy, and resistance to the implementation of generalized community policing. On the whole, these various assessments of the relationship between front-line officers and top organizational managers indicate that the organizational climate and culture were not as "healthy" as they might be.

In the process of implementing and bringing about organizational change, the Motor City Police Department did not capitalize on the potential benefits which might have been realized by tapping key actors, union officials, and mid-level supervisors. Because no efforts were made to incorporate these formal and informal leaders in the change process, it is difficult to conclusively state that they would have helped facilitate a successful transition to generalized community policing. Existing literature and prior experiences suggest that their inclusion might have helped mollify some of the resistance exhibited by MCPD officers. The fact that they were overlooked, however, does not appear to have had a deleterious effect on the change process in the Motor City.

The mechanics of the team-based system also presented problems in the eyes of the study participants. A critical issue was that staffing levels were perceived as too low to support the team-based system. Officers and supervisors felt that there were insufficient personnel resources to manage the Department's reactive policing (calls for service) responsibilities, making it difficult for officers to undertake proactive efforts (problem solving) within their team areas. Analyzing the various data sources supported the argument that officers had little free time during the course of their shifts and spent only a small portion of their time in the team areas. While these findings do not allow for a clear determination of whether staffing levels were sufficient, they do indicate that officers had few opportunities to engage in proactive problem solving during the course of their routine working hours.

The team system itself posed numerous problems for officers and supervisors. Officers had to balance the temporal and geographic responsibilities which the team-based community policing system created. Supervisors and officers had to deal with the tension created by the dual supervision system. Survey respondents indicated that coordination, communication and supervision across the shifts were difficult. The implementation process itself was criticized on several levels. Respondents indicated that in the course of the reorganization, top leaders had provided poor clarity and insufficient information. The team-based system reportedly suffered from a poor workload distribution, insufficient time for problem solving endeavors, and inadequate rewards.

Officers were unsure how to operate under the team-based system. They believed top leaders had not been clear about what the Department expected to achieve, how officers were supposed to work under the system, how they were to balance their temporal and geographic responsibilities, how they were to deal with the tension of dual supervision, and what criteria would indicate "good" performance on their part. Respondents indicated that their problem solving training was inadequate to prepare them to operate under the new system, forcing them to rely on informal (and inconsistent?) means by which to learn these skills. In the absence of clarity, resources, and training, it was difficult for officers to succeed under the team-based system, even if they were committed to its ideals.

A final element of organizational planning which was absent in the Motor City experience was a modified system of accountability, evaluations, and rewards. Community policing alters accountability patterns within police organizations; this alteration necessitates a change in evaluation tools. The quantitative measures traditionally employed by organizations to evaluate police employees do not assess the range of behaviors and actions that need to be captured to make evaluations in a community policing setting. Alternative reward mechanisms may also help encourage employees to make behavioral modifications. In MCPD, these elements were largely overlooked in the implementation process, making it difficult to determine the role they might have played. Based on prior studies, it may be speculated that the use of these three tools would have aided the Department in realizing a more successful change within their organization.

CHAPTER 9

Exploring Officer Attitudes

Based upon the findings from the literature review and the results of the preliminary quantitative and qualitative analysis, it is possible to consider the survey data in a more systematic manner. This chapter uses the results of the officer survey to test the hypotheses proffered in chapter 6. These hypotheses were developed to better understand how the various elements of the study's conceptual framework intersected in the available data. This chapter first discusses the development of those factors used in hypotheses testing. Specifically, factors were developed to represent attitudes about community policing as a philosophy, perceptions of organizational culture, and evaluations of community policing as implemented in the Motor City Police Department.

Using these factors and other salient survey variables the hypotheses are then individually tested. This testing makes it possible to assess how measures of individual socialization, organizational culture, and organizational planning intersect in determining respondent attitudes toward three key issues. Specifically, the issues being targeted are beliefs about how community policing should be organized in the future, perceptions about how community policing was implemented in the Motor City Police Department, and attitudes respondents held about community policing as a philosophy.

DEVELOPMENT OF THE FACTORS

Prior to testing the hypotheses, it was first necessary to construct three factors for use in the analysis. Several concepts of importance in this study (i.e., perceptions of community policing as a philosophy) were not directly addressed through the survey completed by the patrol officers.

The authors of the officer survey instrument were concerned about these concepts; however, the nature of the concepts was such that direct measurement was deemed to be ill-advised. The controversial nature of the concepts was likely to cause respondents to provide answers based on emotions, rather than their actual beliefs. Although the concepts were not directly measured in the survey, important elements were reflected in select items. Through the use of factor analysis, these groups of variables may be combined to represent a single concept (Walker, J.T., 1999). Factor analysis was used to create measures of concepts not assessed through individual survey items.

Given the emotional nature of the term "community policing," (particularly in the context of MCPD at the time of the survey's administration) the officer survey did not ask the respondents to provide a direct evaluation of this concept. The survey authors were concerned that respondents would not be able to separate their attitudes about community policing from their evaluation of community policing as it was instituted in MCPD. Despite the absence of a direct measure of such attitudes, several survey items asked officers to evaluate elements of community policing. These elements were combined to develop a factor for use in the instant study.

Table 19 displays the four variables (including their response options, means, and standard deviations) used to create a factor reflecting attitudes about community policing as a philosophy (CPATT). These variables were used to create an overall community policing attitude scale (Cronbach's alpha = .8093). Factor scores ranged from -1.87 to 2.14; higher scores indicated more positive attitudes about community policing as a philosophy. Factor analysis produced one significant factor with an eigenvalue of 2.583; all remaining factors had eigenvalues at or below .620. These eigenvalues suggest the scale produced by these four items was reflecting only one concept, making the scores suitable for use in further analysis.

It is unclear if a respondent's attitudes about community policing as a philosophy are separate from their evaluation of community policing as it was instituted in the Motor City Police Department. There was no single survey item which directly measured the respondents' evaluation of community policing in MCPD. Despite the absence of a direct measure of such an evaluation, several items asked officers to evaluate elements of community policing as it was instituted in MCPD. The elements were combined to develop a factor suitable for analysis in this text.

Table 19.
Factor composition:
Attitudes about community policing as a philosophy (CPATT).

Variable	Response Options	Mean	S.D.
How would you feel about receiving an assignment to work as a Community Policing Officer during the coming year?	1= Very negative 2= Somewhat negative 3= Neutral 4= Somewhat positive 5= Very positive	2.13	1.26
CPO's make an important contribution toward reducing crime and disorder in the neighborhoods where they are assigned.	1= Disagree strongly 2= Disagree somewhat 3= Agree somewhat 4= Agree strongly	2.57	.95
CPO's make an important contribution toward improving the attitudes of neighborhood residents toward the police department.	1= Disagree strongly 2= Disagree somewhat 3= Agree somewhat 4= Agree strongly	2.90	.86
Doing community policing means that officers will be unable to do more important tasks.	1= Agree strongly 2= Agree somewhat 3= Disagree somewhat 4= Disagree strongly	2.68	.98

The variables used to create a factor reflecting evaluations of community policing as it was instituted in MCPD (CPINMCPD) are displayed in Table 20 (along with variable response options, means, and standard deviations). These five variables were used to create a scale reflecting an overall evaluation of community policing as instituted in MCPD (Cronbach's alpha = .7850). For this factor, scores ranged from -1.50 to 3.27; higher scores indicated a more positive evaluation of community policing as it was instituted in the Motor City Police Department. Factor analysis produced one significant factor with an eigenvalue of 3.100; all remaining factors had eigenvalues at or below .861. Based upon the eigenvalues it is evident that these five items

Table 20.
Factor composition: Evaluation of
community policing as instituted in MCPD (CPINMCPD).

Variable	**Response Options**	**Mean**	**S.D.**
How well has MCPD done in clarifying the role of regular patrol officers in problem solving?	4= Excellent 3= Good 2= Fair 1= Poor	1.90	.80
How well has MCPD done in distributing the workload fairly between problem solving specialists and officers who are responsible for taking calls?	4= Excellent 3= Good 2= Fair 1= Poor	1.84	.77
How well has MCPD done in giving officers enough time for problem solving?	4= Excellent 3= Good 2= Fair 1= Poor	1.86	.88
How well has MCPD done in providing the information officers need on the problems in their assigned areas?	4= Excellent 3= Good 2= Fair 1= Poor	2.34	.92
How well has MCPD done in rewarding officers who do a good job with problem solving?	4= Excellent 3= Good 2= Fair 1= Poor	1.51	.75

produce a scale which reflects a single concept, suggesting that these scores are suitable for use in further analysis.

The officer survey did not attempt to directly measure perceptions of organizational culture held by the respondents. It is important to examine the relationship between perceptions of organizational culture and other variables within the study's conceptual framework. Specifically, are there significant differences on community policing-related measures based upon a respondent's perception of the organizational culture ("healthy" versus "not healthy") in MCPD. Although direct measures of such perceptions are absent in the officer survey data, several survey items reflected perceptions of organizational culture in MCPD. Using these elements, a factor was developed for this analysis.

Table 21 presents the variables (along with variable response options, means, and standard deviations) used to create the factor reflecting perceptions of organizational culture (ORGCULT). These five variables were used to create a scale reflecting overall perceptions of organizational culture (Cronbach's alpha = .7013). For this factor, scores ranged from -1.49 to 2.99; higher scores indicated a more "healthy" perception of the organizational culture in the Motor City Police Department. Factor analysis produced one significant factor with an eigenvalue of 2.305; all remaining factors had eigenvalues at or below .970. These eigenvalues suggest the scale produced by these five items was reflecting only one concept and that it is appropriate for use in further analysis.

These three factors (CPATT, CPINMCPD, and ORGCULT) will be used to reflect their underlying concepts in testing the research hypotheses derived from the conceptual framework. By combining variables which are theoretically and mathematically related, the analysis will provide a better understanding of the relationship between the study's key concepts.

ANALYSIS OF HYPOTHESES

Within the framework described in the preceding chapters, it is possible to consider the relationship between various attitudes/opinions and the three conceptual areas of interest in this study. These relationships are described and tested as a series of research hypotheses. The reader is reminded that all hypotheses are present in the null form. All of the

Table 21.
Factor composition:
Perceptions of organizational culture in MCPD (ORGCULT).

Variable	Response Options	Mean	S.D.
Top department leadership has unrealistically high expectations about how much the current organizational strategies will reduce crime and disorder in the neighborhoods.	1= Agree strongly 2= Agree somewhat 3= Disagree somewhat 4= Disagree strongly	3.34	.74
Top department management has a good understanding of what the work of the rank-and-file police officer is like.	1= Disagree strongly 2= Disagree somewhat 3= Agree somewhat 4= Agree strongly	1.88	.90
Rank-and-file officers do not have enough opportunity to participate in developing policies and planning strategies.	1= Agree strongly 2= Agree somewhat 3= Disagree somewhat 4= Disagree strongly	3.17	.76
Rank-and-file officers are kept well-informed of management's policies and plans.	1= Disagree strongly 2= Disagree somewhat 3= Agree somewhat 4= Agree strongly	1.81	.86
Top leaders have made the department's priorities clear.	1= Disagree strongly 2= Disagree somewhat 3= Agree somewhat 4= Agree strongly	2.17	.92

regression models contained herein originally included the respondents' precinct. This variable was not found to be significant in any of the models. It has been left out of the final models to ensure parsimony.

Ho_1: Measures of individual socialization will not significantly affect the respondents' attitudes about community policing as a philosophy.

OLS regression was employed to estimate the effects of individual socialization on attitudes about community policing. The dependent variable was a four-item factor score (CPATT); higher values on the factor reflected more positive attitudes about community policing as a philosophy. Four measures of individual socialization (education, years of service, race/ethnicity, and gender) were entered into the regression model as independent variables. In addition, based upon their significance in prior research it was necessary to control for rank and experience as a community policing officer.

A significant relationship was found between individual socialization and the respondents' attitudes about community policing. The analytical model was significant with a moderate/strong predictive value. The individual effects of the independent variables are presented in Table 22. Table entries are unstandardized regression coefficients with corresponding *t*-ratios.

Table 22.
Regression of individual socialization on
attitudes about CP as a philosophy (CPATT). †

Variable	***b***	***t*-ratio**
CPO experience	-1.374	-5.700***
rank	.760	2.933***
gender	-.833	-2.888***
years of service	-.155	-2.133**
education	-.086	-.770
race/ethnicity	-.047	-.461

† F= 8.336, $p \leq .001$, $R^2 = .370$; **$p < .05$, ***$p < .01$

Both of the control variables (CPO experience and rank) were significant at the p=.01 level and were the strongest predictors in the model. Two of the four individual socialization predictors were significant. Gender was significant at the p=.01 level and years of service was significant at the p=.05 level. The respondents' attitudes about community policing as a philosophy were more favorable if the respondent had experience as a CPO, held a rank (sergeant or lieutenant), was a female, or had fewer years of service with the Motor City Police Department.

Based on the results of this analysis, the null hypothesis is rejected at the p<.001 level. Measures of individual socialization have a significant effect on attitudes about community policing as a philosophy.

Ho_2: Measures of individual socialization will not significantly affect the respondents' evaluation of community policing as it was instituted in the Motor City Police Department.

OLS regression was used to estimate the effects of individual socialization on the respondents' evaluation of community policing as it was instituted in MCPD. The dependent variable was a five-item factor score (CPINMCPD); higher values on the factor reflected greater support for community policing as it was instituted in MCPD. Four measures of individual socialization (education, years of service, race/ethnicity, and gender) were entered into the regression model as independent variables. Rank and experience as a CPO were controlled for in the model based upon their significance in prior research.

A significant relationship was not found between individual socialization and the respondents' evaluation of community policing as instituted in MCPD. The analytical model was not found to be significant. The individual effects of the independent variables are presented in Table 23. Table entries are unstandardized regression coefficients with corresponding t-ratios.

In addition to the regression model failing to achieve statistical significance, none of the model's independent variables were found to have significant values. The level of significance achieved with both the regression model and individual independent variables still failed to achieve statistical significance, even when the model controlled for the respondents' precinct.

Based on the results of this analysis, the author fails to reject the null hypothesis. The regression model is not significant at or below either the

Table 23.
Regression of individual socialization on evaluation of CP as instituted in MCPD (CPINMCPD). †

Variable	*b*	*t*-ratio ‡
CPO experience	-.228	-.806
rank	.112	.382
gender	-.246	-.719
years of service	-.048	-.582
education	-.117	-.943
race/ethnicity	-.115	.988

† F= .519, p= .792; ‡ No values achieved $p \leq .10$

p=.05 level or the p=.10 level. Measures of individual socialization (taken individually or collectively) do not appear to influence the respondents' evaluations of community policing as it was instituted in the Motor City Police Department.

> Ho_3: Measures of individual socialization will not significantly affect the respondents' belief about how the Motor City Police Department should organize community policing in the future.

The effects of individual socialization on the respondents' belief of how MCPD should organize community policing in the future were estimated using OLS regression. The dependent variable was a single survey question; respondents were asked "what would be the best way for the Motor City Police Department to organize community policing?" Possible responses (recoded from lowest to highest support for the MCPD approach to community policing) were: "do not do community policing at all," "designate specialists to do it," "make it the responsibility of all patrol officers" and "make it the responsibility of both specialists and general patrol officers."

The regression model consisted of four measures of individual socialization (education, years of service, race/ethnicity, and gender) and two control measures (rank and experience as a community policing officer). A significant relationship was found between individual socialization and beliefs about how community policing should be organized in the future. The analytical model was found to be significant with a moderate predictive value. The individual effects of the independent variables are presented in Table 24. Table entries are unstandardized regression coefficients with corresponding *t*-ratios.

Table 24.
Regression of individual socialization on how MCPD should organize CP in the future. †

Variable	***b***	***t*-ratio**
CPO experience	-1.264	-4.044***
rank	.982	3.026***
gender	-.611	-1.735*
years of service	-.164	-1.790*
education	.077	.568
race/ethnicity	-.027	-.207

† F= 5.014, $p \leq .001$, $R^2 = .266$; *$p<.10$, ***$p<.01$

The two control variables (CPO experience and rank) were both found to be significant at the p=.01 level; these variables were the strongest predictors in the model. Of the four individual socialization predictors, none were significant at the p=.05 level; gender and years of service were found to be significant at the p=.10 level. The respondents' belief about how the Motor City Police Department should organize community policing in the future was more supportive of the current strategy if the respondent had experience as a CPO or held a rank (sergeant or lieutenant) and, to a lesser extent, if the respondent was a female, or had fewer years of service with the Department.

Based on the results of this analysis, the null hypothesis is rejected at the p<.001 level. Measures of individual socialization influence beliefs about how the Motor City Police Department should organize community policing in the future.

Ho_4: Respondent demographics will not significantly affect perceptions of the organizational culture in the Motor City Police Department.

Using OLS regression, demographics were used to estimate perceptions of the organizational culture in MCPD. The dependent variable was a five-item factor score (ORGCULT); as the value of the factor increases, the organizational culture in the Department was perceived as more "healthy." The regression model consisted of six independent variables which reflected the respondents' demographic characteristics. These measures were: level of education, years of service, race/ethnicity, gender, rank, and experience as a community policing officer. Demographics were not found to have a significant effect on respondents' perceptions of organizational culture. The analytical model was not found to be significant. The individual effects of the demographic measures are presented in Table 25. Table entries are unstandardized regression coefficients with corresponding *t*-ratios.

Table 25.
Regression of demographics on
perceptions of organizational culture in MCPD (ORGCULT). †

Variable	***b***	***t*-ratio**
CPO experience	-.283	-1.040
rank	.502	1.728*
gender	-.362	-1.062
years of service	-.124	-1.514
education	.021	-.172
race/ethnicity	.145	1.254

† F=1.165, p=.332; *p<.10

In addition to the regression model failing to achieve statistical significance, none of the independent variables were found to have significant values at the p=.05 level. This is consistent with the earlier findings which failed to yield consistent relationships between individual demographic variables and elements of organizational culture. One variable (rank) was significant at the p=.10 level.

Based on the results of this analysis, the author fails to reject the null hypothesis. Perceptions of the organizational culture in the Motor City Police Department are independent of an individual's demographic characteristics.

Ho$_5$: Perceptions of the organizational culture of the Motor City Police Department do not have a significant effect on the respondents' evaluation of community policing as it was instituted in the MCPD.

A basic comparison of perceptions of organizational culture and evaluation of community policing can be made by calculating their bivariate correlation. The two factors were significantly related (p=.000) and highly correlated (r=.659). These findings suggest a strong positive relationship between the variables. Employees who perceived of the organizational culture as "healthy" gave a higher evaluation of community policing in MCPD. Employees who gave high evaluations to community policing in MCPD perceived of the organizational culture as more "healthy."

In order to determine if perceptions of the organization's culture affected evaluations of community policing in MCPD, the factors were analyzed using OLS regression. In light of the results of the first three hypotheses and prior research studies, three independent variables were controlled for in the final regression model (CPO experience, rank, and gender). Initial models included other measures of individual socialization (years of service, level of education, and race/ethnicity); however, these variables were not significant predictors and were eliminated to ensure that the final model was parsimonious.

The final regression model was run with the evaluation of community policing in Motor City (CPINMCPD) as the dependent variable. Perception of organizational culture (ORGCULT) was the independent variable; the control variables were CPO experience, rank, and gender. Analysis indicated that perceptions of organizational culture have an effect on evaluations of community policing as it was instituted in MCPD. The analytical model was found to be significant with a strong predictive value. The individual effects of the independent and control variables are presented in Table 26. Table entries are unstandardized regression coefficients with corresponding *t*-ratios.

Evaluation of community policing as it was instituted in the Motor City Police Department (CPINMCPD) was strongly predicted by the respondents' perception of organizational culture. The three control variables (CPO experience, rank, and gender) were not found to be significant predictors in this regression model. Respondents who perceived of MCPD's organizational culture as more "healthy" tended to provide higher evaluations of the Department's approach to community policing.

Table 26.
Regression of perceptions of organizational culture on evaluation of CP as instituted in MCPD. †

Variable	*b*	*t*-ratio
ORGCULT	.650	8.722***
CPO experience	-.070	-.356
rank	-.164	-.913
gender	.165	.638

† F= 19.092, $p \leq .001$, $R^2 = .448$; ***$p < .01$

Based on the results of this analysis, the null hypothesis is rejected at the $p<.001$ level. Perceptions of organizational culture have a significant effect on how respondents evaluated community policing as it was instituted in the Motor City Police Department.

> Ho_6: Perceptions of the organizational culture of the Motor City Police Department do not have a significant effect on the respondents' beliefs about how MCPD should organize community policing in the future.

Perceptions of organizational culture and beliefs about how MCPD should organize community policing in the future can easily be compared by calculating their bivariate correlation. The two items were significantly related ($p=.001$) with a low correlation (r=.304). These findings reflect a positive relationship between these two items. Employees who perceived of the organizational culture as "healthy" believed that MCPD should continue to organize community policing in its current fashion (making it the responsibility of both specialists and general patrol officers). Employees who believed that MCPD should continue to organize community policing in its current fashion also perceived of the organizational culture as "healthier."

In order to determine if perceptions of the organization's culture affected beliefs about how community policing should be organized in the future, the items were analyzed using OLS regression. Based upon the outcome of the first three hypotheses and prior research studies, three independent variables were controlled for in the final regression model (CPO experience, rank, and gender). Initial models included other measures of individual socialization (years of service, level of education, and race/ethnicity). These variables were not found to be significant predictors and were eliminated to ensure that the final model was parsimonious.

The final regression model was run with beliefs about how community policing should be organized in the future as the dependent variable. The five-item factor score reflecting perception of organizational culture (ORGCULT) was the independent variable; the control variables were CPO experience, rank, and gender. Perceptions of organizational culture affect beliefs about how MCPD should organize community policing in the future. The analytical model was found to be significant with a moderate predictive value. The individual effects of the independent and control variables are presented in Table 27. Table entries are unstandardized regression coefficients with corresponding *t*-ratios.

Table 27.
Regression of perceptions of organizational culture on beliefs about how MCPD should organize CP in the future. †

Variable	***b***	***t*-ratio**
ORGCULT	.281	2.791***
CPO experience	-1.101	-4.054***
rank	.661	2.685***
gender	-.269	-.807

† $F= 8.501, p \leq .001, R^2= .266$; ***$p< .01$

Beliefs about how MCPD should organize community policing in the future were strongly predicted by experience as a community policing officer, perceptions of organizational culture, and rank. Gender was the only control variable which was not found to be a significant predictor in this model. Supervisors (sergeants and lieutenants), those with CPO experience, and those who perceived of the organizational culture as "healthy" tended to believe the Department should continue to organize community policing in the contemporary manner (making it the responsibility of both specialists and general patrol officers).

The null hypothesis is rejected at the $p<.001$ level based upon the results of this analysis. Perceptions of organizational culture have a significant effect on beliefs about how the Motor City Police Department should organize community policing in the future.

Ho_7: Perceptions of the organizational culture of the Motor City Police Department do not have a significant effect on the respondents' attitudes about community policing as a philosophy (CPATT).

Calculating the bivariate correlation for these two factors (ORGCULT and CPATT) allows for a simple exploration of their relationship. The two factors were significantly related ($p< .001$) and moderately correlated ($r=.409$). This calculation reflects a strong positive relationship between the factors. Employees who perceived of the organizational culture as "healthy" provided more positive evaluations of community policing as a philosophy. Employees who gave positive evaluations of community policing perceived of the organizational culture as "healthier."

OLS regression was employed to determine if perceptions of the organization's culture affected attitudes about community policing as a philosophy. Based upon the outcome of the first three hypotheses and prior research studies, three independent variables were controlled for in the final regression model (CPO experience, rank, and gender). Initial models also included other measures of individual socialization (years of service, level of education, and race/ethnicity). These variables were not found to be significant predictors of attitudes about community policing as a philosophy. They were eliminated from the final model to ensure that it was parsimonious.

The final regression model was run with respondents' attitudes about community policing as a philosophy as the dependent variable. The factor reflecting perception of organizational culture (ORGCULT) was the independent variable; the control variables were CPO experience, rank, and gender. According to the regression analysis, perceptions of organizational culture affect how respondents evaluate community policing as a philosophy. The analytical model was found to be significant (F=20.307, $p \leq .001$) with a strong predictive value (R^2= .461). Table 28 provides the individual effects of the independent and control variables. Table entries are unstandardized regression coefficients with corresponding *t*-ratios.

Table 28.
Regression of perceptions of organizational culture on attitudes about CP as a philosophy. †

Variable	*b*	*t*-ratio
ORGCULT	.368	4.707***
CPO experience	-1.294	-6.480***
rank	.422	2.231**
gender	-.575	-2.237**

† F= 20.307, $p \leq .001$, R^2= .461; ***p*<.05, ****p*< .01

Evaluations of community policing as a philosophy were strongly predicted by all of the independent variables in this model. Experience as a community policing officer and perceptions of organizational culture were the strongest predictors; both were highly significant ($p \leq .000$). Gender and rank were also strong predictors and both were significant at the *p*=.05 level. Respondents gave higher evaluations of community policing as a philosophy when they were a supervisor (sergeants and lieutenants), had experience working as a CPO, were female, or perceived of the organizational culture as "healthy."

Based upon the results of this analysis, the null hypothesis is rejected at the *p*<.001. Perceptions of organizational culture have a significant effect on the evaluation of community policing as a philosophy.

Ho_8: Attitudes about community policing as a philosophy do not have a significant effect on the respondents' evaluation of community policing it was instituted in the Motor City Police Department.

The relationship between these two factors (CPATT and CPINMCPD) may be explored by computing their bivariate correlation. Calculation of the correlation indicated that the two factors were significantly related (p= .001) with a low correlation (r=.318). This calculation reflects a positive relationship between the factors. Employees who expressed a more positive attitude about community policing as a philosophy were more favorable in evaluating community policing as it was instituted in MCPD. Employees who gave positive evaluations of community policing as implemented in MCPD held more positive attitudes about community policing as a philosophy.

OLS regression was used to determine if attitudes about community policing affected evaluations of community policing as it was implemented in MCPD. Given their significance in prior research studies and in earlier stages of this analysis, three independent variables were controlled for in the final regression model (CPO experience, rank, and gender). Initial regression models also included other measures of individual socialization (years of service, level of education, and race/ethnicity) as control variables. These variables were not found to be significant predictors of evaluation of community policing as it was instituted in MCPD. In order ensure a parsimonious model, these variables were eliminated from the final analysis.

The final regression model was run with respondents' evaluation of community policing as instituted in MCPD (CPINMCPD) as the dependent variable. The independent variable was the respondents' attitudes about community policing as a philosophy (CPATT); control variables were CPO experience, rank, and gender. Attitudes about community policing affect how the respondents evaluated community policing as instituted in MCPD. The analytical model proved to be significant with a low predictive value. Table 29 presents the individual effects of the independent and control variables. Table entries are unstandardized regression coefficients with corresponding t-ratios.

A respondent's attitude about community policing as a philosophy was a strong predictor of the evaluation of community policing as instituted in MCPD. In this model, the control variables (CPO experience, rank, and gender) did not exhibit a significant effect on the dependent variable. Employees with a favorable attitude about community policing gave more positive evaluations of the Motor City Police Department's efforts to implement generalized community policing.

Table 29.
Regression of attitudes about CP as a philosophy on evaluation of CP as instituted in MCPD. †

Variable	*b*	*t*-ratio
CPATT	.397	3.549***
CPO experience	.417	1.461
rank	-.235	-1.004
gender	.143	.451

† $F = 3.243$, $p \leq .05$, $R^2 = .124$; ***$p < .01$

The results of this analysis allow for the rejection of the null hypothesis at the $p<.05$ level. Perceptions of community policing as a philosophy have a significant effect on the evaluation of community policing as instituted by the Motor City Police Department.

Ho_9: Attitudes about community policing as a philosophy do not have a significant effect on beliefs about how the Motor City Police Department should organize community policing in the future.

These two items (CPATT and community policing in the future) may be compared by calculating their bivariate correlation. The two items were found to be significantly related ($p< .001$) and highly correlated ($r=.611$), reflecting a strong positive relationship. Employees who expressed a positive attitude about community policing as a philosophy tended to believe that MCPD should continue to organize community policing as it had been doing (making in the joint responsibility of specialists and general patrol officers). Employees who believed that MCPD should continue with its contemporary approach to community policing tended to have a more positive attitude about community policing as a philosophy.

OLS regression was used to determine if attitudes about community policing as a philosophy affected beliefs about how community policing should be organized in the future. Based upon their significance in the first three hypotheses and in prior research studies, three independent variables were controlled for in the final regression model (CPO experience, rank, and gender). Other measures of individual socialization (years of service, level of education, and race/ethnicity) were included in initial models, but were not found to be significant predictors of beliefs about how MCPD should organize community policing in the future. They were excluded from the final model to ensure that it was parsimonious.

The final regression model was run with the survey item measuring belief about how MCPD should organize community policing in the future as the dependent variable. The factor reflecting attitudes about community policing as a philosophy (CPATT) was the independent variable; the control variables were CPO experience, rank, and gender. According to the regression analysis, perceptions of organizational culture affect how respondents evaluate community policing as a philosophy. The analytical model was found to be significant with a moderate/strong predictive value. Table 30 provides the individual effects of the independent and control variables. Table entries are unstandardized regression coefficients with corresponding *t*-ratios.

Table 30.
Regression of attitudes about CP as a philosophy on belief about how MCPD should organize CP in the future. †

Variable	***b***	***t*-ratio**
CPATT	.603	5.244***
CPO experience	-.288	-.981
rank	.414	1.736*
gender	-.061	-.199

† F= 14.326, $p \leq .001$, $R^2 = .386$; *$p < .10$, ***$p < .01$

The respondents' belief about how community policing should be organized in the future was strongly predicted by their attitudes about community policing as a philosophy. One control variable, rank, was also found to be significant at the $p = .10$ level; the other control variables did not exhibit significant effects. Respondents were more likely to believe that MCPD should continue to organize community policing as it had been doing if they were a supervisor (sergeant or lieutenant) or expressed a positive attitude about community policing as a philosophy.

Based upon the results of this analysis, the null hypothesis is rejected at the $p<.001$ level. A respondent's attitude about community policing as a philosophy has a significant effect on their belief about how the Motor City Police Department should organize community policing in the future.

Ho_{10}: Evaluations of community policing as instituted in the Motor City Police Department do not have a significant effect on the belief of how MCPD should organize community policing in the future.

Calculating the bivariate correlation for these two items (CPINMCPD and how to organize community policing in the future) allows for a simple exploration of their relationship. The bivariate correlation indicates that the two items are not significantly related ($p=.375$). A respondent's evaluation of community policing as instituted in the Motor City Police Department was independent of their belief about how MCPD should organize community policing in the future.

OLS regression was used to reconfirm that evaluations of community policing as instituted in MCPD did not affect beliefs about how MCPD should organize community policing in the future. Based upon the outcome of the first three hypotheses and prior research studies, three independent variables were controlled for in the final regression model (CPO experience, rank, and gender). Initial regression models also included other measures of individual socialization (years of service, level of education, and race/ethnicity). These variables were not found to be significant predictors of beliefs about how community policing should be organized in the future by the Department. They were eliminated from the final analysis to ensure that the model was parsimonious.

The final regression model was run with belief about how the Motor City Police Department should organize community policing in the future as the dependent variable. The factor reflecting the respondents' evaluation of community policing as instituted in MCPD (CPINMCPD) was the independent variable; the control variables were CPO experience, rank, and gender. A respondent's evaluation of community policing as instituted in MCPD did not affect their belief about how MCPD should organize community policing in the future. The analytical model was found to be significant with a low predictive value; however, CPINMCPD did not have a significant effect on the respondents' belief about how community policing should be organized in the future. Table 31 provides the individual effects of the independent and control variables. Table entries are unstandardized regression coefficients with corresponding *t*-ratios.

Table 31.
Regression of evaluation of CP as instituted in MCPD on belief about how CP should be organized in the future. †

Variable	***b***	***t*-ratio**
CPINMCPD	.043	.379
CPO experience	-1.006	-3.398***
rank	.727	2.800***
gender	-.456	-1.296

† F= 5.282, $p \leq .001$, $R^2 = .188$; ***$p < .01$

Belief about how community policing should be organized in the future was predicted by experience as a community policing officer and rank. There was not a significant relationship between this dependent variable and evaluation of community policing as instituted in MCPD (CPINMCPD) or gender. Respondents tended to believe that the Motor City Police Department should continue its current strategy for organizing community policing (making both specialists and general patrol officers responsible for this activity) if they had experience working as a CPO or if they were a supervisor (sergeant or lieutenant).

Based upon the results of this analysis, the author fails to reject the null hypothesis at the $p<.05$ level. Although the overall analytical model was significant, evaluation of community policing as instituted in Motor City does not affect beliefs about how the Motor City Police Department should organize community policing in the future.

SUMMARY

The results of the review of the literature and these initial study findings facilitated the development of ten hypotheses which were tested using the results of the officer survey. These hypotheses were produced to provide a better understanding of how the elements of the conceptual framework intersected in Motor City. The hypotheses were designed to assess how measures of individual socialization, organizational culture, and organizational planning intersected in determining respondent attitudes toward three issues. Specifically, the issues being targeted were beliefs about how community policing should be organized in the future, evaluation of community policing as implemented in MCPD, and attitudes respondents held about community policing as a philosophy.

The following observations and conclusions are based upon the results of the hypotheses testing. The respondents' attitudes about community policing as a philosophy were affected by experience as a CPO, gender, and rank (and, to a lesser extent, years of service). Females, supervisors, and those with CPO experience held more positive attitudes (as did newer officers). In addition, respondents who perceived of the organizational culture as "healthy" also had more positive attitudes about community policing as a philosophy. Other measures of individual socialization were not found to have an impact on attitudes about community policing as a philosophy.

Measures of individual socialization had an effect on beliefs about how community policing should be organized in the future. Experience as a CPO and rank were significant predictors, while gender and years of service exhibited smaller effects. When other factors were controlled for in regression models, the impact of these individual socialization elements was less pronounced. When controlling for perceptions of organizational culture or evaluation of community policing as instituted in MCPD, only CPO experience and rank were found to be significant. When controlling for attitudes about community policing, only rank was found to be significant (at a questionably low level). Taken as a whole, these results suggest that beliefs about how community policing should be organized in the future were most closely related with attitudes about community policing as a philosophy.

Finally, measures of individual socialization were not found to be related with the evaluation of community policing in the Motor City Police Department. Respondents' evaluation was related with their attitudes about community policing and their perceptions of organizational culture. As expected, this evaluation was correlated with attitudes about community policing as a philosophy. Surprisingly, this evaluation was highly correlated with perceptions of organizational culture; respondents' who saw the culture as "healthy" were more satisfied with how community policing was instituted in MCPD. This might suggest that officers who were content with their work environment and their relationship with top leaders were less critical of change.

Taken as a whole, supervisors, females, and officers with CPO experience held more positive attitudes about community policing as a philosophy. Evaluations of community policing as instituted in MCPD were independent of individual socialization; instead, they were affected by general attitudes about community policing and, more profoundly, by perceptions of organizational culture. Officers who perceived of the organizational culture as "healthy" were more supportive of community policing, both specifically (in MCPD) and generally (as a philosophy). Beliefs about how MCPD should organize community policing in the future were affected by perceptions of organizational culture, evaluations of community policing as implemented in MCPD, and attitudes about community policing as a philosophy. Officers who supported the idea of community policing, supported how it had been implemented, and perceived of MCPD's organizational culture as "healthy" believed that the Department should continue to organization community policing using the team-based system.

In conclusion, it should be noted that the problems experienced in the Motor City Police Department should not be viewed as an indication that it was/is a "bad" Department. As the literature review suggests, the process of bringing about organizational change is challenging and complex. The difficulties and barriers encountered in Motor City are extremely common in a variety of organizational settings. Unfortunately, the Department did not learn from prior failures by incorporating their lessons into the reorganization efforts.

CHAPTER 10

Implications of the Research Findings

The literature review was used to develop a three-prong conceptual framework through which the "big picture" of organizational change in police agencies might be examined. These analyses have considered data from a planned change in a police organization (specifically, from a specialized to a generalized form of community policing) in the context of this framework. Qualitative and quantitative data have been employed to develop a more thorough understanding of the complex nature of resistance to organizational change. The variables and findings reported in this analysis were selected to address both the hypotheses being tested and other areas of interest that either supported these hypotheses or were not suitable for statistical testing.

Police planners and administrators have historically focused their energies on structural issues in initiating organizational change. Those considerations which are more social in nature (such as employee motivation and morale) have frequently been overlooked in the change process. Studies examining community policing have tended to focus on the outcome of community policing efforts, rather than the process of implementing such programs. In addition, community policing has typically been a program, rather than a philosophy in American police agencies. As such, little is known about how officers experience efforts to introduce generalized community policing in their work environment. If community policing is going to continue to revolutionize and redefine American policing, it will be critical to develop an understanding of how front-line employees experience its implementation.

This text has attempted to overcome these various limitations experienced by both practitioners and members of the academy. It has tried to examine the process of implementing community policing in a broader context. It has focused on an agency which was seeking to make the transition from community policing as a *program* to community policing as a *philosophy*. Because few studies have incorporated these elements together, the efforts of the author are, in a sense, largely exploratory. This study has considered an emerging problem (the transition to generalized community policing) in a broader context. As such, the study holds important implications for both scholars and practitioners. The final chapter of this text will provide conclusions, policy implications, and recommendations for future research in light of the results of this study.

This final chapter will consider the implications of the overall research findings in light of the conceptual framework put forth in the literature review. These implications can be derived from two primary sources: (1) based upon the analyses presented in the previous chapter; and (2) based upon the experiences of the SCJ research team and the author. The implications of the research findings may be divided into three categories. First, the study illuminates implications for general organizational change in police agencies. Second, the research findings are of importance for the implementation of generalized community policing. Third, the experiences of the SCJ research team and this author hold implications for future research in the area of community policing and planned change in police agencies. Each category is considered separately in this chapter.

IMPLICATIONS FOR ORGANIZATIONAL CHANGE IN POLICE AGENCIES

Care must be exercised in generalizing this study's findings. The data under consideration only represent the experiences of a single police agency. Issues which were important in the Motor City Police Department may not be important in other agencies; analogously, matters which were not important in MCPD may be important elsewhere. There are, however, a number of consistencies between these research findings and the results of other studies presented in the literature review. These consistencies would suggest that it might be possible to generalize these findings to other police agencies (particularly those agencies of similar size and composition, serving similar communities).

Based upon the issues which emerged in the literature review and the results of this study, it is possible to offer some tentative elements of a general model for organizational change in police agencies. The following model is far from exhaustive, but should serve as a starting point for future planning and research efforts. The nine elements it includes delineate issues which police organizations must incorporate into their plans for organizational change. The applicability of individual elements will vary between agencies; however, on the whole, they would seem to be germane in discussing organizational change.

First, planners and administrators need to take employee attitudes and perceptions into account in the process of planning and implementing organizational change. It is not enough to focus on structural issues. While organizations may be able to "force" change on employees (through strict accountability, evaluations, policies, procedures, etc.), there may be other alternatives to ensuring success. By taking the social needs of employees into account, employers may be able to ensure that employees embrace organizational change, thus enhancing the likelihood of achieving success. Working with employees so they understand why change is being initiated and giving employees time to voice their questions and concerns helps organizations garner support from those most directly affected by change, thus mollifying one source of resistance.

Second, prior research has shown (and this research supports) that employers tend to ignore the psychological contracts held by their employees. It is important for employers to note that many elements of the psychological contract are non-monetary in nature. In other words, it will not cost an employer anything (other than time and effort) to fulfill these expectations of their employees. While individual elements will certainly vary between employees, general elements may be noted. Employers need to legitimately listen to employee needs and concerns; they need to respect an employee's need for clarity, respect, involvement, and understanding. In this study, the Department's lack of clarity not only presented structural challenges, but it was also viewed by some as a violation of their psychological contract. The Department's failure to clarify expectations, demands, and processes was viewed as a sign that the agency did not respect the needs of its employees. In seeking to bring about change, employers must be conscious of how such changes intersect with the elements of their employees' psychological contracts.

Third, the preceding discussion of the psychological contract is closely related to organizational culture. As this analysis revealed, employee perceptions of organizational culture are closely related with their views on organizational change (in the context of community policing). The exact reason is not indicated through this analysis. It might be supposed that employees who feel that they have a good relationship with their supervisors and are respected by their employer may be more open to new approaches to doing their job. Employees who are less satisfied with their employer may resist change simply because it is initiated by their employer. Thus, agencies with a "healthy" organizational culture may have fewer barriers to overcome in seeking to bring about change.

Fourth, as evident in earlier experiments with team policing, change alters traditional reward systems in organizations. Such rewards may include informal benefits granted to officers exhibiting desirable conduct and formal patterns of promotions and specialized assignments. Although this did not appear to make a significant difference in the outcome of this study, there was evidence that this issue was of concern to some officers. The transition to the team-based system modified the role and function of the patrol lieutenant, making this position less desirable. In a more general sense, many officers reported that they no longer knew "what mattered" to the organization. Many transitions in police organizations require agencies to rethink how they will reward desirable behavior by their employees. While organizations must allow time for employees to adjust to new reward and incentive patterns, they must also recognize that such changes can be a powerful tool in resocializing employees to adopt new patterns of behavior.

Fifth, as a product of their excitement to initiate a transition in their organization, planners and managers sometimes rush into and/or do not allow enough time to implement change. The more dramatic the impact of a new program, structure, or philosophy, the longer it will take for successful change to be realized. Change often challenges the *status quo* within an organization. Given this fact it takes time to reorient employees and to modify organizational structure. By giving sufficient forethought to change, implementation and transition, and their impact on an organization, it may be possible to avoid errors, contradictions, resistance, tension, and mistakes.

Sixth, organizations should not expect overnight results in the process of implementing change. Mangers need to have realistic expectations of what change will achieve. Modification of individual socialization and organizational culture may take a great deal of time. The more dramatic the change, the longer this process may take. As some have suggested, the introduction of a new paradigm may take generations to become firmly entrenched. Police managers need to be realistic in what they hope to achieve in the short-term through change. By not setting standards which are too high and by continuing to stay on track in pursuing change, police departments may bring change to fruition with time. If standards are unrealistic and/or change is expected overnight, potentially successful and beneficial efforts may be abandoned with too much haste. Success often takes time.

Seventh, police organizations need to do a better job involving key actors in the resocialization process. By involving those employees who set a tone within an organization and who are formal or informal leaders, other employees may support a new idea, program, or philosophy. If employers take the time to identify key actors and help these employees understand why change is necessary, broader support may be realized within the organization. Too often, employers do not take the time to explain the rationale for change to their employees. Armed with such an understanding, employees may be more likely to support change. By targeting employees who have the respect of their peers, employers may create general support for their efforts with the least amount of effort. In addition, employees may view support for change as having originated among their peers, rather than be forced upon them from the top levels of an organizational hierarchy.

Eighth, in attempting to modify officer behavior, actions and attitudes, employers need to consider how they can incorporate methods which both "push" and "pull" employees. Techniques for "pushing" employees to change their behavior might include structural controls on behavior and actions (i.e., modified evaluation techniques, articulated accountability patterns, new policies and procedures). Methods of "pulling" employees to change their attitudes are focused on altering perceptions and beliefs. In other words, how can an employer make their employee see the value in change so that the employee wants to support that change (winning over the employee's "heart")? It is possible greater success may be realized in implementing change by incorporating both these "pushes" and "pulls" on employees. Not only will employees experience an external push to modify their behavior, but they will also have an internal pull which might further motivate them to do so.

Ninth, in addition to having a realistic idea of what may be achieved through the change process, planners and administrators must provide sufficient clarity, training and resources. Change efforts are likely to be predestined to fail if affected employees lack a clear understanding of the outcomes they are to achieve, the knowledge and skills they need to realize these outcomes, and the resources to reach objectives. Even where all other issues in this text have been resolved, in the absence of clarity, training and resources, fully successful change is unlikely, regardless of employee efforts. When affected employees do not understand the "what" and "how" of change, and do not have the means to operate under a new system or structure, success is highly improbable.

Finally, it must be remembered that change is a process. Not only does it require time and planning, but it also requires assessment and refinement. Regardless of the extent of pre-implementation planning, there are usually a number of "loose ends" which must be resolved after the change process has begun. Once managers have initiated change they typically need to respond to the unanticipated consequences which have emerged. In addition, change must be initiated with clear outcomes in mind. Organizations need to assess their success on such outcome measures and determine if and how they should retool their efforts to maximize the realization of their objectives. The Motor City evaluation project was intended to assist the Department in identifying and responding to the unanticipated consequences which emerged from their efforts at structural and philosophical change. It was initiated based upon the recognition that their efforts were part of a process, not a single event, which required additional consideration and adjustment.

IMPLICATIONS FOR THE IMPLEMENTATION OF GENERALIZED COMMUNITY POLICING

The previous section outlined several key issues which need to be considered in implementing change in police organizations. Building upon these foundation issues, this text suggests implications specifically for police agencies seeking to implement generalized community policing. Community policing was conceptualized as a philosophy which should influence how every officer in a police department performs his/her duties on a daily basis. Rather than pursuing this generalized form of community policing, many American police departments have used community policing as a program carried out by specific employees within their organization. If generalized community policing is going to be realized in a law enforcement agency, the following issues (among others) will need to be considered and addressed.

First, mid-level supervisors may be important lynchpins in implementing generalized community policing. By bringing sergeants and lieutenants "on board" with the philosophy of community policing, departments may be able to overcome much of the resistance offered by line employees. In many police agencies, these mid-level supervisors are the only command officers with whom line officers have routine contact; they represent the administration to the majority of the department. If these supervisors exhibit pro-community policing behavior and set a standard of proactive problem solving for the officers whom they supervise, success may be realized more readily. Mid-level supervisors are in a position to not only enforce new policies and procedures, but also to lead by example. As such, they have a unique capacity to facilitate change in their agency.

Second, a central lesson from the Motor City experience is organizations need to take the time to explain change to their employees. Officers need to understand why an agency is adopting a community policing philosophy, why changes in structure are necessary, how employees should operate under the new structure, and what the organization expects to achieve through its approach to community policing. Officers have no reason to alter their behavior if they do not understand why a change is being initiated. Officers who have not been told how to operate under a generalized community policing paradigm are likely to resort to traditional policing tactics in carrying out their duties. If organizational expectations are not explicit, officers will not know what ends they are supposed to pursue. If success is not defined prior to implementing a change, the department will not know how to assess its progress and make structural and programmatic adjustments. If sufficient explanation is not provided on these and other issues, employees will have a difficult time operating under a generalized community policing structure (even if they want to do so).

Third, prior to implementing generalized community policing, agencies need to ensure that they have sufficient resources. Community policing can be a resource-intensive endeavor. To be done well, it may tax a department's personnel and financial resources. Although community policing may reduce an organization's workload in the long run, in the short term it involves a high number of personnel hours. Beyond these financial and personnel resources, agencies also might question if they have sufficient support resources to aid community policing activities. Examples of such support resources might include crime analysis, employee training, active community residents, and support from other governmental and social service agencies. These financial, personnel, and support resources provide officers with the time, facilities and tools to engage in successful community policing and problem solving efforts.

Fourth, prior to implementing generalized community policing agencies need to consider their future structure and how to best bring about a successful organizational change. Planned change should only occur after sufficient contemplating and consideration; whenever possible, the implementation process should not be rushed. If change is forced, resistance is more likely. If change is slow and incremental, employees have the opportunity to learn new techniques and skills over time while slowly acclimating to a new organizational philosophy. Agencies might consider what types of employees will succeed under their new philosophy. If these types of employees are not abundant within the organization, this might modify how the agency chooses to go about recruiting, selecting, and training employees in the future.

Fifth, community policing requires that officers adopt new patterns of behavior. The traditional "scripts" and "routines" police officers have used in performing their job-related tasks may not support the goals and objectives of community policing. Officers need sufficient training so that they can learn alternative ways to perform their duties. In the absence of such training, officers must turn to peer socialization. While peer socialization is not inherently bad, it may be inconsistent across an organization. MCPD officers indicated that in the absence of uniform and consistent training they learned how to do problem solving from their peers. This informal training is not inherently flawed, yet its quality and consistency are uncertain. Based on this and other studies, it does not appear that community policing is something which police officers can effectively teach to themselves. Agencies wishing to pursue generalized community policing must ensure they provide their employees with sufficient training in the theory and practice of community policing. Such training not only ensures that employees are operating in an informed and consistent manner, but may help resolve issues of clarity and misunderstanding which might further hamper implementation efforts.

Sixth, community policing requires that agencies rethink their accountability patterns, evaluation mechanisms, and reward structures. This is required both to ensure that organizational structure is consistent with organizational demands and to provide another means by which agencies may "push" officers to exhibit certain behaviors in the performance of their duties. Community policing alters officer accountability and modifies the criteria upon which employee performance is assessed. By rewarding and recognizing officers who exhibit pro-community policing behavior, employers may be able to encourage other employees to exhibit similar actions. These issues must be modified so that they are consistent with the needs of a police organization operating under a generalized community policing paradigm. Their modification may also serve to help agencies encourage officers to embrace a community policing approach in the performance of their duties.

Seventh, despite the critical tone of this text, the Motor City Police Department did experience some gratifying successes through its team-based approach to community policing. Quality of life concerns were addressed in many neighborhoods. Community groups and neighborhood associations were empowered to take control of their social environment. Bridges were built between the Department and the community. Unfortunately, these successes (which could have become models for the "best practices" in resolving certain concerns) rarely received sufficient attention from the Department. If the Department had worked harder to record successful problem solving efforts, these efforts might have served as a starting point for other teams confronting similar challenges. By creating and disseminating a catalog of resources and strategies agencies can increase the efficiency of subsequent problem solving efforts. Taking the time to recognize successful problem solving initiatives compounds the overall success of community policing by setting an example of appropriate techniques and by recognizing desired behavior among employees (thus improving morale).

Finally, for nearly a decade, MCPD had been struggling to improve the services it provides to the community. Despite their extensive efforts the Department found that other governmental and social service providers were not always interested in collaborating to improve the quality of life in the community. Other government agencies were typically ill prepared to act as partners in proactive problem solving efforts. Broader problem solving success might have been realized if the employees of these other agencies had been willing and able to assist in problem solving endeavors. Agencies seeking to institute generalize community policing must consider the fundamental question of whether the police are properly trained and equipped to spearhead community transformation. If such efforts are appropriate, are other government and social service agencies prepared to assist in such endeavors?

IMPLICATIONS FOR FUTURE STUDIES OF ORGANIZATIONAL CHANGE IN POLICE AGENCIES

The experience of studying the implementation of generalized community policing in Motor City illuminated several implications for similar efforts. Paying attention to the methodological issues described in chapter six may enhance the success and efficacy of future research endeavors. Although this study has attempted to understand how a broad set of issues intersects in the process of changing police organizations, there are limitations to its findings. Further research will be needed to better understand this phenomenon and to devise strategies to deal with the challenges of effective organizational change.

First, the data available in the present study was not a perfect fit with the conceptual framework developed through the literature review. One of the greatest limitations was the lack of a full range of measures which might reflect individual socialization. Future research may devise mechanisms to better assess the role individual socialization plays in the process of organizational change. Such efforts present practical challenges to a researcher as it may be pragmatically difficult to separate socialization on individual and organizational levels in studying police officers. Despite this challenge, future research might consider how elements of individual socialization might be assessed in a more comprehensive manner.

Second, future research efforts using this conceptual framework might consider how individual socialization and organizational culture can be analytically separated to allow better understanding of their relative impact. Simply assessing an employee's expressed attitudes, beliefs, and values is not sufficient to understand how these expressions have been molded through various socialization processes. Ideally, a researcher could assess attitudes, beliefs and values before an employee began a new job and make comparisons after some duration of service. Such an assessment would provide the most complete picture of individual socialization experiences. Pragmatically, such methodologies would rarely be possible in this type of organizational research. As an alternative, future studies could attempt to structure questions in such a way that a respondent's individual socialization could be separated from the impact of organizational socialization and culture on their attitudes, beliefs and values.

Third, this study's method of operationalizing organizational culture allows one way to assess the impact of this factor on the process of change. Future studies might seek to compare multiple agencies attempting analogous change. This would allow for another way of assessing the role of organizational culture. The advantage of using a single agency to study organizational culture, however, is that it limits reliability concerns which may arise in a multi-agency study. Using data from different agencies does create methodological concerns; each agency will have a different "starting point" for their culture, organizational climate, efforts to bring about change, etc. By using only one agency there is not a question of whether the way in which agencies move through the change process may complicate this conceptual model.

Fourth, future research needs to give more consideration to the way generalized community policing is experienced by those charged with carrying it out. Studies might assess how this alternative philosophy affects how police officers experience their jobs. Do the officers engaged in generalized community policing experience the same benefits reported by specialized community policing officers in prior research? What new challenges and stresses might this paradigm create for officers operating under this approach? How can agencies which are pursuing generalized community policing better meet the various needs of their employees? These and other issues will need to be addressed if generalized community policing is going to take hold in American law enforcement agencies.

Fifth, a key implication of the SCJ research project was the need for researchers and police organizations to engage in long-term projects to better understand the "big picture" of organizational change. Outside evaluators cannot enter an organization, make a quick assessment of select factors, and produce an accurate report about the "state of affairs" in that organization. Although there was a time when this latter approach was the norm, it is becoming evident that if academics are going to understand organizations and the process of change, research involvements need to be longer in duration. An enduring presence allows researchers to better understand the nature and scope of problems, demonstrates commitment to employees, and provides a more thorough and accurate understanding of the issues under consideration.

Finally, in seeking to understand the "big picture" of organizational change, future research should attempt to assess changes in attitudes, beliefs and values over time. This text utilized longitudinal interviews and focus groups, but the available quantitative data were gathered as a snapshot in time. Administering a variation of the officer survey several times during the course of implementing change might provide researchers with a more thorough understanding of trends and shifts in employee attitudes during the course of this process. Armed with a more thorough understanding of the implementation of organizational change, managers might be able to mollify resistance from their employees.

CONCLUSION

Based upon the data presented in this text, the reader should not view the Motor City Police Department pejoratively. While the Department and its leaders made mistakes, their behavior was typical of managers planning for change. The agency's most serious shortcoming was its failure to learn from the lessons of the past. It is possible that the Department's efforts to implement generalized community policing might have been more successful if top leaders had given more attention to the issues illuminated by this research

Although the data used in this text were derived from a specific agency attempting a specific change, the findings have broader implications. Departments which are analogous to the Motor City Police Department (i.e., size of agency, size and nature of jurisdiction, resources, etc.) may have similar experiences in the process of attempting to introduce planned organizational change. In addition, these challenges may create barriers in attempts to initiate other forms of change in police organizations. Above all else, police planners and administrators need to understand the myriad of structural and humanistic issues which must be addressed in the process of bringing about change. Failure to give due consideration to these issues may result in the failure of future efforts.

Future research endeavors which take the preceding factors into consideration will greatly contribute to the understanding of planned change in police organizations. Realistically, it is difficult to study change in depth while accounting for diverse elements such as individual socialization, organizational culture, and organizational planning. It may often be difficult to do so in the course of conducting research in dynamic and changing organizational environments. If, however, the issues addressed in this research are of genuine importance then this is a challenge which researchers must bear in the future.

Some might label community policing as a concept which is a "simple theory" but a "harsh reality." Although the ideas associated with the philosophy would seem to be laudable goals for police organizations to pursue, realizing these ideas can be very difficult, as this text has demonstrated. For a variety of reasons, police officers tend to resist efforts to implement community policing within their agencies. Where implementation has been attempted, true success if often illusive. If the promise of generalized community policing is ever to come to fruition in American policing, the issues, challenges and barriers identified in this text must first be understood, confronted and overcome.

APPENDIX A

Methodology for Systematic Social Observation Data

Three instruments were used in the original evaluation study: the officer survey, systematic social observation tools, and a community survey. The methodology section of this text provided a detailed description of the processes used to obtain data in the officer survey. This appendix provides a brief discussion of the methodologies used to develop the systematic social observation data. The community survey is not used in the instant study. While not providing the same depth found in the methodology section, this discussion should orient the reader with the means by which these data were derived.

Student observers were used to conduct a series of field observations of MCPD road officers during the course of their normal shifts. The central purpose of these observations was to obtain data about where officers were spending the bulk of their time (in their team area or in other team areas). Officers were not informed of this purpose because the issue of where officers spent their time was of significant concern in determining if the team area system was successful. A consistent complaint heard from officers was that they could not support the problem solving needs in their team area because they were continually being dispatched to handle calls for service in other portions of the City. Also of interest was general information on what officers did during the course of their shifts and how they interacted with the public.

Student observers were used to conduct systematic social observations of Motor City police officers. These observers were being trained for another project being operated, in part, by SCJ (the Project on

Policing Neighborhoods, sponsored by the National Institute of Justice). They used the customized data program and instruments developed for this other project to "code" their field observations in Motor City. Based on decades of collective experience in conducting systematic social observations of police officers in the field, researchers from the four institutes operating POPN[1] had developed a standardized instrument. This instrument had successfully been used by project observers for over a year; no significant instrument modifications were required. This instrument was designed to provide both quantitative and qualitative data about where police officers spend their time, the types of activities in which they engage, with whom they interact, and how they interact with citizens.

The population for this portion of the study was Motor City (MI) police officers assigned to the patrol division. Due to logistical problems, it was not possible to establish a systematic sampling protocol. Ideally, students would have been assigned to a random date, shift, and officer to provide truly randomized sampling. Observations were being done during the academic year, making it impossible to randomize the date and shifts during which students made their observations. In addition, the Department was not willing to allow students to be assigned to random officers. Instead, they felt it would be better if students were assigned to officers who shift sergeants felt would be open to having a student observer. These officers were not selected because of the area they worked, their operational style, or their views or attitudes. Officers were selected because they would cooperate with these neophyte observers who were not necessarily ready to deal with difficult officers.

At the beginning of each ride along student observers provided their assigned officer with a cover letter from the SCJ POPN director. This letter briefly explained the purpose of the student's presence and assured the officer that confidentiality would be maintained under all circumstances. During the course of the ride along, the student observer took short-handed field notes about where the officer went, what the

---

[1] Dr. Albert Reiss at Yale University, Dr. Roger Parks at Indiana University, Dr. Robert Warden at the State University of New York– Albany, and Dr. Stephen Mastrofski at Michigan State University (now with George Mason University).

officer did, with whom the officer interacted, and how the officer carried out their duties. Students went with their assigned officer on the vast majority of that officer's activities, ceasing observations when officers were handling an activity which posed an imminent threat to the observer's safety. After the ride along was over, the observers used these field notes to write a detailed narrative report describing what was observed.

This narrative report was then used to complete a computerized data entry program. This customized program had been written for the POPN project to guide observers through a series of questions for each activity, encounter, and citizen interaction observed during the ride along period. The program prompted students to provide specific information to ensure that the data were consistent and reliable. The observer answered a series of questions which captured a vast amount of information about how officers spend their time, do their job, and interact with the public. Once completed, reviewed, and corrected, these narrative reports and data files provided useful insights into the job of being a Motor City police officer.

APPENDIX B

Officer Survey Cover Letter[1]

Who is conducting the survey?

The survey is being conducted by Michigan State University's School of Criminal Justice for the Motor City Police Department. The study is funded by the National Institute of Justice, the research agency of the United States Department of Justice. It is being directed by Professor Timothy Bynum. The survey questions were developed with the assistance of a panel of police officers and sergeants of the Motor City Police Department.

Survey's Purpose

This study is intended to obtain a comprehensive picture of the views and experiences of Motor City Police Department's patrol officers and their supervisors. It asks a wide variety of questions about police work, the Motor City Police Department, and the community it serves.

Who is being surveyed?

The survey is intended for all police officers, sergeants, and lieutenants working in the patrol division, both the North and South Precincts.

Survey Procedure

Your participation is completely voluntary. You may decline to participate entirely. If you do participate, you may still decline to answer

---

1 This letter accompanied each officer survey packet.

any questions on the survey. Please keep this sheet for your information. Once you have completed the survey, place it in the unmarked envelope provided and seal the envelope. Return the envelope to the person who distributed it. He or she will deliver all of the surveys unopened to Lieutenant X. Lieutenant X will deliver the unopened surveys to the Michigan State University research team. If you do not wish to participate, please place the blank survey form in the envelope, seal it, and return it to the person who distributed it.

Confidentiality of survey responses is guaranteed.

All survey responses are anonymous and will be kept in confidence. Do not write your name or any other identification number on the survey. The results of the survey will be presented in statistical groupings. No individual's responses will be singled out for reporting. The data will remain in the possession of the research team. Only the summary report will be given to the department.

Uses of the Survey

The survey will be delivered to the department to assist in assessing existing policies and practices and to develop or modify new ones. A short summary of the report will be prepared for all officers who participated.

Contact Persons

If you have any questions, call: Dr. Timothy Bynum (355-XXXX) or Dr. Stephen Mastrofski (353-XXXX).

APPENDIX C

Officer Survey Instrument

First we would like to learn your views on topics about police work generally. For each item, please check the box of the response that best indicates your opinion (agree strongly, agree somewhat, disagree somewhat, or disagree strongly) about the statement.

1. Enforcing the law is by far a patrol officer's most important responsibility.
2. Police officers have reason to be distrustful of most citizens.
3. A good patrol officer is one who patrols aggressively by stopping cars, checking out people, running license checks, etc.
4. Assisting citizens is just as important as enforcing the law.
5. A good patrol officer will try to find out what residents think the neighborhood problems are.
6. In order to do their jobs, patrol officers must sometimes overlook search and seizure laws and other legal guidelines.

Here are some different kinds of incidents or conditions citizens sometimes ask police to handle. We'd like to know how often (always, much of the time, sometimes, or never), in your view, patrol officers should be expected to do something about each of these situations. For each one, please check the box indicating how often patrol officers should be expected to do something about that situation.

7. Public nuisances
8. Neighbor disputes
9. Family disputes
10. Litter and trash

11. Parents who don't control their kids
12. Nuisance businesses that cause lots of problems for neighbors

13. How frequently (often, sometimes, rarely, or never) would you say there are good reasons not to make an arrest or issue an appearance summons to someone who has committed a minor criminal offense?

Here is a list of goals that police are sometimes expected to accomplish. Please look these over and mark with an "X" the TWO that you believe are the MOST important for patrol officers.

Then please mark with an "O" the TWO that you believe are the LEAST important for patrol officers.

14. _____ Handling the calls for their assigned area
15. _____ Making arrests and issuing citations
16. _____ Reducing the number of repeat calls to the same address
17. _____ Seizing drugs, guns, and other contraband
18. _____ Reducing the level of public disorders
19. _____ Getting the public involved in improving the neighborhood
20. _____ Reducing the public's fear of crime

For the questions in this section please think about the district or other geographic area in which you have worked the most in the last 6 months. If you were not assigned to a district or other geographic area during the last 6 months, please skip this section and go to Question 49.

21. What kind of geographic area (District, Team area, or Other [Please describe]) are you referring to?
22. Over the last 2 years, how many months (Less than 1 month, 1 - 2 months, 3 - 4 months, 5 - 6 months, 7 - 12 months, 13 - 18 months, or 19 - 24 months) have you routinely worked in this geographic area?

Here are some conditions that might be problems in some neighborhoods. For each one, please check whether YOU think that it has been a major problem, a minor problem, or not a problem in the geographic area you've routinely worked over the last 6 months.

23. Theft or burglary
24. Litter and trash
25. Vandalism of cars & property
26. Drug dealing
27. Gangs
28. Loitering
29. Abandoned buildings
30. Assaults in public
31. Domestic violence
32. Traffic violations

33. In this geographic area, what kind of reputation (a reputation for being hard-nosed, a reputation for being approachable, or don't know) is it better for a patrol officer to have?

For each of the following, please indicate how many citizens (most, some, few, or none) in this geographic area would fit the described action or situation.

34. Would call the police if they saw something suspicious?
35. Would provide information about a crime if they knew something and were asked about it by police?
36. Are afraid to cooperate with the police because of what other citizens might do to them?
37. Are willing to work with the police to try to solve neighborhood problems?
38. In most districts there are people who repeatedly cause trouble or make work for the police. How many of these people in your geographic area could you identify by name if you saw them on the street?

Here is a list of some ways to get information about public safety problems. For each one, please check the number that best indicates how frequently (often, rarely, sometimes, or never) you find out about problems in your geographic area.

39. From your supervisor
40. By talking with citizens who live and work there
41. By talking with other officers

42. By looking at statistics on crime and calls for service
43. By attending meetings of community groups

44. On a typical busy shift, what portion of your work shift (0 - 20%, 21 - 40%, 41 - 60%, 61 - 80%, or 81 - 100%) do you spend in your team area?
45. On a typical slow shift, what portion of your work shift d (0 - 20%, 21 - 40%, 41 - 60%, 61 - 80%, or 81 - 100%) o you spend in your team area?
46. How many members of your assigned team (all, most, some, a few, or none) do you know well enough to feel that you can depend upon them when working on team projects?
47. The supervisor for my team (always, usually, sometimes, rarely, or never) provides subordinates adequate guidance on problem-solving projects.
48. How often (daily, one or two times a week, one or two times a month, less than once a month, or never) does your supervisor communicate with you about team projects?

Here are some questions about your work unit--the officers who work in your precinct on your shift. For each item, please indicate the number that best indicates your opinion.

49. Compared to other police shifts, how would you rate the job (better than most others, about the same as most others, or not as good as most others) your shift does?

For each of the following, please check the box that shows how many officers on your shift (all or most, about half, a few, or none) best fit the description.

50. Would you consider to be your friend?
51. If you obtained some hard-to-get information about the identity of an offender causing a lot of trouble in your precinct, with how many officers on your shift would you share this information?
52. Would say that enforcing the law is by far a patrol officer's most important responsibility?
53. Would say that police officers have reason to be distrustful of most citizens?

54. Would say that assisting citizens is just as important as enforcing the law?
55. Would say that in order to do their jobs, they must sometimes overlook legal guidelines?

Here are some questions about the role of Community Policing Officers.

56. In your opinion, which of the following best describes the workload of Community Policing Officers (it is greater than it should be, it is at about the level it should be, it is lower than it should be, or don't know)?
57. Are you now or have you ever served as a Community Policing Officer (yes or no)?
58. How would you feel (very positive, somewhat positive, neutral, somewhat negative, or very negative) about receiving an assignment to work as a Community Policing Officer during the coming year?

59. Below is a list of things which are sometimes mentioned as <u>advantages</u> of working as a Community Policing Officer. Please place an "X" by any of these that you think apply to those who receive assignments as Community Policing Officers in Motor City. Check as many as apply.

    ___ Independence to do the job as you see fit
    ___ Good work schedule
    ___ Enough time to work on long-term projects
    ___ Opportunity to work closely with the public
    ___ Leeway to try new things to get the job done
    ___ Getting positive feedback from the public
    ___ High status of the job among other police
    ___ Diversity in the kinds of tasks and skills required
    ___ Opportunities for promotion and career advancement

60. Below is a list of things that are sometimes mentioned as <u>disadvantages</u> of working as a Community Policing Officer. Please place an "X" by any of these that you think apply to those who receive assignments as Community Policing Officers in Motor City. Check as many as apply.

___ Insufficient department direction about what you are expected to do
___ Poor work schedule
___ Not enough time to get the work done
___ Having to work closely with members of the public as "partners"
___ Inadequate training to do the job expected
___ Not enough leeway to do the things that are necessary to get the job done
___ Having to pay too much attention to keeping the public happy
___ Low status of the job among other police
___ Spending too much time on work that is not really police work
___ Poor prospects for promotion or career advancement

61. When a crime problem is displaced from one neighborhood to another inside Motor City, what impact (reduces over all crime and related problems for a time by disrupting the criminal activity, no effect on overall crime and related problems; it just moves the problem from one area to another, or makes it harder to monitor and track criminals for a while in the new neighborhood) do you believe that has on Motor City as a whole?
62. Where is the greatest need for coordination among police officers who are working on a problem-solving effort (among officers working different shifts, among officers working the same shift, or about the same for both)?
63. What would be the best way for the Motor City Police Department to organize community policing (designate specialists to do it, make it the responsibility of all patrol officers, make it the responsibility of both specialists and general patrol officers, or do not do community policing at all)?

Now we have some questions about your experiences with problem solving in the Motor City Police Department.

By "problem solving," we mean doing something to reduce the frequency or seriousness of an ongoing problem in a given area. That area may be an address, a street or block, a team area, or the entire precinct.

Please think about the last problem-solving effort you have completed. A completed effort is one on which you are no longer working, regardless of how successful it was. Do not select something that is currently under way. Answer each of the following questions with this effort in mind.

64. How long ago did you complete this effort (I have completed no problem-solving effort [GO TO Q-81], within the last week, within the last month, within the last two months, within the last four months, within the last 6 months, within the last 12 months, or longer than 12 months ago)?
65. How long a time period (a day, a week, 2-3 weeks, a month, 2-6 months, or longer than 6 months) did this effort last?
66. What was the problem that this effort was aimed at? Select the one that best describes the problem if more than one applies.
    1 Drugs
    2 Burglary and Breaking & Entering (residential)
    3 Burglary and Breaking & Entering (business)
    4 Larcenies
    5 Auto theft
    6 Loud parties
    7 Retail fraud
    8 Physical deterioration of neighborhood
    9 Traffic problems
    10 Disorderly people in public places
    11 Violent crime against strangers
    12 Domestic violence
    13 Other (Please describe):______________________________

67. In a typical work week, how many hours did you devote to working on this effort?
68. What percent of the time that you worked on this effort did you work closely with one or more other officers?
69. To the best of your knowledge, how many other officers made a significant contribution to this effort?
70. What was the scope (Single address or street corner, block, 2-4 blocks, a quarter to half of your assigned district or area, more than

half of your assigned district or area, or an area larger than your district or assigned area) of this effort?

71. How would you assess the success (very successful, somewhat successful, or not at all successful) of this effort?
72. On what basis (personal impressions, views of other officers, feedback from supervisor or manager, feedback from citizens, feedback from public officials outside the department, or data or study) do you form your view of the degree of effort success? Select the most important if more than one applies.
73. What would have made the effort more successful? Select the <u>one</u> that would have had the biggest effect.
    1 More police time or resources devoted to it.
    2 Better analysis of the problem before implementing solution
    3 Different tactic for solving the problem
    4 More citizen participation
    5 More participation from other government agencies
    6 Better coordination of police efforts
    7 Clearer definition of project goals and objectives
    8 None of the above. The project was as successful as possible

Please indicate how useful (not received, not helpful, somewhat helpful, or very helpful) each of the following has been to you in developing problem-solving skills.

74. Formal training in department
75. Formal training outside department
76. College course work
77. Field Training Officer
78. Supervisor
79. Informal training from other officers
80. Personal experience

Below are a few questions about Motor City Police Department's efforts to implement problem solving. For each item, please select the response that best reflects your view.

81. How well (excellent, good, fair, or poor) has MCPD done in clarifying the role of regular patrol officers in problem solving?

82. How well (excellent, good, fair, or poor) has MCPD done in distributing the workload fairly between problem solving specialists and officers who are responsible for taking calls?
83. How well (excellent, good, fair, or poor) has MCPD done in giving officers enough time for problem solving?
84. How well (excellent, good, fair, or poor) has MCPD done in providing the information officers need on the problems in their assigned areas?
85. How well (excellent, good, fair, or poor) has MCPD done in rewarding officers who do a good job with problem solving?

Following is a list of functions that supervisors are sometimes expected to perform. Please indicate how much effort (much, some, a little, or none) you believe sergeants in the Motor City Police Department should give each of these.

86. Being present at the scene when a subordinate is involved in a potentially dangerous or difficult situation.
87. Reviewing subordinates' written reports.
88. Dealing directly with citizens who are complaining about problems in their neighborhood.
89. Keeping superiors advised of what is going on during their shifts.
90. Dealing with personnel matters (paperwork, discipline, counseling).
91. Attending meetings with the public and giving talks to the public.
92. Coordinating and scheduling the work of team members.
93. Getting other public and private organizations to cooperate with the police to solve community problems.
94. Identifying projects for subordinates and monitoring their progress with those projects.
95. Evaluating the performance of individual officers and giving them feedback.

FOR POLICE OFFICERS: Think about the sergeant on this shift with whom you have the most contact. How good a job (very good, good, fair, poor, or very poor) do you think that sergeant is doing on each of the following things?

FOR SERGEANTS & LIEUTENANTS: Think about the <u>immediate supervisor</u> with whom you have the most contact. <u>How good a job</u> (very good, good, fair, poor, or very poor) do you think that supervisor is doing on each of the following things?

96. Being present at the scene when a subordinate is involved in a potentially dangerous or difficult situation.
97. Reviewing subordinates' written reports.
98. Dealing directly with citizens who are complaining about problems in their neighborhood.
99. Keeping superiors advised of what is going on in their shifts.
100. Dealing with personnel matters (paperwork, discipline, counseling).
101. Attending meetings with the public and giving talks to the public.
102. Coordinating and scheduling the work of team members.
103. Getting other public and private organizations to cooperate with the police to solve community problems.
104. Identifying projects for subordinates and monitoring their progress with those projects.
105. Evaluating the performance of individual officers and giving them feedback.

FOR POLICE OFFICERS: Now we would like you to think about your <u>team sergeant</u>. For each of the following statements, please check the box (agree strongly, agree somewhat, disagree somewhat, or disagree strongly) that best indicates your experience or opinion about your team sergeant.

FOR SERGEANTS & LIEUTENANTS: Now we would like you to think about the <u>immediate supervisor</u> with whom you have the most contact. For each of the following statements, please check the box (agree strongly, agree somewhat, disagree somewhat, or disagree strongly) that best indicates your experience or opinion about that immediate supervisor.

106. The decisions or judgments I make are seldom criticized or modified by my supervisor.
107. My supervisor lets officers know what is expected of them.

108. My supervisor's approach tends to discourage me from giving extra effort.
109. My supervisor has a lot of professional experience to help officers do their jobs.
110. My supervisor looks out for the personal welfare of his/her subordinates.
111. I have complete faith in my supervisor.

Please check the box that indicates for each of the following how often (always, much of the time, sometimes, or never) the statement is applicable to the supervisor you selected in the previous section.

112. When you try a new approach to doing your job and it doesn't work, how often does your supervisor treat it as an honest effort and not a disciplinary matter.
113. When your team has a problem that higher-ups could straighten out, how often is your supervisor able to get those higher-ups to actually do something about the problem?

Now we have a few questions about your <u>precinct's management</u>. First think about the priorities of the precinct's management here. Please look these over and mark with an "X" the TWO that you think Precinct MANAGEMENT would say are the MOST important for patrol officers.

Then please mark with an "O" the TWO that you think Precinct MANAGEMENT would say are the LEAST important for patrol officers.

114. _____ Handling the calls for their assigned area
115. _____ Making arrests and issuing citations
116. _____ Reducing the number of repeat calls to the same address
117. _____ Seizing drugs, guns, and other contraband
118. _____ Reducing the level of public disorders
119. _____ Getting the public involved in improving the neighborhood
120. _____ Reducing the public's fear of crime

For the following items, please indicate how likely (very likely,

somewhat likely, somewhat unlikely, or very unlikely) each is to occur.

121. When there is an alleged rule violation, how likely is it that an officer will be treated fairly?
122. When an officer contributes to a team effort rather than look good individually how likely is it that top management here will recognize it?

Below are statements about a variety of issues concerning the Motor City Police Department and the community of Motor City. For each one, please check the box that best indicates your opinion (agree strongly, agree somewhat, disagree somewhat, disagree strongly).

123. Community Policing Officers make an important contribution toward reducing crime and disorder in the neighborhoods where they are assigned.
124. Community Policing Officers make an important contribution toward improving the attitudes of neighborhood residents toward the police department.
125. The neighborhoods that complain the loudest are the ones mot likely to receive a Community Policing Officer.
126. There are not enough officers assigned to patrol functions to handle the demands from calls for service.
127. Top department leadership has unrealistically high expectations about how much the current organizational strategies will reduce crime and disorder in the neighborhoods.
128. It is rare for the activities and projects of my team to be well coordinated across shifts.
129. Sergeants working on another shift are unable to effectively supervise officers who work on this shift.
130. A precinct lieutenant is usually available when he/she is needed on this shift.
131. Precinct lieutenants do not have enough contact with the officers and sergeants on the street.
132. There are not enough citizens in my district who are willing to exercise the necessary initiative to make their neighborhood a nicer place to live.

133. Citizens in my district do not call upon the police nearly as much as they should to solve neighborhood problems.

134. Most of the time, neighborhood associations pretty accurately reflect the views of the majority of citizens on my district about what police priorities for the district should be.

135. Decentralization to the precincts has improved communication between patrol officers and detectives.

136. The department should put more resources into the general patrol function and less into specialist functions.

137. Rookie officers should have their assignments rotated through different districts around the city before receiving a permanent assignment.

138. Top department management has a good understanding of what the work of the rank-and-file police officer is like.

139. Rank-and-file officers do not have enough opportunity to participate in developing policies and planning strategies.

140. Rank and file officers are kept well-informed of management's policies and plans.

141. On the whole, the department's system of promotion to sergeant selects the best qualified people.

142. On the whole, the department's system of promotion to lieutenant selects the best qualified people.

143. Top leaders have made the department's priorities clear.

144. Commendations are given too easily for tasks and accomplishments that really do not contribute to improved police service.

145. Doing community policing means that officers will be unable to do more important tasks.

Finally, we have a few questions about your background. This information is for statistical purposes only. Individual responses will not be reported.

146. How many years (less than 1 year, 1 - 2 years, 3 - 5 years, 6 - 10 years, 11 - 15 years, or 16 years or more) have you worked as a sworn officer for the Motor City Police Department?

147. How many years (not applicable - have only worked in MCPD,

less than 1 year, 1 - 2 years, 3 - 5 years, 6 - 10 years, 11 - 15 years, or 16 years or more) have you worked elsewhere as a sworn law enforcement officer?

148. How important (very important, somewhat important, somewhat unimportant, or very unimportant) to you is getting promoted?

149. How important (very important, somewhat important, somewhat unimportant, or very unimportant) to you is moving from patrol to a specialized unit, such as special operations, Metro, or motorcycle?

150. What is the highest level of formal education you have completed?

1 high school or lower (include GED)
2 some college, but did not earn a bachelors (4-year) degree
3 bachelors (4-year) degree
4 some graduate or law courses but did not earn a degree
5 graduate or law degree (masters, doctorate, J.D., L.L.D.)

151. To what precinct (north or south) are you assigned?

152. What shift (0630 - 1630, 1100 - 2100, 1630 - 0230, 2100 - 0700, or other) are you currently working?

153. What is your rank (police officer or supervisor [sergeant/lieutenant])?

154. What is your race/ethnicity (White/Caucasian, Black/African-American, Hispanic/Latino, Asian-American/Pacific Islander, Native American, or other)?

155. What is your gender (male or female)?

Thank you very much for completing the survey. If you have any other comments to make, please do so in the space provided below and on the reverse side. Then place the questionnaire in the plain envelope, seal the envelope, and give it to your supervisor.

BIBLIOGRAPHY

Angell, J.E. (1971). Toward an alternative to the classic police organizational arrangements: A democratic model. *Criminology,* 9, 185-206.

Babbie, E.R. (1973). *Survey research methods.* Belmont, CA: Wadsworth.

Babbie, E.R. (1992). *Practicing social research* (6th ed.). Belmont, CA: Wadsworth.

Bachman, R., & Paternoster, R. (1997). *Statistical methods for criminology and criminal justice.* New York: McGraw-Hill.

Bahn, C. (1984). Police socialization in the eighties: Strains in the forging of an occupational identity. *Journal of Police Science and Administration,* 12, 390-394.

Barkdoll, G.L. (1998). Individual personality and organizational culture or "let's change this place so I feel more comfortable." *Public Administration and Management: An Interactive Journal,* 3(2) [Online] Available: http:www/hbg.psu.edu/Faculty/jxr11/barkdoll.html [1998, Aug. 15].

Barker, J.C. (1999). *Danger, duty, and disillusion: The worldview of Los Angeles police officers.* Prospect Heights, IL: Waveland.

Bartollas, C., Hahn, L.D. (1999). *Policing in America.* Boston: Allyn & Bacon.

Bies, R.J., & Tyler, T.R. (1993). The "litigation mentality" in organizations: A test of alternative psychological explanations. *Organizational Science,* 4, 352-366.

Bittner, E. (1970). *The function of police in modern society.* Washington, DC: National Institute of Health.

Bittner, E. (1990). *Aspects of police work.* Boston: Northeastern University Press.

Blau, P.M. (1963). *The dynamics of bureaucracy: A study of interpersonal relations in two government agencies.* Chicago: University of Chicago Press.

Buzawa, E.S. (1981). The role of race in predicting job attitudes of patrol officers. *Journal of Criminal Justice,* 9, 63-77.

Carey, M.A. (1994). The group effect in focus groups: Planning, implementing, and interpreting focus group research. In J.M. Morse (Ed.), *Critical issues in qualitative research methods* (pp. 225-241). Thousand Oaks, CA: Sage.

Carpenter, B.N., & Raza, S.M. (1987). Personality characteristics of police applicants: Comparisons across subgroups and with other populations. *Journal of Police Science and Administration,* 15, 10-17.

Carte, G.E., & Carte, E.H. (1975). *Police reform in the United States: The era of August Vollmer, 1905-1932.* Berkeley, CA: University of California Press.

Carter, D., Sapp, A.D., & Stephens, D.W. (1988). *The state of police education: Policy direction for the 21st century.* Washington, D.C.: Police Executive Research Forum.

Cordner, G.W. (1978). Open and closed models in police organizations: Traditions, dilemmas, and practical consideration. *Journal of Police Science and Administration,* 6, 22-34.

Crank, J.P. (1998). *Understanding police culture.* Cincinnati, OH: Anderson.

Dantzker, M.L. (1995). *Understanding today's police.* Englewood Cliffs, NJ: Prentice Hall.

Deal, T.E., & Kennedy, A.A. (1982). *Corporate cultures: The rites and rituals of corporate life.* Reading, MA: Addison-Wesley.

Dey, I. (1993). *Qualitative data analysis.* London: Routledge.

Eck, J.E. (1992, June). Helpful hints for the tradition-bound chief. *Fresh Perspectives,* 1-8.

Eck, J.E., & Spelman, W. (with Hill, D., Stephens, D.W., Stedman, J.R., & Murphy, G.R.) (1987). *Problem-solving: Problem-oriented policing in Newport News.* Washington, D.C.: Police Executive Research Forum.

Findley, K.W., & Taylor, R.W. (1990). Re-thinking neighborhood policing. *Journal of Contemporary Criminal Justice,* 6, 70-78.

Fletcher, C. (1995). *Breaking and entering: Women cops talk about life in the ultimate men's club*. New York: Harper Collins.

Fogelson, R. (1977). *Big-city police*. Cambridge, MA: Harvard University Press.

Franz, V., & Jones, D.M. (1987). Perceptions of organizational performance in suburban police departments: A critique of the military model. *Journal of Police Science and Administration,* 15, 153-161.

Gaines, L. (1993). Community-oriented policing: Management issues, concerns, and problems. *Journal of Contemporary Criminal Justice,* 10, 17-35.

Glaser, B.G. & Strauss, A.L. (1967). *The discovery of grounded theory: Strategies for qualitative research.* Chicago: Aldine.

Goffman, E. (1959). *The presentation of self in everyday life.* Garden City, NY: Doubleday Anchor.

Goldstein, H. (1990). *Problem-oriented policing.* New York: McGraw-Hill.

Goodman, P.S., Bazerman, M., & Conlon, E. (1980). Institutionalization of planned organizational change. In B.M. Straw and L.L. Cummings (Eds.), *Research in Organizational Behavior: Volume 2* (pp. 215-246). Greenwich, CT: JAI Press.

Greene, J.R. (1981). Organizational change in law enforcement. *Journal of Criminal Justice,* 9, 79-91.

Greene, J.R., Alpert, G.P., & Styles, P. (1992). Values and culture in two American police departments: Lessons from King Arthur. *Journal of Contemporary Criminal Justice,* 8, 183-207.

Greene, J.R., Bergman, W.T., & McLaughlin, E.J. (1994). Implementing community policing: Cultural and structural change in police organizations. In D.P. Rosenbaum (Ed.), *The challenge of community policing: Testing the promises* (pp. 92-109). Thousand Oaks, CA: Sage.

Greene, J.R. & Klockars, C. (1991). What police do. In C. Klockars and S. Mastrofski (Eds.), *Thinking About Police: Contemporary Readings* (pp. 273-284). New York: McGraw-Hill.

Greene, J.R., & Mastrofski, S.D. (Eds.). (1988). *Community policing: Rhetoric or reality?* New York: Praeger.

Guyot, D. (1991). *Policing as though people matter.* Philadelphia: Temple University Press.

Guzzo, R.A., Noonan, K.A., & Elron, E. (1994). Expatriate managers and the psychological contract. *Journal of Applied Psychology,* 79, 617-626.

Hagan, F.E. (1997). *Research methods in criminal justice and criminology* (4th ed.). Boston: Allyn and Bacon.

Hagan, F.E. (2000). *Research methods in criminal justice and criminology* (5th ed.). Boston: Allyn and Bacon.

Haney, C., & Manzolatti, J. (1981). Television criminology: Network illusions of criminal justice realities. In S. Soronson (Ed.), *Readings about the social animal* (pp. 125-136). San Francisco, CA: W.H. Freeman & Co.

Harrison, S.J. (1998). Police organizational culture: Using ingrained values to build positive organizational improvement. *Public Administration and Management: An Interactive Journal,* 3(2) [Online] Available: http:www/hbg.psu.edu/Faculty/jxr11/harrison.html [1998, Aug. 15].

Haught, L. (1997). *Organizational change in a sheriff's department: The implementation of community oriented policing.* Unpublished doctoral dissertation, Gonzaga University.

Hewitt, W.H., Sr. (1978). Current issues in police collective bargaining. In A.W. Cohn (Ed.), *The future of policing* (pp. 205-223). Beverly Hills, CA: Sage.

Hoover, L.T. (1992). Police mission: An era of debate. In L.T. Hoover (Ed.), *Police management: Issues and perspectives* (pp. 1-30). Washington, DC: Police Executive Research Forum.

Hudzik, J.K., & Cordner, G.W. (1983). *Planning in criminal justice organizations and systems.* New York: Macmillan Publishing.

Jermier, J.M., & Berkes, L.J. (1979). Leader behavior in a police command bureaucracy: A closer look at the quasi-military model. *Administrative Science Quarterly,* 24, 1-23.

Johns, E.A. (1973). *The sociology of organizational change.* Oxford, UK: Pergamon Press.

Kappeler, V.E., Sapp, A., & Carter, D. (1992). Police officer higher education, citizen complaints, and departmental rule violations. *American Journal of Police,* 11(2), 37-54.

Kappeler, V.E., Sluder, R.D., & Alpert, G.P. (1998). *Forces of deviance: Understanding the dark side of policing* (2nd ed.). Prospect Heights, IL: Waveland.

Katz, D., & Kahn, R.L. (1978). *The social psychology of organizations* (2nd ed.). New York: John Wiley & Sons.

Kelling, G.L., & Bratton, W.J. (1993). *Perspectives on policing (no. 17): Implementing community policing: The administrative problem* (NCJ 141236). Washington, DC: U.S. Department of Justice.

Kelling, G. & Moore, M. (1988). From political reform to community: The evolving strategy of police. In J. Greene & S. Mastrofski (Eds.), *Community policing: Rhetoric or reality?* (p. 3-25). New York: Praeger.

Kilmann, R.H., Saxton, M.J., Serpa, R., & Associates. (1985). *Gaining control of the corporate culture.* San Francisco: Jossey-Bass.

King, N. (1994). The qualitative research interview. In C. Cassell & G. Symon (Eds.), *Qualitative methods in organizational research* (pp. 14-36). London: Sage.

Klockars, C.B. (1985). *The idea of police.* Newbury Park, CA: Sage.

Klockars, C.B. (1991). The rhetoric of community policing. In C. Klockars and S. Mastrofski (Eds.) *Thinking about policing* (2nd ed.) (pp. 530-542). New York: McGraw-Hill.

Kobler, A. (1975). Police homicide in a democracy. *Journal of Social Issues,* 31(1), 163-184.

Kraska, P.B., & Kappeler, V.E. (1997). Militarizing American police: The rise and normalization of paramilitary units. *Social Problems,* 44, 101-117.

Kruger, R.A. (1994). *Focus groups: A practical guide for applied research* (2nd ed.). Thousand Oaks, CA: Sage.

Kuykendall, J., & Roberg, R.R. (1982). Mapping police organizational change. *Criminology,* 20, 241-256.

Kuykendall, J., & Usinger, P.C. (1982). The leadership styles of police managers. *Journal of Criminal Justice,* 10, 311-322.

Lipsky, M. (1980). *Street-level bureaucracy: Dilemmas of the individual in public services.* New York: Russell Sage Foundation.

Lurigio, A.J., & Rosenbaum, D.P. (1994). The impact of community policing on police personnel: A review of the literature. In D.P. Rosenbaum (Ed.), *The challenge of community policing: Testing the promises* (pp. 147-163). Thousand Oaks, CA: Sage Publications.

Lurigio, A.J., & Skogan, W.G. (1994). Winning the hearts and minds of police officers: An assessment of staff perceptions of community policing in Chicago. *Crime & Delinquency,*40, 315-330.

Manning, P.K. (1997a, July). *Authority, loyalty, and community policing: An organizational and dramaturgical analysis.* Paper presented at the conference on crime and social organization in honour of Albert J. Reiss, Jr., Rutgers University.

Manning, P.K. (1997b). *Police work: The social organization of policing* (2nd ed.). Prospect Heights, IL: Waveland Press.

Marsh, C. (1982). *The survey method: The contributions of surveys to sociological explanation.* London: George Allen & Unwin.

Mastrofski, S.D. (1993). Eyeing the doughnut: Community policing and progressive reform [review of the book *Beyond 911: A new era for policing*]. *American Journal of Police,* 12, 1-21.

Mastrofski, S.D., Schafer, J.A., DeJong, C., & Bynum, T.S. (1997). *Information from systematic observation of police (A report to the Motor City Police Department).* East Lansing, MI: School of Criminal Justice, Michigan State University.

Maxfield, M.G., & Babbie, E. (1998). *Research methods for criminal justice and criminology* (2nd edition). Belmont, CA: West/Wadsworth.

McNamara, J.H. (1967). Uncertainties in police work: The relevance of police recruits' backgrounds and training. In D.J. Bordua (Ed.), *The police: Six sociological essays* (pp. 163-252). New York: John Wiley and Sons.

Meagher, M.S., & Yentes, N.A. (1986). Choosing a career in policing: A comparison of male and female perceptions. *Journal of Police Science and Administration,* 14, 320-327.

Merton, R.K. (1936). The unanticipated consequences of purposive social action. *American Sociological Review,* 1, 894-904.

Miles, M., & Huberman, M. (1984). *Qualitative data analysis*. Thousand Oaks, CA: Sage.

Moore, M.H., & Stephens, D.W. (1991). *Beyond command and control: The strategic management of police departments*. Washington, D.C.: Police Executive Research Forum.

Moorhead, G., & Griffin, R.W. (1998). *Organizational behavior: Managing people and organizations* (5th ed.). Boston: Houghton Mifflin.

More, H.W. (1998). *Special topics in policing* (2nd ed.). Cincinnati, OH: Anderson.

Morgan, D.L. (1997). *Focus groups as qualitative research* (2nd ed.). Thousand Oaks, CA: Sage.

Moser, C.A., & Kalton, G. (1972). *Survey methods in social investigation* (2nd ed.). New York: Basic Books.

Neuman, W.L., & Wiegand, B. (2000). *Criminal justice research methods: Qualitative and quantitative approaches.* Boston: Allyn & Bacon.

Oettmeier, T.N., & Brown, L.P. (1988). Developing a neighborhood-oriented policing style. In J.R. Greene and S.D. Mastrofski (Eds.), *Community policing: Rhetoric or reality* (pp. 121-134). New York: Praeger.

Ogawa, R.T., & Malen, B. (1991). Towards rigor in review of multivocal literatures: Applying the exploratory case study method. *Review of Educational Research,* 61, 265-286.

Ott, J.S. (1989). *The organizational culture perspective.* Pacific Grove, CA: Brooks/Cole Publishing.

Ouchi, W.G. (1981). *Theory Z: How American business can meet the Japanese Challenge.* Reading, MA: Addison-Wesley.

Payne, D.M., & Trojanowicz, R. (1985). *Performance profiles of foot versus motor officers.* [Online] Available: http://www.cj.msu.edu/~people/cp/perform.html [1999, September 16].

Peters, T.J., & Waterman, R.H., Jr. (1982). *In search of excellence: Lessons from America's best-run companies.* New York: Harper & Row.

Pogrebin, M.R., & Poole, E.D. (1988). Humor in the briefing room: A study of the strategic uses of humor among police. *Journal of Contemporary Ethnography,* 17, 183-210.

Polzin, M.J. (1997). *A labor-management approach to community policing.* [Online]. Available: http://www.cj.msu.edu/~outreach/cp/labman.html 1998, October 12].

Radelet, L.A., & Carter, D.L. (1994). *The police and the community* (5th ed.). New York: MacMillan College Publishing.

Rea, L.M., & Parker, R.A. (1997). *Designing and conducting survey research: A comprehensive guide* (2nd ed.). San Francisco: Jossey-Bass.

Reiss, A.J., Jr. (1971). *The police and the public.* New Haven, CT: Yale.

Reuss-Ianni, E. (1983). *Two cultures of policing: Street cops and management cops.* New Brunswick, NJ: Transaction Books.

Reynolds, P.D., & Sponaugle, G.C. (1982). *A guide to survey research: How to plan a survey, estimate costs, and use a survey research service.* Minneapolis, MN: Center for Urban and Regional Affairs, University of Minnesota.

Riechers, L.M., & Roberg, R.R. (1990). Community policing: A critical review of underlying assumptions. *Journal of Police Science and Administration*, 17, 105-114.

Robinson, S.L., & Rousseau, D.M. (1994). Violating the psychological contract: Not the exception but the norm. *Journal of Organizational Behavior*, 15, 245-259.

Rosenbaum, D.P. (Ed.). (1994). *The challenge of community policing: Testing the promises*. Thousand Oaks, CA: Sage.

Rousseau, D.M. (1995). *Psychological contracts in organizations: Understanding written and unwritten agreements*. Thousand Oaks, CA: Sage.

Rubinstein, J. (1973). *City police.* New York: Farrar, Staus & Giroux.

Sadd, S., & Grinc, R. (1994). Innovative neighborhood oriented policing: An evaluation of community policing in eight communities. In D.P. Rosenbaum (Ed.), *The challenge of community policing: Testing the promises* (pp. 27-52). Thousand Oaks, CA: Sage Publications.

Sadd, S., & Grinc, R. (1996). *Implementation challenges in community policing: Innovative Neighborhood-Oriented Policing in eight cities*. Washington, D.C.: National Institute of Justice.

Salant, P., & Dillman, D.A. (1994). *How to conduct your own survey*. New York: John Wiley & Sons.

Schein, E.H. (1985). *Organizational culture and leadership: A dynamic view*. San Francisco: Jossey-Bass.

Schermerhorn, J.R., Jr., Hunt, J.G., & Osborn, R.N. (1994). *Managing organizational behavior* (5th ed.). New York: John Wiley & Sons.

Seagrave, J. (1996). Community policing: The views of police executives in British Columbia. *Policing and Society,* 6, 163-180.

Skogan, W.G., & Hartnett, S.M. (1997). *Community policing, Chicago style.* New York: Oxford University Press.

Skolnick, J.H. (1994). *Justice without trial; Law enforcement in a democratic society* (3rd ed.). New York: Macmillan.

Skolnick, J.H., & Bayley, D.H. (1986). *The new blue line: Police innovation in six American cities.* New York: Free Press.

Skolnick, J.H., & Fyfe, J.J. (1993). *Above the law: Police and the excessive use of force.* New York: The Free Press.

Sparrow, M.K. (1988). *Perspectives on policing (no. 9): Implementing community policing* (NCJ 114217). Washington, DC: U.S. Department of Justice.

Sparrow, M.K., Moore, M.H., & Kennedy, D.M. (1990). *Beyond 911: A new era for policing.* New York: Basic Books.

SPSS Inc. (1997). *SPSS® Base 7.5 applications guide.* Chicago: SPSS.

Stamper, N.H. (1992). *Removing managerial barriers to effective police leadership: A study of executive leadership and executive management in big-city police departments.* Washington, DC: Police Executive Research Forum.

Steinman, M. (1986). Managing and evaluating police behavior. *Journal of Police Science and Administration,* 14, 285-292.

Strauss, A.S., & Corbin, J. (1990). *Basics of qualitative research: Grounded theory procedures and techniques.* Newbury Park, CA: Sage.

Swanson, C.R., Territo, L., Taylor, R.W. (1998). *Police administration: Structures, processes, and behavior* (4th ed.). Upper Saddle River, NJ: Prentice Hall.

Taylor, R.W., Fritsch, E.J, & Caeti, T.J. (1998, May/June). Core challenges facing community policing: The emperor still has no clothes. *ACJS Today,* 17(1), 1-5.

Territo, L. (1980). Planning and implementing organizational change. *Journal of Police Science and Administration*, 8, 390-398.

Trice, H.M., & Beyer, J.M. (1993). *The cultures of work organizations.* Englewood Cliffs, NJ: Prentice-Hall.

Trojanowicz, R.C. (1980). *The environment of the first-line police supervisor.* Englewood Cliffs, NJ: Prentice-Hall.

Trojanowicz, R.C., & Carter, D. (1988). *The philosophy and role of community policing.* [Online] Available: http://www.cj.msu.edu/~people/cp/cpphil.html [1999, September 16].

Trojanowicz, R.C., Kappeler, V.E., Gaines, L.K., Bucqueroux, B. (1998). *Community policing: A contemporary perspective* (2nd ed.). Cincinnati, OH: Anderson.

Trojanowicz, R.C., & Pollard, B. (1986). *Community policing: The line officers' perspective.* [Online] Available: *http://www.cj.msu.edu/~people/cp/communit.html* [1999, September 16].

Van Maanen, J. (1974). Working the street: A developmental view of police behavior. In H. Jacob (Ed.), *The potential for reform in the criminal justice system*, (pp. 83-130). Beverly Hills, CA: Sage.

Van Maanen, J. & Schein, E. (1977). *Toward a theory of organizational socialization.* Cambridge, MA: Alfred P. Sloan School of Management, Massachusetts Institute of Technology.

Vito, G.F., & Latessa, E.J. (1989). *Statistical applications in criminal justice.* Newbury Park, CA: Sage.

Walker, J.T. (1999). *Statistics in criminal justice: Analysis and interpretation.* Gaithersburg, MD: Aspen.

Walker, S. (1977). *A critical history of police reform.* Lexington, MA: D.C. Heath.

Walker, S. (1993). Does anyone remember team policing? Lessons of the team policing experience for community policing. *American Journal of Police,* 12(1), 33-55.

Walker, S. (1999). *The police in America: An introduction* (3rd ed.). Boston: McGraw-Hill.

Wanous, J.P. (1977). Organizational entry: Newcomers moving from outside to inside. *Psychological Bulletin*, 84, 601-618.

Weisburd, D., McElroy, J., & Hardyman, P. (1988). Challenges to supervision in community policing: Observations on a pilot project. *American Journal of Police,* 7(2), 29-50.

Weisel, D.L., & Eck, J.E. (1994). Toward a practical approach to organizational change: Community policing initiatives in six cities. In D.P. Rosenbaum (Ed.), *The challenge of community policing: Testing the promises* (pp. 53-72). Thousand Oaks, CA: Sage Publishing.

Wilkinson, D., Stemen, D., & Allen, M. (1997, March). The patrol officer's view of community policing: Experiences from Aurora and Joliet, IL, from 1991-1996. Paper presented at the annual meetings of the Academy of Criminal Justice Sciences, Louisville, KY.

Wilkinson, D.L., & Rosenbaum, D.P. (1994). The effects of organizational structure on community policing: A comparison of two cities. In D.P. Rosenbaum (Ed.), *The challenge of community policing: Testing the promises* (pp. 110-126). Thousand Oaks, CA: Sage Publishing.

Wilson, J.Q. (1968). *Varieties of police behavior: The management of law & order in eight communities.* Cambridge, MA: Harvard University Press.

Wycoff, M.A. (1991). The benefits of community policing: Evidence and conjecture. In J.R. Green & S.D. Mastrofski (Eds.), *Community policing: Rhetoric or reality* (pp. 103-120). New York: Praeger.

Wycoff, M.A., & Kelling, G.L. (1978). *The Dallas experience: Organizational reform.* Washington, DC: Police Foundation.

Wycoff, M.A., & Skogan, W.G. (1994). Community policing in Madison: An analysis of implementation and impact. In D.P. Rosenbaum (Ed.), *The challenge of community policing: Testing the promises* (pp. 75-91). Thousand Oaks, CA: Sage Publications.

Yin, R.K. (1993). *Applications of case study research.* Newbury Park, CA: Sage.

Zhao, J. (1996). *Why police organizations change: A study of community-oriented policing.* Washington, D.C.: Police Executive Research Forum.

Zhao, J., Thurman, Q.C., & Lovrich, N.P. (1995). Community-oriented policing across the U.S.: Facilitators and impediment to implementation. *American Journal of Police*, 14(1), 11-28.

INDEX